RABBI YACOV BARBER

Sparks
of Wisdom

from
Rabbi Yehonatan Eybeshitz

Gerber's Miracle Publishers LLC
FORT LAUDERDALE, FLORIDA

Published by:

Gerber's Miracle Publishers LLC
FORT LAUDERDALE, FL
sparksofwisdom.com

Copyright © 2022 Gerber's Miracle Publishers LLC

ISBN-13
Paperback: 979-8-218-07924-6
Hardback: 979-8-9872698-1-7

Copyediting by Carol Killman Rosenberg

Interior production by Gary A. Rosenberg

**A portion of the sales of this book
will be donated to Colel Chabad**

Contents

About the Menorah

The menorah featured on the cover of this book was bequeathed in 1762 to the main synagogue in Altona where Reb Yehonatan Eybeshitz was the chief rabbi, two years prior to the rabbi's passing.

In November of 1938, during Kristallnacht (the Night of Broken Glass), the menorah, which was housed in the Bornplatz Synagogue in Hamburg, was partially destroyed. In 1989, the base and the attached middle pole of the menorah were found in the storage of the Altona Museum, at which point the menorah was restored to its former glory.

The menorah stands over three feet tall and weighs approximately 220 pounds. It is presently housed in the Hohe Weide Synagogue in Hamburg. Four lines of embossed Hebrew appear on the base:

לכבוד הבורא ולכבוד התורה, אשר היא לנו לאורה

התנדבו החבורה זאת המנורה, בירה ואלף מוווילנא,

ר׳ אנשיל שפץ, ר׳ נתן בן פרנקפורט, ר׳ ירמיה מפולדא,

ר׳ זעליגמן מנארדן, ר׳ וייבש סגל, משה בהר״ז, ר׳ חיים סגל,

שנת תכ״ב לפ״ק

The translation reads:

*In honor of the Creator and in honor of the Torah, which is our
    source of light.*
This menorah has been donated by the following:
*Bira Wolf from Vilna, Rabbi Anshil Shpatz, Rabbi Nosson from
    Frankfurt,*
Rabbi Yermiyahu from Fulda, Rabbi Zeligman from Nardan,
*Rabbi Feivish Segal, Moshe son of Rabbi Z. and Rabbi Haim
    Segal.*
Year 1762.

While biographical information from the time is scant, research provides a brief history of the lives of these few donors:

Bira Wolf from Vilna was a well-known Torah scholar; he was a grandson of the Rema[1] and a son-in-law of the Shach.[2]

Reb Haim Segal was the husband of Glückel of Hameln, a very well-known figure in Hamburg and Germany. She was born into a wealthy family in 1746. When she was twelve years old, Glückel was betrothed to Haim Segal, whom she married in 1760 at the age of fourteen. After the marriage, the couple lived in the groom's parents' home in Hameln. A year after their marriage, the couple moved in with Glückel's parents in Hamburg. Glückel and Haim had a total of fourteen children, and after Haim's death she was known as Glückel the Widow. She was a well-known Jewish philanthropist.

We would like to offer special thanks to Rabbi Bistritsky and Rabbi Havlin for their help regarding the Menorah's history.

It is with great reverence and honor that we adorn the cover of this book with this revered symbol of Jewish history and faith.

---

1. Rabbi Moshe Isserles (b. 1530 d. 1572) was an eminent Polish Ashkenazic rabbi, Talmudist, and *posek* (expert in Jewish law).

2. Rabbi Shabtai HaCohen (b. 1621 d. 1662) was a noted seventeenth-century Talmudist and Halakhist.

Publisher's Note

Rabbi Yehonatan Eybeshitz was a towering intellect during his lifetime: a charismatic rabbi, an expert on Jewish law, a master Kabbalist, a prolific writer, a peacemaker, and so much more. His direct descendant Julie Gerber grew up in Havana, Cuba, aware of her family lineage. Though she knew Eybeshitz was a famous last name, she never gave it much thought; it was simply her grandfather's last name and her mother's maiden name. However, as the years passed and maturity set in, Julie started to find the genealogical connection compelling.

Richie Gerber, Julie's husband, realized the significance of his wife's incredible family tree and was so honored by this connection that he never hesitated to mention Julie's ancestor to anyone who would listen. The Gerbers noticed how excited some people were to actually meet a direct descendant of this celebrated Torah Giant. Most often, people who knew of Rabbi Yehonatan were Orthodox rabbis who would go on to describe studying his work during their Yeshiva days. They would always share how very impressed they were with his complex writings and sermons.

Craving to know more, Julie and Richie searched and searched for Rabbi Yehonatan's works, realizing that most of it was in Hebrew. Moreover, very little had been written about him or his writings in English and very little had been translated from the Hebrew. It became the Gerbers' mission to make Rabbi Yehonatan's works available in English. Fast-forward to the present, and the reader can be assured that this is happening, as this second book focusing on Rabbi Yehonatan's writings is being published.

The first book, *Pearls of Wisdom*, has been critically acclaimed and acknowledged to be a noteworthy translation of Rabbi Yehonatan's

Torah interpretations and his thoughts on the weekly Torah Reading and Jewish holidays. Since Rabbi Yehonatan's ideas can be lofty and complex, *Pearls of Wisdom* can be a challenging book for some readers to follow. In this second book, *Sparks of Wisdom*, Rabbi Eybeshitz's words have been translated, interpreted, and explained by Rabbi Yacov Barber, the translator of Rabbi Yehonatan's writings for *Pearls of Wisdom*.

Rabbi Barber shares the Gerbers' passion in bringing Rabbi Yehonatan's teachings to a wider readership. Rabbi Barber is known to use ancient and modern wisdom to inspire and motivate through his easy-to-understand lectures. This way, he makes the complex understandable to those with less of a background in Jewish studies. In this book, Rabbi Barber injects his own insights regarding the thoughts and ideas expressed in Rabbi Eybeshitz's writings on Torah, Kabbala, Talmud, Jewish law, and so on, succeeding in making them accessible to a much larger audience.

In furthering Rabbi Barber's objective, he conveys the message of Rabbi Yehonatan through the lens of the twenty-first-century perspective, connecting complex concepts into accessible modern-day understanding, thus inspiring the reader to gain wisdom into the *Sparks of Wisdom* that Rabbi Eybeshitz intended more than 250 years ago.

Rabbi Yehonatan Eybeshitz's deep and esoteric writings are finally revealed for all to enjoy. Be forewarned—reading this book may change your life.

Introduction

Like *Pearls of Wisdom* **which came before it,** this book is devoted to the teachings and writings of the great Reb Yehonatan Eybeshitz. While both books present the teachings of Reb Yehonatan in English, they are quite different in style and intention.

Pearls of Wisdom is a direct translation of the original writings of Reb Yehonatan Eybeshitz; the challenge with that book was ensuring accurate translation and conveyance of Reb Yehonatan's thoughts. It follows the weekly Torah reading, the festivals, and major events in Jewish history. While it gives the English-speaking world an authentic glimpse into the richness and profound wisdom of Reb Yehonatan Eybeshitz, its style and format preclude it from reaching a wider readership. Many readers are unfamiliar with the content of the weekly portion as well as the deeper themes of the festivals and may therefore struggle to find a topic of interest to explore.

Nevertheless, *Pearls of Wisdom* has been read and appreciated here and in such far-reaching places as Germany and Japan, but perhaps the book's impact can best be crystalized by the following incident: A senior rabbi from Sau Paulo, Brazil, was visiting New York, and he went into a Jewish bookstore to purchase a bar mitzvah present for one of his congregant's sons. The family did not have a very strong connection with Judaism, and he was looking for a gift that would inspire the young man. When he saw *Pearls of Wisdom* on the shelf, he knew this was the bar mitzvah present he had to buy. You see, the bar mitzvah boy's name is Yehonatan Eybeshitz, as he is a direct descendant of Reb Yehonatan.

Sparks of Wisdom takes a different approach from *Pearls* in a few important ways to reach a wider readership: First, the book is topic based with alphabetical entries, making it user friendly and practical. Second, I have taken the liberty of focusing more on the spirit and ideas that Reb Yehonatan wished to convey rather than on a more literal translation. And, third, each section concludes with modern-day application of Reb Yehonatan's insights (see the italicized copy).

There is an erroneous belief that the teachings of our great rabbis do not speak and address the issues that we face in the twenty-first century. Hopefully, *Sparks of Wisdom* goes someway in rectifying this. Please note that if there are any inaccuracies in the text or ideas presented, the fault lies squarely on my shoulders and my inability to understand and correctly convey Reb Yehonatan's teachings.

The Life of Reb Yehonatan Eybeshitz

Reb Yehonatan Eybeshitz was born on the 6th of Cheshvan, 1696, in Pintshov, Poland. His father was Reb Nossan Nota, a descendent of the Megaleh Amukos.[1] His mother was Shaindel, the daughter of Reb Yehuda Leib Tzuntz, who was the Av Beit Din of Helishoi and Pintshov. Reb Yehuda Leib was a descendant of the Mahra"m Schiff.[2] He is mentioned a number of times in Reb Yehonatan's writings.[3]

When Reb Yehonatan was a young boy, his mother passed away. While he was growing up, it was evident that he possessed great intelligence. His father hired a private tutor to teach him. The teacher asked Reb Nossan Nota which tractate he should teach the boy. Reb Nossan Nota suggested the tractate Beitza. (The word *beitza* means egg.) However, the teacher felt that a boy with such a keen mind should learn a more difficult tractate. Having overheard the conversation, Reb Yehonatan said, "Beitza may not be that challenging, but just as an egg can be boiled until it is hard, similarly the tractate can be learnt in a manner that it will be hard."

When Reb Yehonatan was eleven years old, his father was appointed the Av Beit Din in the city Eybeschutz (Morovia), and the family adopted the name Eybeshitz as their surname. About a year

---

1. *Rabbi Nossan Nota Spira lived in Poland 1585–1633. He was a Torah scholar and master Kabbalist, and Reb Yehonatan's paternal grandfather. He authored the "Megaleh Amokus." He was the son of Reb Shlomo, who was a son of Reb Nossan Shapiro of Hurodna, author of "Movoi Shearim." The Megaleh Amukos (Rabbi Nossan Nota Spira) was chief rabbi and head of the Yeshivah in Krakow. On his tombstone, it is written that he spoke with Elijah the Prophet.*

2. *Rabbi Meir ben Ya'akov Schiff 1605–1641*

3. *Tumim 33,3 92,1 Pleisi 97,1 109,2*

later, Reb Nossan Nota passed away, leaving Reb Yehonatan without a father or mother.

In the introduction to his sefer *Kreisi U'Pleisi*, Reb Yehonatan writes, "My father passed away while I was still young, and I did not have the opportunity to sufficiently study with him and absorb the teachings of my illustrious forefather the Megaleh Amukos."

With the passing of Reb Nossan Nota, the yeshivah closed. The heads of the community sent Reb Yehonatan to learn at the yeshivah in Pruznitz, which was in close proximity to Eybeschutz. The yeshivah was headed by the Av Beit Din Reb Meir Eizenshtate, known as the Maharam Ash. Reb Meir authored the work *Shu"t Ponim Meirot* and held his new *talmid* (disciple) in great esteem.

In 1709, Reb Meir Eizenshtate left Pruznitz. Reb Yehonatan then traveled to the yeshivah of his great uncle Reb Eliezer Segal Itinga. A year later, in 1710, Reb Yehonatan married Elkeli, the daughter of Reb Moshe Yitzchak Shapiro.

Reb Moshe was the Av Beit Din of Amsela and the chief rabbi of Bohemia. Prior to Reb Moshe taking Reb Yehonatan as his son-in-law, he examined him extensively in his learning. Reb Yehonatan also gave a lengthy *pilpul* (discourse) on the Thirteen Principles through which the rabbis understand the Torah verses. After Reb Yehonatan's marriage, he joined his father-in-law's yeshivah, where he was appointed a teacher. He was only fifteen years old and was teaching students who were older than him.

Reb Yehonatan's father-in-law passed away on the 18th Tevet, 1750. Reb Yehonatan eulogized his father-in-law and said that he had been like a father to him. "I must give him credit for my Torah knowledge," he stated.

In 1713, Reb Yehonatan decided to move to Hamburg where his wife's grandfather Reb Mordechai HaCohen lived. Reb Mordechai was a man of great stature who supported Reb Yehonatan in his studies. Reb Yehonatan writes[4] that during this time period, he reached great heights in his Torah studies.

---

4. Introduction Kreisi U'Pleisi

In 1714, Reb Shimon Reisher, the preacher of Prague, passed away. The heads of the community offered the position to Reb Yehonatan, who was not yet twenty years old. They still recalled the very deep and profound Torah discourse he had given at his wedding. Reb Yehonatan would speak every Shabbat, and his sermons would last five to six hours at times.

At that time, Reb Avraham Fasilberg was the *rosh yeshiva* (dean of Talmudic studies) in Prague. He had asked his talmidim a very difficult question. Reb Yehonatan gave each student a different answer. When Reb Avraham heard the various answers and who had given them, he informed the heads of the community that he was abdicating his position and they should appoint Reb Yehonatan in his stead.

When Reb Avraham passed away, Reb Yehonatan gave a eulogy and said that on many occasions Reb Avraham helped him reach the correct understanding in his studies.[5]

At that time, the Prague government did not allow the Jews to print the Talmud. Reb Yehonatan traveled to Vienna to seek permission for its printing. After ten years of due diligence, he received permission to print the Talmud on the condition that the government could delete any sections they saw fit to omit. In 1727, the Tractate Brachot and the Mishnayot Zeraim were printed for the first time in Prague.

In 1736, Reb Dovid Openheim, the Av Beit Din of Prague, passed away. Reb Yehonatan was chosen to fill the position. Reb Yehonatan held three prestigious positions in Prague. He was the preacher, head of the yeshivah, and Av Beit Din.

In 1742, Reb Yehonatan was appointed Av Beit Din of Mintz. In Mintz, he began writing the sefer *Urim V'Tumim*. His student Reb Yedidya Vayl writes that he rarely saw his teacher sleeping in a bed; rather, he would catnap while sitting in his chair—and that he was so engrossed in his learning that he would only eat just before *mincha* (afternoon prayer). And, at times, he would give a *shiur* (study session) that lasted seven hours.

In 1746, the Av Beit Din of Fourda passed away, and Reb

---

5. *Yaaroth Devash 1,12*

Yehonatan was offered the position. He found the offer very attractive since there was a printing house in Fourda, and he very much wanted to print his *seforim* (holy books). However, the congregation of Mintz did not allow him to leave since he had signed a contract with the congregation, and the contract had not yet concluded.

Three years later, in 1749, the Av Beit Din of Altona, Reb Yechezkel Katzenelenbogen, passed away, and the community wanted to appoint Reb Yehonatan as his successor. Altona was a very prestigious appointment, and it also had a very large printing house. A year later, Reb Yehonatan accepted the position, and he became the Av Beit Din of Altona, Hamburg, and Wanzinbeck. When he arrived, he was greeted with great pomp and glory. Many of his students from Mintz joined him in Altona.

It was in Altona that the controversy between Reb Yaakov Emden and Reb Yehonatan broke out. The conflict was over amulets that Reb Yehonatan had written for a woman who had miscarried. Reb Yaakov Emden accused him of being part of the Shabtai Zvi sect.[6] The conflict ended in 1756 when the king made a decree against anyone who disagreed with Reb Yehonatan.

During this period, Reb Yehonatan was offered the position of Av Beit Din of Cracow, Poland, and of Nikolsberg. He declined both offers and preferred to remain in Altona. In the year 1753, he personally fundraised and built a new shul and beit midrash, and four years later, he built another one in Hamburg.

On the 10th of Tevet, 1756, Reb Yehonatan's wife passed away. In the year 1761, he became ill; however, he continued to learn with great self-sacrifice. He writes, "There were a number of occasions when I did not feel well; however, thanks to Hashem, my learning was not interrupted."[7]

---

6. *Shabtai Zvi, a rabbi from Smyrna, had claimed to be the messiah. However, it soon became evident that Shabtai Zvi was a fraud; nonetheless, he had created havoc among the Jewish people. Those who were opposed to Rabbi Yehonatan claimed that he was a secret follower of Shabtai Zvi, which was completely false.*

7. *Yaaroth Devash p. 148*

Two years later, in 1763, Reb Yehonatan once again became extremely ill. He made a vow that if Hashem would bless him with good health, he would print his seforim. His condition improved, and he printed the first section of the *Kresi U'Pleisi*. Printing at the time was extremely expensive, and Reb Yehonatan did not have the funds to print the whole sefer. In his will, he instructed his grandson to print the rest of the sefer. Ten years later, in 1773, the *Kresi U'Pleisi* was printed in full.

On the 21st of Elul, 1764, at the age of sixty-nine, Reb Yehonatan Eybeshitz returned his soul to his creator.

His Students

Ten years before his passing, Reb Yehonatan had more than 20,000 students. He considered educating the next generation his fundamental purpose in life. He writes, "The best years of my life was when I was given the opportunity to educate and bring Jews back to the service of Hashem."[8] Reb Yehonatan also instructed others to follow in such a calling.

While he was the Av Beit Din of Altona, he once gave a public address marking the conclusion of the study of the tractate Baba Metziah. He implored the members of the community to see to it that they should always have a yeshiva student at their meal. And in that merit, they would be safeguarded from all evil.

Personality

Reb Yehonatan was beloved by all. People would say, "Happy is the woman who gave birth to such a child." He was loved and greatly respected by kings and princes, who would often visit him at his home. Many times, Reb Yehonatan would use his close connections with various heads of state to nullify evil decrees that had been placed on the Jewish community.

---

8. *Yaaroth Devash 1, Drush Aseret Yemei Tshuvah 1740*

Reb Yehonatan writes, "My nights are dedicated to the study of Torah, and during the day, I need to present myself to various ministers and priests to defend the Yidden against false accusations leveled against us."[9] It is well known that on one occasion Reb Yehonatan wrote an amulet to nullify an evil decree that had been placed upon them. The amulet was presented to the king, and on it was written 76,052 times, "The Jewish people will live for eternity."

Toiling in Torah

We cannot fathom the extent of Reb Yehonatan's diligence when it came to Torah study. By way of illustration, his students described how on one occasion in the middle of winter late at night, Reb Yehonatan had left the beit midrash. A number of hours later, they realized he had not yet returned.

They went outside to look for him and saw him standing under a tree covered in snow. They screamed his name, and he shook off the snow. He told his students, "I have the answer to a difficult question posed on the Rambam."

Reb Yehonatan writes, "The truth be told, I have devoted myself with all my energy to study Torah. I slept little, my nights were like day when it came to study."[10]

Reb Naftoli Hirsh Vashirtrayling, the Av Beit Din of Chesin writes, "May heaven and earth be my witness that Reb Yehonatan did not go to sleep the whole week. And when everyone else was sleeping, he would be learning with great enthusiasm. And I wonder if anyone else in our generation learns Torah with such effort and toil. Shabbat morning, I took Mishnayot Seder Zeroim and he recited it by heart without making a single error. The following week the scene repeated itself, except this time it was Seder Moed. This continued until Reb Yehonatan had recited all six sections of Mishnayot. From the day I have known Reb Yehonatan I have never seen him interested in any

9. *Introduction Kreisi U'Pleisi*

10. *Introduction Kreisi U'Pleisi*

worldly pleasures. He also never had a designated time when he would sit and eat his meal."[11]

Halacha

Whenever a halachic decision needed the opinion of a medical practitioner, Reb Yehonatan personally would go and discuss the matter with the doctor.[12] He would personally check to ensure that the *shochtim* (ritual slaughterers) were righteous and trustworthy individuals.

He writes, "Initially when I gave a certificate to allow an individual to become a shochet I limited the certificate to a three-year period. And after that they would have to be retested in order to continue practicing. Unfortunately, I faced strong opposition to my position, and I had to forgo it." [13]

He also writes, "The situation of the credibility of the shochtim in Prague is such that anyone who is God fearing should not eat from their shechita." On another occasion, he writes, "There was a particular individual who was in charge of removing the non-kosher veins from the animal. He erroneously concluded which veins were kosher and which were not. As a result, I no longer relied on him, and I personally would remove the non-kosher veins from the meat that I would eat."[14]

Writings

Reb Yehonatan explained why he felt that it was important to publish his writings.[15] He said, "When I was teaching my students sections of the Shulchan Aruch, I would share with them my insights; they then would record what had been taught. As a result, there were many

---

11. *Luchos Eidus p. 113*

12. *Kreisi U'Pleisi 40,4*

13. *Kreisi 1,11: 39,13:*

14. *Kreisi 65,15*

15. *Introduction Kreisi U'Pleisi 33,5*

versions of what had been said, and at times, they seem to contradict themselves. I therefore felt it was important to publish exactly what I had said. I also feel it is important that I only publish that which has practical halachic application."

Pronouncements

Reb Yehonatan enacted various rulings for his community, including:

Avoiding expensive brit milahs, pidyon habens, and bar mitzvahs.

A bride and groom should make a firm undertaking that they will be careful in all matters relating to modesty during the engagement period.

The first five years after marriage the couple should be supported by the wife's father to enable the groom to devote himself solely to the study of Torah. After five years, the husband then can begin to earn a livelihood.

On the eve of Rosh Hashanah and Yom Kippur, men and woman should not go to the same cemetery.

A person should learn a half hour each day *sifrei mussar* (Jewish ethical literature).

Adam—The First Human Being

God's Creation

God created Adam. No other human being was created solely by God. As such, Adam was endowed with unique gifts. Adam was able to discern which parts of planet earth were suitable for man to successfully inhabit and which parts of the globe would remain uninhabitable for all time.[16]

The human species is a composite of the physical and the spiritual. God took earth to make Adam's body, and He then blew into it a Godly soul. The human needs both elements—the physical and the spiritual—to be considered truly human. Without a soul, we are lifeless, nothing more than a chunk of clay. And missing a body, we are purely angelic. Just as our physical self needs certain conditions to function properly and truly excel, our spiritual element also needs the right environment to be able to blossom.

We should pitch our tent amongst upright God-fearing individuals who show compassion and care for the stranger and the needy. Living in such an environment will only enhance what it means to be truly human.

Overenthusiasm: The Downfall of Man

There are times when we are so excited about something that we don't pause for a moment to consider the necessary steps we need to take to achieve it. It is like someone who is so excited by the sight of a swimming pool in the heat of the summer that he jumps into the deep end, forgetting for a moment that he doesn't know how to swim. We can appreciate how dangerous that may be and the tragic outcome that might result.

---

16. *Chidushei Rabbi Yehonatan Brochos 31*

The first sin of mankind was the sin of Adam and Chava. Their sin was a consequence of their overenthusiasm. Adam and Chava were given two instructions: The first that they were not permitted to eat from the tree of knowledge of good and bad. The second that they were to protect and work in the Garden of Eden.

God's plan was to eventually allow Adam and Chava to eat from the tree. However, prior to their receiving permission, they had a bridge to cross first. They had to protect and work the Garden.

By eating the fruit of the tree of knowledge, one of the greatest mysteries known to man would be unlocked. Adam and Chava would be privy to understanding how good and evil can emanate from the same source. However, Adam and Chava would not be able to comprehend and appreciate this unless they had previously worked and protected the Garden.

Adam and Chava's overexuberance, as noble and well intentioned it was, led to their downfall. [17]

There is an ancient saying perhaps as old as the city itself and that is, "Rome wasn't built in a day." If we want something to be permanent and everlasting, we need to take it in small increments. We must never forget that we need to learn how to walk before we can begin to run.

Resolving Conflict

At first glance, it seems difficult to understand the severity of Adam and Chava's sin. All they did was eat fruit they shouldn't have. It would seem to be analogous to a parent telling their child that they can't have dessert after dinner, but the child takes it anyway.

Since the beginning of time and it would seem till the end of days, there is one constant: the inability for mankind to live harmoniously with one another—whether it is man against his neighbor or nation against nation. At the very outset of the world's existence, mankind was embroiled in conflict and disagreement. It reached a point of great

---

17. *Yaaroth Devash* 1,2

tragedy when brother killed brother—that is, when Cain took the life of Abel, both the sons of Adam.

The inability for mankind to find a way to create a society where humanity can live in peace and harmony was a direct result of Adam and Chava's sin. Is it any wonder then why they were punished so severely? [18]

How do we resolve conflict? The very first step is to be aware of an ancient statement made by the rabbis in the Talmud. The Talmud states that just as no two people look alike, likewise no two people think alike. Whenever we interact with another human being, we need to remember we will not agree on everything. And there is a possibility that we will not agree on anything.

The second step is to recall the dictum "Derech eretz kadma l'Tora." (Good manners are prerequisites for a Torah life.) Even if we disagree, we need to be gracious about it. Conflicts arise more because of how something is said rather than by what is said.

The third step is to look at other people not only as physical beings but also as having an inner Divine soul. If we can see beyond their superficial faults to the core of their beautiful soul, it will be easier to accept and love them, and avoid conflict with them.

There are more steps that need to be taken. However, if we begin with these three steps, we will be definitely going in the right direction.

---

18. *Yaaroth Devash* 2,12

Adulthood

At What Age?

Different countries permit a person to buy alcohol at different ages. For example, in the United States, the legal age is twenty-one, and in Australia, it is eighteen. The discrepancy in age is due to how each country assesses the age at which an individual has reached a certain level of maturity.

Is there a Jewish understanding not necessarily of the age when one can purchase alcohol but rather when a person would be considered to have reached an age of maturity? Or to pose the question somewhat differently, we often hear people say, "You are old enough to know better," so when is that magical age?

The answer is very much dependent on the particular scenario. Does Jewish law shed light on a particular age whereby we can be confident that a person has reached maturity?

The Talmud states that if a child inherits his father's properties, he will not be allowed to sell any of them until he has reached the age of twenty. Since, before the age of twenty, we consider the person's intellect to not have fully matured, we should not rely on the choices he makes.

It is the age of twenty that Jewish law considers someone as having reached complete intellectual maturity. This will explain why the heavenly courts punish the individual only from the age of twenty. Prior to the age of twenty, the person's intellect has not matured sufficiently and therefore he cannot be punished—not twenty-one nor eighteen but twenty.[19]

---

19. *Yaaroth Devash 2,11*

Adolescence is a stage in a person's life that doesn't exist in Jewish law. According to Jewish law, we begin life as a minor and we bear no responsibility for our actions. Then, we go from being a child to immediately being an adult who carries full responsibility for our actions.

In a sense, adolescence is no-man's-land; we are no longer considered a child and therefore feel we can no longer be told what to do. Yet, on the other hand, we play the adolescence card whenever we don't want to take responsibility for our actions.

Judaism is of the firm belief that, if we are old enough to no longer be called a child, then we are old enough to be an adult and responsible for our actions.

Advice

The Best Piece of Advice You Will Ever Receive

There are times in our lives when we are overcome with emotion—whether it is anger, fear, love, or hate. At that moment, it is extremely difficult to think rationally. Therefore, it is in our best interest to have somebody we can confide in to seek their advice. This person does not need to be smarter than us. They just need to be someone who cares about us and has our best interests at heart. And since they are not emotionally involved, they are able to think clearly and offer sound advice.[20]

We have all experienced giving someone else sound advice. However, when we experience the same situation, we are constantly second-guessing ourselves and we seem to be unable to find an appropriate course of action. The reason is simple: when we are involved personally, our emotions come to the fore. We would have to be a unique type of a person where we could compartmentalize our emotions and view the matter from a purely cerebral perspective.

It is in our best interest then to have someone we can bounce our ideas off to help us find clarity. Seeking outside counsel does not show weakness; on the contrary, it shows that we are in tune with our psyche and know how to constructively move forward.

---

20. *Yaaroth Devash 2,9*

Ahavat Yisrael/Love Your Fellow Jew

We Make the Same Mistake

Reb Yehonatan laments the fact that during his lifetime many people derived great satisfaction and pleasure when they heard about someone's misfortune. He writes that these individuals would then tell as many people as possible, making no difference if the information was true or not. In a sense, it became their calling to share someone's downfall with whomever would listen day in and day out.[21]

Tragically, it seems we haven't learnt from our predecessors and many of us find glee in following in their footsteps and perpetuating their behavior. What steps can we take in helping ourselves overcome this negative trait?

Imagine you are walking down the street and you trip over and hurt yourself. After getting up and wiping the dirt off your clothing, would you begin to chastise your legs for tripping? Would you go and tell your friends how stupid your legs are for causing you to fall over?

Of course not. Because our legs are part of us. If we make fun of our legs, we are really making fun of ourselves. The same is true when it comes to our fellow Jew. The Jewish people are considered as one body. Collectively, we are one person.

The first step may be the hardest step to take but necessary nonetheless. And that is to internalize the eternal truth that we are all one. And who in their right mind would make fun of themselves?

---

21. *Yaaroth Devash 1,11*

Love Your Brother, Physically and Spiritually

We have all experienced it: We are in the middle of nowhere and meet a total stranger that we discover is Jewish, and we become all excited, as if we have met a long-lost brother. There is an unbreakable bond between us. It is as if we are connected at the hip. We will roll up our sleeves to help a Jew we have never met.

Reb Yehonatan writes that our spiritual soul is eternal, while our physical self resides on earth for a limited time. He therefore laments that we don't seem to have that same level of brotherly love and concern when we see a fellow Jew who is facing a spiritual crisis and we may not even realize how spiritually unwell that person is.

Reb Yehonatan explains his position as being based on a deeper understanding of the Talmud's rationale for the destruction of the second Beit Hamikdash. The second Temple was destroyed because of *sinat chinam* (unwanted hatred between Jews). He asks, "If the Jewish people at the time had tragically transgressed some of the most severe sins in the eyes of God, why then were they punished for the lack of *Ahavat Yisrael* (the love between one Jew and another)?"

The root of all the evil at that time was their lack of interest and concern for the spiritual well-being of their fellow Jew. If they truly loved their fellow Jew, they would have tried to be a positive influence on their brethren who had drifted from God and His Torah.

While there were more grievous sins than sinat chinam, by showing no concern and interest in their fellow Jews' conduct, the end result was a proliferation of truly hideous sins in the eyes of God.[22]

Five of the top-six spots in an annual list of givers in the United States are Jews. The Talmud states that every Jew is compassionate and caring as part of their DNA, and if they are not, you should question their pedigree.

Reb Yehonatan impresses upon us that there are two types of giving, since there are two types of needs. And, in Reb Yehonatan's lifetime, if he was

---

22. *Yaaroth Devash* 1,10

troubled by the deficiency in Jewish knowledge and in Jewish observance, imagine how he would be reflecting on the state of affairs in the Jewish world today.

A great rabbi once said that the way to combat Jewish ignorance is by each and every one of us becoming teachers of our faith. If you know the first letter of the Hebrew aleph bet, which is the letter aleph, and you meet a Jew who doesn't even know that, then you must become a teacher and teach them the letter aleph.

Remember, every Jew is a long-lost brother. We must love every Jew unconditionally and help them equally with their physical and their spiritual needs.

Angels

Beyond the Letter of the Law

An agent who has been selected to fulfill a particular task cannot deviate from the explicit instructions they have received. Angels are God's agents who are given specific tasks to accomplish, and they are given very defined instructions they need to follow. An angel cannot decide on its own to deviate from the path it needs to follow. Therefore, an angel does not have the ability to act beyond the letter of the law and act favorably and compassionately with a person who is not deserving.[23]

If we behave in a manner where we go beyond the letter of the law and we are treated in kind, we need to realize that it is God Himself who is pulling the strings and not an angel.

We should always be willing to go beyond the letter of the law when we interact with our fellow human beings. We should be willing to forgive even though we may find it very challenging. And we should extend our hand in friendship even though it isn't reciprocated.

Reb Yehonatan shares with us an added incentive that should further motivate us in wanting to extend ourselves beyond the norm and beyond that which is expected. Since, when we do, we merit that God Himself interacts directly with us and not via an angel.

---

23. *Ahavat Yehonatan Voetchanan*

Anger

A New Approach

An angry person is not a happy person. How can you be happy if you walk around all day being mad at the world?

Anger can also have grave medical repercussions. Studies have shown that in the two hours after an angry outburst, the chances of having a heart attack double.[24] It also increases chances of having a stroke and weakens the immune system.

We all want to be healthy and happy, and a lot has been written about how we can deal with our anger and ways we can control it. They include "Think before you speak" and "Delay your response till you have calmed down somewhat."

Most approaches accept the premise that a human will get angry, and we need to learn how to deal with our anger. Reb Yehonatan offers a novel approach—one where he offers us the tools how not to become angry in the first place. He says that if you don't want to become an angry person, you need to become a humble person.

Have you ever seen someone who is truly humble become angry? The question we need to find an answer to is, how can we become humble?

The more spiritual we become and the more we expose ourselves to holiness, the more we feel a sense of humility. The reason being, when we feel the presence of God in our lives, we begin to comprehend to a degree the awesomeness of God and the insignificance of man. This will evoke within us a sense of humility. And humility and anger are not bed partners.[25]

---

24. University of Sydney. "Keep calm, anger can trigger a heart attack!" *ScienceDaily*. www.sciencedaily.com/releases/2015/02/150224083819.htm (accessed March 2, 2022).

25. *Magen Aleph*

Self-help is the most popular book genre. It is a billion-dollar industry. What we don't realize is that the greatest self-help book is the one authored by God Himself. You couldn't get a better writer, since who knows man better than He Who created him? The book, of course, is the Torah. The Hebrew word Torah translates to "teaching." The Torah not only teaches what we can and cannot do but also teaches and guides us in dealing with all aspects of human endeavors. It is the ultimate guide for human development.

Since the Torah is not written in the traditional format of a self-help book, it is difficult to navigate. When seeking answers to a specific issue, such as overcoming anger, it is a challenge to know exactly where to look. We need to understand that the answers are all there, and we may need to seek help and guidance in uncovering the pearls of wisdom found in it.

Remember the cardinal rule laid out by our rabbis: "Search and you shall find."

Assimilation

Age-Old Problem

Every one of us seek two things: we want to feel safe, and we want to be successful. Unfortunately, many of us are of the understanding that we can only achieve these goals by not highlighting our Jewishness and the need to appear and present ourselves as being no different from the rest of society.

Reb Yehonatan points out that this attitude was prevalent among the Jewish people from the beginning of our nationhood. And this was the motivating factor behind a rather strange instruction given by Yoseph, the son of Yaakov, to the Egyptian people. Yoseph was appointed as the viceroy of Egypt, and he was given the task of dealing with the famine that had engulfed the civilized world. Yoseph decreed that all Egyptian males needed to circumcise themselves prior to receiving their ration of grain.

A non-Jew is not obligated to be circumcised. Why then did Yoseph insist that they do so? Yoseph knew that the Jewish people would make their way to Egypt, and he was concerned that they would try to blend in with the locals to the extent the Jewish male would not want to be circumcised just as the Egyptian men were not circumcised. By insisting that all men be circumcised, this would encourage the Jewish men to be circumcised as well.[26]

History has shown this not to be the case. By trying to become like the rest of society, we have not stopped the rising tide of anti-Semitism. We all know the saying, "People respect those who respect themselves." When we are proud of our Judaism and we are willing to display it to the general populace, we garner respect and not derision.

---

26. *Yaaroth Devash 1,2*

Aura

According to some spiritual beliefs, every human being has an aura, or an energy field, said to enclose the human body. How does Judaism understand this phenomenon?

After Adam and Chava ate from the Tree of Knowledge, they realized that they were naked. Have you ever come across a person unknowingly walking in the street naked? If so, your immediate reaction would likely be that the person needs psychiatric intervention.

By eating from the tree, Adam and Chava became conscious of their nakedness. They became aware that they were not like animals and needed to be clothed. Why then was it forbidden for them to eat the fruit when it led them to realize the importance of modesty?

Every human being is surrounded by an *oir makif* (a spiritual garment that protects the person). Animals also possess spiritual clothing but not to the same degree as a human being. Prior to Adam and Chava's sin, their spiritual clothing was so powerful and intense that they did not appear naked and had no need to wear physical garments. However, once they sinned, the spiritual garments were removed, and Adam and Chava became conscious of their nakedness.[27]

The Hebrew word for "modesty" is tzniut. The idea of modesty extends beyond how we dress. How we speak and how we behave are also governed by the laws of tzniut. We need to be vigilant in ensuring that what leaves our mouth is kosher, just as we are careful in ensuring that what enters our mouth is kosher. We need to refrain from using foul and vulgar speech. Likewise, how we act falls under the rubric of modesty. We shouldn't flaunt our wealth. We should try to lead a modest lifestyle.

---

27. *Yaaroth Devash* 2,2

Behavior

Can We Change?

We are all familiar with the many quotes that contain the words, "What happens behind closed doors." For example, one is "No one knows what is happening behind someone else's closed doors." Very often this is understood to mean that appearances mean nothing. A person may be a nice, pleasant individual in public, but in the privacy of his home, he may be a tyrant and a bully. Or in public he may be a despicable character, while at home he may be a wonderful caring individual.

Repetition plays an important part in our lives. We pray three times a day, we put on tefillin every day, and the list goes on. The rabbis saw the significance in this as God's desire that His commandments should become second nature—since the more we do something, the more it becomes part of our very selves, and this will have a positive effect on our spiritual growth.

Reb Yehonatan extends this idea to our behavior. The more we behave in a certain way, the more likely it will impact our behavior overall. He writes that if a person is very opinionated and intolerant at home and it becomes part of his nature, he will behave like that in public. Similarly, if a person is very kind and caring at home, this will influence his conduct in public as well.[28]

While it is true that we don't know what happens behind closed doors, it is hard to envision that a person who is a nasty piece of work in public will suddenly become an angel when he walks over the threshold of his home. Since our actions feed off each other, the more we act in a certain way, the more likely it will be that we will always act in that manner.

---

28. *Yaaroth Devash* 1,3

The upside of this is that if we want to, we can change any negative behavior we may have. It will be an arduous, lengthy process, but it can be done. For example, if we are struggling with anger issues and are constantly yelling and screaming and inevitably feel terrible about ourselves afterward but don't seem to have the willpower to stop, our anger seems like a mountain we cannot traverse. However, we can conquer that angry mountain one small step at a time.

When we reach our front door, before we go inside, we should make a firm commitment that no matter what, for the next fifteen minutes, we will not raise our voice. Once we have conquered that first fifteen minutes, we will add another fifteen minutes until we are at a point when we don't raise our voice at home at all.

Remember Rome wasn't built in a day, and neither do we reach perfection in a day.

Bet Din/Jewish Court of Law

Judge with Great Care

A bet din is comprised of three judges. When a bet din hands down its decision, it doesn't need to explain the basis for it. There are circumstances when a single judge can adjudicate a case.

Whenever Rabbi Meir of Rothenberg, a thirteenth-century scholar, would act as a single judge, he would always give the rationale for his decision. He felt by doing so he would not err in judgment as the litigants would be in a position to query and question his verdict.

In fact, this was the practice of Moshe. Moshe explained to his father-in-law, Yitro, "If any of them has a claim, he comes to me, and I judge between a man and his fellow. I make known the statutes of God and His teachings."

Moshe's words can be understood to mean that since I am judging on my own, I always explain my judgment to ensure I do not make a mistake.[29]

When passing judgment, don't believe that it is below your standing to seek a second opinion or bounce your ideas off others. Take a leaf out of Moshe's and Rabbi Meir of Rothenberg's conduct and follow the necessary steps to ensure your decision is correct.

Walking a Tightrope

The position of a *dayan* (judge) is an extremely challenging one. The dayan needs to be proficient in areas of Jewish law that are not normally studied in the regular Yeshivah curriculum.

Besides the extensive amount of knowledge that the dayan needs to possess, his ability to apply that knowledge is equally as crucial. The

---

29. *Tiferet Yehonatan Yitro*

dayan has to walk a fine line between two seemingly conflicting rabbinic statements.

On the one hand, the rabbis state, "The city of Jerusalem was destroyed because the dayanim's rulings were based on the letter of the law, and they did not seek a ruling [that shows compassion] and goes beyond the letter of the law."

The other rabbinic statement is, "A dayan should not be merciful when judging a case."

How does the dayan reconcile the two distinct approaches when it comes to judging a case?

If the case is black and white, the dayan cannot circumvent the law by showing compassion. If, however, the case is not that clear cut and there is room to maneuver, the dayan should show compassion and go beyond the letter of the law when determining a case.[30]

We may not be judges sitting in a court of law; however, we do judge and pass judgment on people's behavior and conduct. Before we judge someone's actions, we need to ask ourselves two questions: One, do I have sufficient knowledge and information to pass judgment? And two, does this situation warrant a decision based on the letter of the law, or perhaps showing mercy and compassion should be the basis of my decision?

---

30. *Tiferet Yehonatan Yitro*

Benefit of the Doubt

Emulating God

Reb Yehonatan shares perhaps one of his most important ideas when he writes the following: We need to learn from the ways of God and emulate His behavior. Every morning when we wake, God has returned our soul in pristine condition, and every night when we go to sleep, we return our soul to God. More often than not, our soul isn't in the same condition as we had received it that morning only a dozen hours earlier. Yet God gives us the benefit of the doubt, returns our soul, and gives us another chance.

When we are faced with a situation where a person is seemingly conducting themselves contrary to the will of God, we need to find every reason and redeeming factor to justify and explain their actions and conduct. Unfortunately, that is not the case. More often than not, we seek to find reasons why a person should be considered a sinner and their conduct unacceptable. And we don't stop there; we take it to the next level, and we rejoice and are happy when we see someone failing.[31]

Reb Yehonatan was one of the great Torah giants of his era. He wrote scholarly works that are studied in the most advanced yeshivot to this very day. However, this does not in any way curtail him from sharing and impressing upon the Jewish people the need for moral growth—how we need to be honest with our own failings and seek avenues on how to improve ourselves.

---

31. *Keshet Yehonatan*

Challenges

My Challenges and Your Challenges

A person goes to the doctor because he is worried about a discolored area of his skin. After the doctor examines it, he feels it needs to be removed.

On the one hand, the patient is upset and apprehensive about the pain he will need to endure. Yet the patient has complete confidence in the doctor and knows he only has his best interest at heart. He is therefore extremely happy that he can be healed and will be able to live a healthy, long life.

This is how we need to understand and deal with life's challenges. God is the source of all goodness, and only goodness emanates from Him. And the trials and the tribulations we endure is a means by which we can atone for our sins.

While this is true when a person is reflecting on his own predicament and circumstance, this is not the way he should view another person's difficulties. When he sees another person going through a tough time, he shouldn't make light of it and attribute it to a process of atonement. Rather, he should be pained by his friend's situation to the extent that it impacts him physically.[32]

A great rabbi who preached the need to learn from every encounter and every life experience was once asked what we can learn from a heretic, a nonbeliever.

The rabbi responded that when you see someone going through a crisis, you shouldn't think everything is part of God's master plan and that there is a reason why the person is poor or sick. And when God sees fit to reverse

---

32. *Yaaroth Devash 1,7*

the person's predicament, He will do so. Rather you need to believe that there is no God and you have to help the person by alleviating his pain and suffering.

In a sense, God is telling us, "I want you to play God."

Circumcision

At Age Ninety-Nine

Which student should receive more credit?

Two students hand over their work to the teacher. One student had been given mandatory work while the other was given a voluntary assignment. On reflection, we could argue the student who had no obligation to do the work but did it anyway is to be lauded for his commitment.

Abraham, the first of our forefathers, kept all the laws of the Torah even before they were given to the Jewish people on Mount Sinai. Why then did Abraham wait until he was ninety-nine years old and instructed by God to be circumcised to fulfill this commandment?

The mitzvah of circumcision is unique in the sense that once it has been performed, it can never be repeated, unlike all other mitzvot. For example, when Abraham, based on his own recourse, fulfilled the mitzvah of giving charity, this would not negate the possibility of fulfilling this mitzvah if specifically instructed by God to do so.

However, once Abraham circumcised himself, he would no longer be in a position to circumcise himself again if instructed by God to do so.

Why did Abraham want to fulfill the mitzvah of circumcision only after being directly instructed by God?

The Talmud states a fascinating law: If we are instructed to do something and carry through, our reward is far greater than if we simply decide to do the same thing in a voluntary capacity. This law seems counterintuitive. One of the rationales offered to explain what seems counterintuitive is how we deal with responsibility and expectations. If we know we must accomplish something, it weighs us down; it makes the task more challenging and more demanding. If, however, we have no responsibility at all and we are under no pressure or time frame and the task becomes too challenging, we can simply quit. Being that we have no pressure, it becomes easier to fulfill the task and our reward will not be as great.

Abraham wanted to be instructed by God to be circumcised as this would place an added level of responsibility and therefore his reward would be far greater.[33]

Which student should get more credit?

While initially we may have had absolutely no doubt which student rightfully deserved the accolades, after being exposed to the Talmudic viewpoint, it places somewhat of a different slant on how we view things.

What I think is crucial in this back and forth is that we should never take things at face value and understand that what we may find nothing more than a skip in the park may be extremely difficult for someone else.

And perhaps both students are deserving of extra brownie points?

A Partnership

A group of scientists proclaimed that they could create a human being just as God had. They went down to the beach to collect sand to make the physical body. A heavenly voice came forth and said, "That is My sand. Get your own."

The created can never become a creator. A human can never become a creator. However, God explicitly requests that we become His partner in creation. The verse reads, "Let us make man." The *us* refers to you and me. It is as if God is saying, "Take a kernel of wheat, place it in the ground, and water it. You will harvest the crop, grind it, and make flour, and you will have food to sustain yourself." We become partners with God in ensuring that we have the food we need to sustain ourselves.

---

33. *Tiferet Yehonatan Lech Lecha*

The role we play in bringing perfection to the world is crystalized in the very first commandment given by God to Abraham: the mitzvah of circumcision. If Abraham and his descendants needed to be circumcised to reach perfection, why were they not born circumcised?

God wanted man to play an active role in bringing himself and the world to a level of perfection.[34]

The animal kingdom and the human being both evolve from the moment of birth; both become larger, stronger, and self-reliant. Unlike the animal who seeks self-preservation, man has been given the task of seeing beyond his needs and charged with changing the world as we know it. To accomplish this, mankind must also mature emotionally and mentally.

This is both an incredible opportunity and, at the same time, an awesome responsibility. If we are God's partners, then we have to fulfill our side of the partnership.

Perfection

Reb Yehonatan shares a very profound insight concerning Abraham's circumcision at the age of ninety-nine. Until Abraham was ninety-nine, he was not considered as having reached the level of perfection. As a result, whenever the Torah speaks of God conversing with Abraham, it was not God who was communicating with him directly; rather, God spoke to Abraham via an intermediary an angel. The angel was considered an angel of strict justice.

However, once Abraham was circumcised and reached the level of completeness, God began to communicate directly with Abraham with the attribute of *rachamim* (compassion).[35]

No matter the level of adherence a person may have, one of the commandments that has never wavered in terms of observance is the mitzvah of

---

34. *Tiferet Yehonatan Lech Lecha*

35. *Tiferet Yehonatan Lech Lecha*

circumcision. If at Mount Sinai we had been asked, "What are the chances the commandment of circumcision will withstand the test of time?" I am not sure how we would have responded. Removing the foreskin of an eight-day-old baby boy is not something that makes sense or something we would naturally gravitate toward.

However, our souls see the eternal truth and recognize that a Jewish male cannot be considered complete without fulfilling the commandment of circumcision. And, as a result, this commandment has withstood the test of time.

Insights

Reb Yehonatan shares a number of profound insights concerning the commandment of circumcision. The following are a number of these ideas.

Every person is born under particular *mazal* (a spiritual energy flow). This impacts the person's persona and inclination. One of the *mazalot* is called *mazal madim* (mazal of blood). The nature of someone born under *mazal madim* is to be a person who spills blood. If such a person becomes a *shochet* (ritual slaughterer) or a *mohel* (one who performs the circumcision), he has used his spiritual energy in a positive manner.

Yitzchak stated that his son Esau would live by the sword. The star of *madim* (of bloodshed) is the star of Esau. However, by the Jewish people fulfilling the mitzvah of circumcision, this will protect us against the sword of Esau.[36]

Prior to the exodus from Egypt, the Jewish people were commanded to circumcise themselves and the blood was placed on the doorframe. By following this instruction, God was opening the door to receive our repentance.[37]

---

36. *Yaaroth Devash 2,11*

37. *Tiferet Yehonatan Voera*

The act of circumcision has two aspects: the external and the internal. The external removal of the foreskin and the internal removal of spiritual impurity. The descendants of Abraham, Yitzchak, and Yaakov possess three innate qualities: compassion, bashfulness, and kindheartedness. These qualities come to the fore after circumcision. It is for this reason that the child receives his Jewish name after circumcision, as it is at that time that his inner essence has been revealed.[38]

The basis for fulfilling God's commandments is because God instructed us to do so. It is irrelevant if we fathom and comprehend the underlying reason for the command. At the same time, it behooves us to use our God-given gift of our intellect to explore and understand the spiritual workings of the commandments we fulfill.

The reason is obvious; the more we understand something, the more we can appreciate it. The flow-on effect is an increase in our desire to accomplish God's given task.

---

38. *Yaaroth Devash 2,11*

Conflict

The Litmus Test

As the old saying goes, "Two Jews, three opinions." Or think about conflict like this: a Jew was rescued from a deserted island. His rescuers saw that he had built two synagogues and were curious to know why he needed two. The rescued man explained, "One synagogue I go to, and the other I wouldn't be caught dead in."

No one likes conflict or disagreements. How are we to know which conflict can be viewed as healthy and appropriate and which conflict we should run from just as we would run from a raging fire?

The rabbis explain that if the argument is similar to the disagreements between Hillel and Shammai of the Mishnaic period, it is one worth pursuing. The question that needs to be addressed is what ground rules did Hillel and Shammai play by to ensure that their conflicts remained healthy?

Even though they disagreed vehemently, Hillel and Shammai never took their scholarly disagreements personally; they always remained the best of friends. This is the litmus test: Does the dispute impact how you feel about your adversary, has your friendship diminished, and/or have you lost respect for him? If your answer is yes, then you need to cease and desist. If your answer is no, then having healthy robust discussions is always a positive thing.[39]

The prime minister of Israel and the president of the United States were commiserating on how challenging their jobs were. The U.S. president commented, "I am president of hundreds of millions of people, while you are prime minister of only a few million people. Why do you think your

---

39. *Yaaroth Devash 2,8*

position is more challenging?" The Israeli prime minister responded, "I am prime minister to three million prime ministers."

We will always have differing opinions. As long as it is played out with a strong sense of comradery, it is healthy, but as soon as you notice that it is becoming personal and is impacting your friendship, it no longer is following the ground rules of Hillel and Shammai and should be halted immediately.

Shalom (peace) is one of the founding principles of the Jewish faith. Remember, being right is not always right.

From the Latin Word to Strike

Very rarely does a criminal begin his "career" with a violent crime. More often than not, he will have a lengthy rap sheet of priors before committing a violent crime. The *Yetzer Hara* (evil inclination) works in a similar fashion. If it would whisper in your ear that you should embarrass someone publicly or you should cause someone grave financial loss, of course you wouldn't listen. The evil inclination wouldn't be able to get a leg in.

What does it do? In a cunning move, it tells you that another Jew's behavior or actions are disrespecting God and His Torah, and it is encouraging you to protect God's honor. You think to yourself, "What could be greater than sanctifying the name of God by defending His honor?" In truth, the person may be behaving badly. However, the evil inclination is hoping that you will rise to the occasion and act. Initially, you will be respectful and cordial, but as time drags on and each party becomes more entrenched in their position, you may, without even realizing you have done so, embarrass the person and perhaps even cause grave financial loss. It is a slippery slope that is hard to get off once on.

Reb Yehonatan was so opposed to conflict that he offered a novel and highly ingenious interpretation of a statement of our rabbis. They write, "How does one know if an argument and conflict is for the sake of heaven and therefore should be sanctioned and even applauded?"

They explained, "If it is like the arguments between the two great rabbis Hillel and Shammai." The accepted understanding of the rabbis' answer is that any argument between two individuals that is similar to the disagreements between Hillel and Shammai can be considered for the sake of heaven.

Reb Yehonatan understood the rabbis' statement to be very limiting. They are conveying that the only two people whose arguments could be considered for the sake of heaven were Hillel and Shammai. Anyone else should never get into an argument since they are neither Hillel nor Shammai.[40]

Conflict comes from the Latin word for striking. When was the last time we hit anyone, if ever? When was the last time we became embroiled in a nasty dispute? We may not need to dig deep into our memory to answer the question. Let us remember that there is a correlation between conflict and striking and how vigilant we need to be to not allow conflict to spiral into striking.

Role of the Mediator

There are times when a disagreement or conflict between two people is such that they are unable to resolve their differences. The reason they cannot come to some form of an agreement is because each party cannot see beyond their own self-interest. In such a situation, it would be helpful to present the dispute to a qualified mediator. The reason being the mediator has no bias in the dispute and therefore can view both sides without any emotional involvement. Hence, it is more likely that he will be able to come to a solution that is both fair and equitable.[41]

We can all agree that seeking the help of a mediator is advantageous. What we need to be extremely cautious of is when we are asked to fill the role of a

---

40. *Yaaroth Devash 2,5*

41. *Tiferet Yehanatan Maatot*

mediator. Our ability in resolving the disagreement in a manner that both parties can live with is very much dependent on our impartiality. Therefore, if prior to the mediation, we feel swayed to one party more than the other, it would be prudent on our part to recluse ourselves from the role of mediator. The reason is self-understood, as our decision would more than likely exacerbate the conflict rather than resolve it.

There could be no greater accomplishment than bringing peace and harmony between conflicting parties. However, we need to ensure that we are part of the solution and not part of the problem.

Contentment

Living within Your Means

After the Jewish people left Egypt, they wandered in the desert for forty years. During that time, they ate the manna (bread that fell from heaven). One of the interesting laws pertaining to the eating of the heavenly bread was that you could not leave any leftovers for the next day.

One of the reasons given for this instruction is that God wanted to teach this new fledgling nation one of the most important qualities they should strive to achieve. That being a sense of contentment. As long as we have what to eat today, we should feel gratified and not worry about tomorrow.

How do we achieve such a lofty level?

In Ethics of the Fathers, it says one should return to God the day before one passes away. Since no one knows the day they will pass away, a person repents every day of their lives. If we live each day thinking this is our last, this will put things into perspective, and we will have no need or desire for anything that could be considered excessive.[42]

Many studies have shown a strong link between extreme wealth and depression.[43] Wealthier children tend to be more distressed than lower-income kids and are at a higher risk of anxiety and depression. There are many theories presented why this is so. Torah literature offers two amazing statements that shed light on this issue. The first states, "He who has $100 wants $200; someone who has $200 wants $400." The second states, "Who is wealthy? Someone who is happy with his lot."

---

42. *Yaaroth Devash* 1

43. Luthar, Suniya S. "The Culture of Affluence: Psychological Costs of Material Wealth." *Child Development* 74, no. 6 (November 2003): 1581–1593. doi. org/10.1046/j.1467-8624.2003.00625.x.

The wealthier we are, the more we want and think we need. We all would love to be able to say, "I am wealthy and happy at the same time." We can achieve that by developing and working on the very important quality trait of contentment and being able to honestly say, "I have everything I truly need."

Bread and Water

Reb Yehonatan relates a discussion he had with a gentile. The gentile quoted Jewish sources stating that one should be satisfied with the bare minimum, such as bread and water. The gentile added that the Torah praises the Land of Israel as being a country flowing with water, and it will have an abundance of bread. The gentile was bemused by this and asked, "Why be satisfied with bread and water? There are so many other more enjoyable and pleasant foods a person can eat for their well-being. Secondly, if Israel is the Promised Land, why isn't it blessed with deposits of rich minerals such as gold and silver?"

Reb Yehonatan directed the questioner to the writings of King Solomon where it says, "Whoever loves silver will not be satisfied with silver."

We will never be content no matter how much we have. What we need to do is come to an understanding that happiness is directly related to being satisfied with what we already possess. Bread and water are used as a metaphor for this life view. Likewise, Israel is not blessed with natural resources such as gold and silver to impress upon us that true richness is found in the flowing spring and a land that produces grain and fruits.[44]

King Solomon teaches us that if we crave for more, we will never be satisfied with the more. We will spend our whole lives trying to acquire and accumulate wealth and possessions. Once we have acquired the wealth and possessions that we set out to attain, we won't be content. We will want more wealth and more possessions. It is a destination that can never be reached.

---

44. *Yaaroth Devash 1*

What will ensue is that we will become miserable and unhappy. And the more we cannot have what we want, the more miserable and unhappier we will become.

We live in a world where we define ourselves and value who we are based on what we have. That is not a recipe for true happiness. The key to happiness is being content with what we have and not pursuing what we have not.

Converts

Kiss Their Feet

Throughout our history the Jewish people have been the target of anti-Semitism. Even when their lives were not endangered, they were treated as second-class citizens. A gentile who witnesses all of this and with sincerity wants to become part of the Jewish people and convert to Judaism needs to be treated with the greatest level of respect. The convert is walking in the footsteps of the first convert, that being Abraham. Just as Abraham was able to see the light of God within a world of darkness, so too does the convert.

One is obligated to love the convert to the extent that they should kiss their feet for what they have done. One needs to remember that the love of a convert is intertwined with the love of God.[45]

A great rabbi once said that it isn't sufficient for a non-Jew to embrace all of the 613 commandments in order to become Jewish. The convert must also feel the pain and suffering that the Jewish people have experienced since they became a nation.

No Honor

No less than thirty-six times, the Torah instructs the Jewish people to love converts and not to cause them any pain or suffering. Why then is the convert not allowed to be appointed to a position of authority? There may be reason to believe that the gentile wants to convert, hoping to assume a position of stature. This may tarnish the convert's sincerity. To ensure that the convert's reputation remains squeaky clean, they were not allowed to be appointed to any position of importance.[46]

---

45. *Yaaroth Devash 1,1*
46. *Yaaroth Devash 1,14*

To show true love does not always mean giving, allowing, and permitting. The convert is a case in point.

I Want to Convert

Within Judaism, certain divisions can never be crossed. For example, if a man's father is a cohen, then he is also a cohen. One cannot disown the position. Likewise, a person cannot purchase the role. And no matter how holy a person is, he can never become a cohen.

However, with regard to becoming a Jew, this is not the case. One can be born a Jew if one's mother was Jewish, or one can become a Jew by converting to Judaism. A fundamental question can be posed: Why do we accept converts? If God wanted the person to become a Jew, He could have orchestrated that he would be born to a Jewish mother.

Life is about growth. Life is about climbing the ladder of spirituality. Conversion to Judaism reflects this belief. Therefore, we embrace the righteous convert.[47]

Judaism is distinct in the sense that it is the only religion that does not insist that its adherents proselytize those not of the faith. It is also unique in the belief that one does not need to be of the Jewish faith to have a place in heaven. As long as a person keeps the seven Noahite laws and recognizes that they are divinely inspired, they will have a place in heaven. Perhaps this is another way to understand why we should embrace and love the convert.

---

47. *Medrash Yehonatan Kedoshim*

Creation

Who Created the World?

Some erroneously believe that there was no creator, and some accept the notion of a creator, though they believe that this creator created the world without purpose or reason and that the world functions without Divine interest or intervention.

Judaism is of the firm understanding that God created the world for a purpose. This is evident when we speak about prophecy and the role of the prophet. The Torah and the Books of the Prophets are replete with communications that took place between God and man. If there was no purpose or importance in creation, there would be no need for prophecy and the role of the prophet.

One of the basic tenets of the Jewish faith is God's constant involvement with His creation. This is clearly apparent in the process of recognizing an individual as a prophet. For a person to be accepted as a prophet, they must foretell the future to the minutest of detail. If they make even one tiny error, they cannot be considered a prophet.

The institution of prophecy could not exist unless the hand of God was involved in the running of the world. For otherwise, how could any human ever accurately predict the future without Godly input.[48]

Miracles are another indicator of God's constant involvement in worldly affairs. When the Jewish people crossed the Reed Sea as they escaped from Egypt, the waters split at the exact moment they needed to enter, and the waters returned to normal the instant the Egyptian army entered after them.

We may no longer have prophets of old. But we do experience miracles. We just have to open our eyes and see them.

---

48. *Chidushei Rabbi Yehonatan*

What Took so Long?

Many people believe that the world always existed. Their rationale is that if God is pure goodness and is the ultimate source of all goodness, why didn't He create the world earlier? In truth, if time preceded creation, then the question would be a legitimate one. Why wait so long?

However, the process of creation began with the creation of time. Prior to creation, there was no concept of time. Before creation, you could not speak in terms of earlier or later. Therefore, the question "What took so long?" is an illegitimate one, as it is based on a false premise.[49]

It is interesting to note that the very first mitzvah the Jewish people received as a nation was the command to sanctify time. There have been countless number of books written and lectures given on the topic of time management.

Recognizing that time is precious and needs to be sanctified will go a long way in helping us manage time in the most productive manner possible.

On the Small Size

The diameter of the earth is approximately 8,000 miles (about 12,874 km). The diameter of the sun is 864,000 miles (1,392,000 km). The sun is 109 times the size of earth. And the solar system is about 36 billion times larger than earth.

The purpose of creation was to create earth to be inhabited by mankind. Why then is earth so small in comparison to the sun and the rest of the universe?

The nature of a person is that they are astounded when they see an exact miniature version of a larger type. The craftsman who built it is considered far more talented than the person who built the large one.

---

49. *Yaaroth Devash 1,12*

God therefore created the earth small but containing all that it needs to further demonstrate His greatness.[50]

If we think about the smallness of planet earth and how it compares to the rest of our galaxy, and we understand that we are one single human being amongst almost 8 billion people, this may lead us to feel inadequate and of little significance. What we need to focus on is the manner by which God created mankind. Unlike all other existences, God created only one human being because every person is considered as a whole world. And what is insignificant about a whole world?

Justice or Kindness

By definition, if you label something you define it. If you call a specific object a pen, it is a pen and not a ruler. Likewise, if someone has a specific name, they are identified by that explicit name and by no other. A person called Moshe will not respond if you call out David.

Only a finite object or being can be given a name or labeled. God is infinite. How then is it that in the Torah and our prayers we refer to God by different names such as Adonai (God) and Elokim (Lord)?

When we refer to God by a particular name, we are not referring to God's essence; rather, we are referring to the specific quality and character trait that God is expressing at that particular moment. The name Adonai is used when God's manifestation is one of kindness and compassion. The name Elokim refers to God revealing Himself with the attribute of strict justice.

Why then did God create the world using the Hebrew name Elokim, which means that God's connection with the world is based on strict justice? The world as we know it is called in Hebrew *Olam Hazeh* (this world). At its conclusion, we will usher in the Messianic era and *Olam HaBa* (the world to come). This world is to be understood as a preparation or conduit for the ultimate purpose of existence, the world to come.

---

50. *Ahavat Yehonatan Tzav*

Kindness in its purest and most pristine form is to give without boundaries. If God would have created the world with God's attribute of kindness, it could never draw to a close to allow *Olam HaBa* (the world to come) to commence. Therefore, God created the world with the trait of justice, which would allow the conclusion of one world and the beginning of another.[51]

Parenting is perhaps the most challenging thing a human being can do. The repercussions are enormous. How the next generation conducts themselves is very much dependent on how their parents raised them. There is a school of thought that says that the recipe for raising healthy, well-adjusted children is to shower them with unconditional love.

Is this a formula for success? While love, kindness, compassion, and gentleness are all wonderful character traits, there needs to be a healthy amount of discipline.

King Solomon in Proverbs (13:234) writes, "Spare the rod spoil the child." We are not suggesting corporal punishment; we are, however, encouraging parents to say no. How often do we hear parents say that they are scared to tell their child no to something they want?

There is an expression, "Kill with kindness as fond apes do their young," referring to the notion that such animals sometimes crushed their offspring by hugging them too hard. If we want our children to move from one stage of life to another—from the realm of childhood to adolescence and then to adulthood—there needs to be a balancing act of appropriate measures of kindness and discipline.

---

51. *Ahavat Yehonatan Voetchanan*

Death

When the Righteous Pass Away

When a great *tzaddik* (righteous person) passes away, the whole Jewish world is plunged into mourning, and even if one didn't know the tzaddik personally, the loss is palatable. Why is this so?

The Talmud states that when the Beit Hamikdash was destroyed, the *Shechina* (part of God's presence) was removed. Where is God's manifestation to be found after the destruction?

The Talmud answers in the four cubits of Halacha (Jewish law). Rambam understands the statement to mean that God's presence is found resting on the *tzaddikim* (the righteous) of each generation.

Can we then question the Jewish people's reaction to the passing of a tzaddik? When a tzaddik leaves this world, it is as if the Beit Hamikdash has been destroyed, and we grieve and mourn accordingly.[52]

A great rabbi once explained that there are three responses to death and mourning; the third being you sing a song. When asked to elaborate, he said every day of our lives, we play another note. Sometimes they are the high notes, highlighting the happy times. Then there are the low notes that symbolize the difficult life experiences. When a person passes away, their doing does not conclude. The family and friends must continue to play that person's song.

As the Day He Died

We read about great tzadikkim whose bodies have been brought to Israel and reinterned, and even though they may have passed away many years ago, their bodies remain intact, and it appears as if they

---

52. *Yaaroth Devash 2,3*

had only recently passed away. We are well aware that the body once placed in the ground begins to decompose. Is there any significance that the body of the tzaddik doesn't seem to decay?

When we are alive, our body and soul combine to create the human being. The soul needs the body, and the body needs the soul. At the time of death, the two life partners separate. When the soul sees what has become of the body that it once called home, it becomes very pained. To alleviate the suffering of the tzadik's soul, God ensures that the tzadik's body does not deteriorate, and it is in the same condition as when the soul and body were one living entity.[53]

We cannot control what happens to our bodies after 120 years. However, while we are alive, we are very much in control. The very first thing we have to consider is that our soul sees the physical body as its partner. The soul realizes that it cannot accomplish its God-given task on earth without it. We therefore need to do whatever we can to remain healthy and well. We need to respect our bodies; we need to treat them with great care. We cannot inflict our bodies with any unnecessary type of pain.

People say cleanliness is next to Godliness. Perhaps we can add to that and say that healthiness is next to Godliness.

Atonement

The rabbis state that a person's passing is to be considered an atonement for their transgressions. How are we to understand this statement? We are not given the choice whether or not we should be born. Likewise, we are not given the choice if and when we will pass away. If we have no say or control when our last day on earth will be, how then can death be an atonement?

A person's passing in and of itself cannot be considered an act of atonement, as the person had no say in the matter. In their statement, the rabbis are impressing upon us that if a person, prior to their

---

53. *Yaaroth Devash 1*

passing, will seek forgiveness from God for all their inequities during their lifetime, then their passing will be considered an atonement.[54]

As Jews, we strongly believe in Olam HaBa (the world to come, the eternal afterlife). In a sense, this world is considered a world of preparation a transient existence that leads to the everlasting reality.

Death enables the soul to move from one form of existence to another—from being part of this physical world to becoming one with the spiritual world. There could be no greater moment and opportunity for atonement than at the time the door to one world closes and the door to another opens.

It is not by chance that there are specific prayers to be recited by a person who feels his days are numbered, or if they are not in a position to do so, the prayers are recited by family members in their presence.

---

54. *Yaaroth Devash* 1,12

Disagreements

Resolving

It is the age-old question: Should we bottle it up inside or should we let it all out?

Finding inspiration from a Biblical verse, Reb Yehonatan is of the school of thought that it is unhealthy to keep things close to one's chest. He writes that if you are angry or upset with someone, the longer you delay dealing with the matter, the more the anger will fester and the animosity will grow.

He suggests you should confront the person who you feel hurt or slighted by. This will allow the other person to explain themselves, and it may very well be that you misunderstood what they were saying, and there is no reason for you to have become angry. Or they may not have even realized that they had caused you pain, and by addressing the matter with them, you will have afforded them the opportunity to make amends. This will go a long way to building bridges and clearing the air between you.[55]

The Hebrew word "Torah" translates to "a teaching" or "an instruction." Every verse of the Torah has four basic interpretations. The literal, the homiletic, the hinted, and the mystical interpretation. The Torah giants such as Reb Yehonatan were able to penetrate the depths of the Torah's teachings and bring to the fore the richness and the multifaceted understanding of the word of God.

As important as it is to read the holy scriptures, we lose so much if we don't accompany our reading with the vast scholarly insights of the rabbinic giants of the generations.

---

55. *Tiferet Yehonatan Vayeshev*

Divine Communication

How?

The Five Books of Moshe, the Books of the Prophets, and the Books of the Writings are replete with great men and women, spiritual giants who were able to communicate with God. Such an individual was known as a *navi* (prophet). The greatest of all prophets was Moshe. Below the navi was a person called a *Baal Ruach Hakodesh*, a person on whom the spirit of God rested and who was able to see and know things beyond the human grasp.

What would we need to do to reach such levels of insight and revelation?

Reb Yehonatan writes that the early Greek philosophers such as Aristotle were of the opinion that there is no such thing as a prophet and God does not communicate with mere mortals. They came to this understanding based on the firm belief that the greater a person's intellectual capacity is and the more they had stripped themselves of earthly and physical pleasures, the more likely they could become a prophet. And since they felt that they had reached the highest level of intellectual pursuit and they had not experienced any Divine revelation, the logical conclusion was that prophecy was a manmade phenomenon.

Their mistake was in identifying the wrong path that would lead a person to prophecy and *Ruach HaKodesh* (the Divine Spirit). A key criterion in attaining the lofty heights of prophecy is not by removing oneself from the world but being part of it. When a person is intimately involved in the physical world through the performance of the mitzvot, and they are performed with great simcha and joy, a crucial step has been taken toward becoming a prophet.[56]

---

56. *Yaaroth Devash 1,11*

Jewish mysticism is fundamentally different from other forms of mysticism. The mystic of other faiths sees spiritual growth in terms of separation. The mystic will not marry, they will take vows of silence, they will fast, and they will live as hermits with minimal interaction with other human beings.

Jewish mysticism, on the other hand, says that the mystical experience is when we can see the Divine spark in the worldly and the holy in the mundane. We don't separate from the physicality of this world and all of its beauty; rather, we attempt to reveal God's presence within it.

When we make a blessing before eating food and we use the energy acquired from the foods nourishment in serving God, then we have raised the mundane to the realm of the spiritual. The prophet has reached a level where he does not see the physical nature of existence as a barrier to God's presence; rather, he sees it as a conduit.

Divine Providence

Bank Account

Maimonides writes that Divine Providence applies to every human being individually. With regard to the animal kingdom, it applies to the species as a whole (that is, whether the species should remain in existence or become extinct), and there is no Divine Providence for each specific animal.

The Zohar, however, states that Divine Providence extends to every animal individually. The Zohar records an incident in which Rabbi Shimon bar Yochai (the author of the Zohar) heard a heavenly voice that declared, "This bird shall live, and this bird shall die." All opinions, however, agree that Divine Providence applies to every human being. We need to always remember that whether we experience difficulties or success, it is all part of the Divine plan.

Our financial successes are also part of the Divine plan. It therefore makes no sense in acting contrary to the will of God, thinking that we will be successful if we bend the rules by cheating, stealing, or lying.[57]

We all want to be successful; we all want to do well financially. We spend many years in study to earn a degree or years learning the ins and outs of what it takes to do well in the business world.

There is the well-known statement that all is fair in love and war. And, by extension, the same is true in the race to become wealthy, better known as the rat race. This of course is not a Jewish perspective. We need to realize that the foundation of any successful venture and the springboard for financial growth is the understanding that God is the source of all blessings. And God and God alone is the ultimate decider of how much money we will

---

57. *Ahavat Yehonatan Shlach*

have in our bank account. That being the case, the first thing we need to study and know is the Torah's guidelines for what is considered moral and ethical when it comes to making a living.

The Long View

After the destruction of the first Temple, the Jewish people went into exile for seventy years. At the conclusion of the exile, they returned to Israel. During this period, not only were there no Jews living in Israel; there were no animals or birds there either. We could imagine that when the Jews in exile heard that even the animal kingdom had forsaken the land, they would feel that this was a further punishment meted out against this once holy and vibrant land.

However, after the seventy years had elapsed and the Jewish people had returned, they understood that the land being bereft of animals was a blessing in disguise. If the animals and birds had remained, they would have destroyed the crops and the fields, and when they came back, there would be no vegetation to speak of. By ridding the land of its animals, this protected the crops and ensured that there would be a source of food when they returned.[58]

Getting lost in a maze is half the fun. Getting lost in a maze for hours on end isn't fun. Sometimes life seems to be leading us through a maze that we cannot understand or explain. We have no idea why things happen as they do. If we could place a very tall ladder in the middle of the maze, we would be able to see both the entrance and exit. And we would be able to figure out the path we need to take. At times the path may be taking us back to the entrance, and there may be stages where the pathway is difficult to traverse. However, we are assured and confident that we are on the right track because our view extends far and wide. We can see the path that leads us out of the maze.

---

58. *Ahavat Yehonatan Shemot*

As humans, we have a very limited view of the tapestry of existence. At best, we can span a period of up to 100 years. If we could only see the big picture, we may begin to understand the whys of life.

We should, however, find a level of solace in the knowledge that God is the Master of History, and there is rhyme and reason for anything and everything. And God is with us as we traverse the maze called life.

Dreams

To Dream the Impossible Dream

Close to one-third of our lives is spent sleeping. We may not remember our dreams, but everyone is thought to dream between three and six times per night. It is thought that each dream lasts between five and twenty minutes. Around 95 percent of dreams are forgotten by the time a person gets out of bed.

The Talmud has a lengthy discussion concerning the Jewish understanding of dreams. The Torah shares with us many dreams of our forebearers, including the dreams of Pharaoh, the butler, and the baker.

One of the dreams recorded is the dream of Yaakov. While sleeping at the site where the Beit Hamikdash was built, Yaakov dreamed of angels going up and down a ladder. Yaakov interpreted the dream in a prophetic manner. How did Yaakov know that the dream was a lofty revelation and not a dream of little or no significance?

The rabbis tell us that Yaakov had immersed himself in an intense period of Torah study prior to going to sleep. Therefore, Yaakov knew that his dream had to be a dream of significance.

What we think about intensely prior to going to sleep will impact what we will dream about.[59]

Most of us struggle to make sense of what happens when we are awake and can control our actions. We could confidently say that virtually no one has a real understanding of what significance, if any, we should give to our dreams. However, what we can deduce from Yaakov's thought process is that what we think about, what we delve into intensely, impacts us. We may not even realize it, but something that we have studied, learned, and focused on deeply becomes very much part of who we are.

---

59. *Tiferet Yehonatan Vayeitzei*

Embalming

Why?

The ancient Egyptians embalmed or mummified the deceased, primarily due to their belief that the physical body would be important in the next life. Thus, preserving the body in as lifelike a way as possible was the goal of mummification. Another rationale given was that the ancient Egyptians believed that the soul lives on after a person has died. They believed that a mummified body was a place or house for the person's spirit to return to after death.

Rabbi Yehonatan felt the reason the Egyptians had this practice was based on the second explanation given. The Egyptians believed that as long as the body was intact, the soul would reside within the body. Once the body had decayed, the soul would depart.

The ancient Egyptians practiced witchcraft. They would speak to the dead in an attempt to predict the future. As long as the soul was still connected to the body, it was easier for them to connect to the soul of the departed. The Egyptians of old were not interested in preserving the body for the betterment of the deceased. Their motivation was based on self-interest. By having the soul remain connected to the body, it would allow them to communicate with the departed.[60]

Judaism not only strongly believes in the sanctity of life but also places great emphasis on the respect and honor we need to bestow on the departed. After the chevra kaddisha (the Jewish burial society) conclude preparing the body for internment, they ask forgiveness from the departed. As perhaps they may not have treated the body with the utmost respect. All the laws pertaining to burial are based on the premise that the body needs to be sanctified and revered. It is for this reason that Jewish law

---

60. *Yaaroth Devash 1*

mandates that the funeral should take place as soon as humanely possible after a person has passed away, as the departed can only find peace after it is buried. Delaying a funeral without cause is considered disrespectful to the deceased.

Embarrassment

Like a Passing Shadow

There are times when we know what we need to do, but we are embarrassed to do so. We are worried what people will think and what people will say. While this may be so, we should still do what is right and accept the fact that we may become somewhat uncomfortable and perhaps even mortified.

Reb Yehonatan offers us a unique perspective that will galvanize us into doing what is right even in the face of becoming embarrassed. He writes that life is a fleeting shadow occupied by mere mortals. Hence, the embarrassment is minimal.

True embarrassment will be experienced in the world to come, an eternal world filled with the souls of the righteous and the angels. Therefore, we should choose to be embarrassed in this world rather than being embarrassed in the world to come.[61]

There is the ten-year rule that many people live by, and it makes a lot of sense. The rule is to frame whatever happens in your life over a ten-year period. For example, if we become upset and angry that someone took our parking spot, we need to ask ourselves if, ten years from now, it will make any difference that we had to drive around the block to find another spot. If we live by the ten-year rule, many of the things that make us angry and upset would be non-events. While it is said that rules are made to be broken, this one may be worth holding on to.

---

61. *Yaaroth Devash 1,1*

Exile

Am I Unwell?

There is a saying that is somewhat ambiguous in terms of its source. While this may be true, heeding it could be a life saver. The saying is this: "Knowing the illness is half the cure." If the doctor knows what is wrong with a patient, then the doctor can begin the healing process. However, if the doctor is unable to diagnose the illness, it will be extremely difficult to know the appropriate treatment that needs to be implemented.

This is true not only when we speak of physical illness; it is equally correct when we speak of spiritual ailments. If we would only sense that we are living in exile, that we don't have the glory of the *Beit Hamikdash* (the Temple) with all its grandeur, and that we no longer have the miracles that occurred in the Beit Hamikdash, we would mourn and cry over its destruction day and night.

To merit the end of our exile, the first step is to recognize that we are indeed in exile.[62]

Mr. Cohen had borrowed money from everyone in the synagogue and then went bankrupt. All the members were crestfallen, as they had each lost a small fortune. There was one member who seemed to be unperturbed by the events. When asked why this was so, as he too had lent the person money, he explained, "Lately, when Mr. Cohen came to the prayer service, he would constantly pray and cry out that we should merit the arrival of the Messiah. When I heard that, I knew something was going sour, and I immediately asked for the return of my loan."

We should want Moshiach even when things are going well. Because no matter how good things are now, they will pale into significance when compared with what awaits us when Moshiach comes.

---

62. *Yaaroth Devash 1*

Faith

Doubt versus Certainty

The word "religion" is at times substituted with the word "faith." We speak of the Jewish religion and the Jewish faith—likewise, the Christian religion and the Christian faith. The word "faith" means belief. When a person says, "I believe the world is round," what they are really saying is, "I am not hundred percent sure that the world is round; however, I believe that it is."

A non-Jewish intellectual once approach Rabbi Yehonatan and asked, "In your Bible, it states that when in doubt, one should follow the majority. The Jewish people make up a very small percentage of the world's major religions. Why don't *you* embrace *our* faith?"

Rabbi Yehonatan responded, "The law that one must follow the majority is applicable only in a situation of uncertainty. However, our religion is not based on belief or uncertainty; we are one hundred percent sure of the validity of the Jewish religion; therefore, we do not follow the majority."

We may speak of the Jewish faith; however, it is a religion based on certainty and not on faith.[63]

Judaism is the only religion that is founded on national revelation—meaning that Moshe proclaimed that all Jews heard God speak on Mount Sinai. As it is written in the Torah, "Only beware for yourself and greatly beware for your soul, lest you forget the things that your eyes have beheld. Do not remove this memory from your heart all the days of your life. Teach your children and your children's children about the day that you stood before the Lord your God at Horev [Mount Sinai]. . ."

---

63. *Yaaroth Devash 1*

If this, in fact, did not occur, how do you think the Jewish people would respond to Moshe's claim? No one in their right mind would believe that Moshe could get away with a claim that everyone knew was an outright lie.

In truth, Judaism is not faith based. We don't need to believe that God spoke and gave us the Torah on Mount Sinai. We know it to be true because our parents told us who had heard it from their parents, going all the way back to our collective ancestors who stood at the base of the mountain and heard the word of God.

Fear

Reacting to Fear

One of God's commandments is that we are to fear God. The more we reflect on God's awesomeness and how God created the world and that we are truly insignificant in comparison, this will awaken within us a sense of fear of God. And the more we reflect on these ideas, the greater our fear of God will become.

How do we understand this positive commandment when our experience is that fear can be counterproductive?

We are familiar with the phrase, "To be paralyzed with fear." For example, we wake up in the middle of the night because we hear a strange sound in the house. Very often, we are so afraid we can't move. Fear can be debilitating; it doesn't allow us to function properly.

There is a difference between fearing God and fear of the unknown. In a sense, fearing God is part of our DNA; it is part of our nature. Since it is not something foreign to us, we are comfortable with this type of fear. In fact, it is something we happily embrace. Fear that stems from an experience or an incident that is foreign to us can cause us to become petrified to the extent that we can't function properly.[64]

Fear in and of itself is not a bad thing. It is our mind telling us to be careful, that what we are attempting to do could be dangerous, such as walking across a tightrope fifty feet off the ground with no netting below. We also need to be aware that certain fears are truly unhealthy, and we would need to seek professional help—such as in the case of agoraphobia, the fear of not wanting to leave our home.

---

64. *Yaaroth Devash* 1,4

However, when it comes to the fear of heaven, it is very easy to discern whether or not our fear is healthy. If our fear is an impetus in coming closer to God and performing more commandments, then we know it is a healthy and proper fear of heaven. If, however, the fear causes us to feel down and lethargic and diminish our interest and desire to reach out to God, then we know that the fear is unhealthy and cannot be considered a true fear of heaven.

Fish

Brain Food

Of all the animals, the fish has the most spiritual energy and spiritual life force. In this respect, the fish is the most similar to the human; therefore, when a person eats fish, it improves his mental capacity. So, when people say that fish is brain food, they have the backing of the rabbis.[65]

People say that fish is brain food. Is there any truth to this? Studies have shown that certain fish are a good source of omega-3 fatty acids. Omega-3s help build membranes around each cell in the body, including brain cells. They can, therefore, improve the structure of brain cells called neurons. A 2017 study found that people with high levels of omega-3s had increased blood flow in the brain. The researchers also identified a connection between omega-3 levels and better cognition, or thinking abilities. These results suggest that eating foods rich in omega-3s, such as oily fish, may boost brain function.[66]

---

65. *Ahavat Yehonatan Sukkot*

66. Amen, Daniel G., William S. Harris, Parris M. Kidd, Somayeh Meysami, and Cyrus A. Raji. "Quantitative Erythrocyte Omega-3 EPA Plus DHA Levels are Related to Higher Regional Cerebral Blood Flow on Brain SPECT." *Journal of Alzheimer's Disease* 58, no. 4 (2017); 1189–1199. doi: 10.3233/JAD-170281.

Flattery

Will Get You Nowhere

Flattery was always viewed in a strong negative manner by the rabbis. Flattery is generally understood to mean excessive and insincere praise or compliments, given especially to further one's own interest.

Reb Yehonatan offers another very insightful understanding of what flattery means. Flattery is not just when you say something that is insincere and excessive. Flattery can occur even when you don't say something. When you see someone doing something wrong and you remain quiet and don't intervene and impress upon the person that their behavior is unacceptable falls under the rubric of flattery.

The reason for this is that when the person who has transgressed sees that you say absolutely nothing, he takes that to mean that you are condoning his behavior. Unfortunately, what very often happens is that we don't remain silent, and we praise the person for what they have done, even though we know that it is wrong.[67]

We are familiar with the well-known saying, "The darkest places in hell are reserved for those who maintain their neutrality in times of moral crisis." This is very much in line with the sentiment expressed by Reb Yehonatan. If we remain silent when we see inappropriate behavior occurring, we become part of the problem and not part of the solution.

It really makes no difference how we define flattery. What does make a difference is how we respond when confronted by evil. We have three options: we can applaud the evil, we can remain silent, or we can shout from the rooftops in the strongest of terms that we condemn the evil. The choice is clear; no one wants to end up in hell.

---

67. *Yaaroth Devash* 1,15

Food

Nonkosher

The saying "You are what you eat" means that it is important to eat good food in order to be healthy and fit. Nutrients from the foods we eat provide the foundation of the structure, function, and wholeness of every cell in our body—from the skin, hair, and bones to the muscles, digestive system, and immune system.

"You are what you eat" is correct from a spiritual sense as well. God, in His infinite wisdom, knows what foods are spiritually healthy for us and those that are not.[68]

When a doctor treats a patient with blocked arteries, one of the first steps the doctor will take is to modify the person's diet. They will encourage the patient to increase their eating of avocados and asparagus, among others as both are considered to be natural artery-clearing. We all understand that if someone wants to become an elite athlete, it is important they follow a regimented diet to enhance their ability to perform at the highest level.

We all have, in a sense, spiritual arteries that allow us to absorb holiness and spirituality. By eating nonkosher food, we are blocking our spiritual arteries, and it becomes very difficult to receive and absorb holiness. And by eating kosher food, this will enhance our spiritual self and we will be primed for spiritual greatness. We are what we eat, in more ways than one.

The Why Is as Important as the How

We can likely all recall our parents impressing upon us as children the need to have good table manners, like making sure our elbows are not

---

68. *Yaaroth Devash 1*

on the table. Equally and perhaps of more importance is the why: Why do we eat?

If we eat to be healthy and use our good health to serve God, then the mundane act of eating becomes a holy endeavor and the food consumed becomes elevated to a higher spiritual plane. A person who eats simply because he enjoys the food or because he wants to have the energy to indulge in personal pleasure is no better than an animal. Animals also eat because they like the food and need the energy to pursue their desires.[69]

Life's experiences can be divided into three categories: black, white, and gray. Black represents all forbidden acts, such as stealing. White signifies all acts that we are obligated in doing, such as giving charity. And gray represents everything in between, acts that are neither sinful nor obligatory.

Most of our lives are spent in the gray zone. However, we have the ability to turn gray into white. We can elevate the mundane and the ordinary to make it holy. Most of our waking hours are spent trying to make a living. What we do with our hard-earned incomes will very much impact in which category all those hours will end up. Will they stay in the gray or will they be elevated to the white? If we use our disposable earnings to indulge in personal pleasure, then the many hours we spent working will remain ordinary and mundane. If, however, we will use those funds to help those less fortunate than ourselves, our working hours will be elevated and viewed as a noble and righteous endeavor.

Good Table Manners

Different cultures set different priorities in terms of table etiquette. In Thailand, it is considered rude to put food in your mouth with a fork. In parts of India, it is deemed bad manners to touch your plate with your left hand.

---

69. *Yaaroth Devash*

Judaism also has guidelines of what is considered inappropriate behavior around the dining room table. For example, we must do our utmost not to become angry and allow the meal to descend into a shouting match.

Reb Yehonatan has a number of suggestions of what should take place when the family sits down to a meal. When everyone is relaxed and eating their meal, it is a perfect opportunity to share words of Torah or initiate a stimulating discussion. He also suggests that we could initiate a discussion about moral behavior.

Our eating can be a holy exercise when we eat to garner strength to serve God.

Finally, it would be considered a great virtue if we could ensure that seated at the table would be a person of lesser means and, at the very least, to make sure that the poor have food to eat.[70]

Much has been written about the positive impact that occurs when a family sits down and eats dinner together. It is a wonderful opportunity for the family to bond and reconnect.

There is, however, another dimension worth considering. One of the beauties of Judaism is how it enables us to take a mundane everyday occurrence and give it meaning and substance. The Talmud writes that the table we eat at is considered an altar. If that understanding becomes the backdrop to our eating experience, it enables us to see our consumption of food not simply to satisfy our hunger or to indulge in culinary pleasure but also as fuel to enable us to serve God.

Food for the Mind

We are constantly bombarded by what foods are good for us and which foods are deemed to be harmful. Oily fish is considered good for the brain, as it is a good source of omega-3 fats.

---

70. *Yaaroth Devash*

The *Cohanim* (the priests) were considered more scholarly than the rest of the Jewish people. This was attributed to the fact that they consumed meats of the animal that had been brought as a sacrifice in the Temple, and as a result, their food was saturated with sparks of holiness.[71]

God, in His infinite wisdom, shared with us which foods are kosher and which are not kosher. Kosher food is beneficial for our spiritual well-being, while nonkosher food is considered detrimental to our spiritual state. Nonkosher food is for the soul what poison is for the body.

71. *Ahavat Yehonatan Toldot*

Free Choice

Man's Greatest Gift

Rambam writes that one of the main obstacles to a person repenting is the false notion that God predetermines our behavior and actions. Hence, we cannot be held responsible for our actions. There are three rationales that would seem to justify this view.

The first is a belief that sounds like this: "I was born like that, and there is nothing I can do about it." The second is the belief that the zodiac sign under which we were born influences who we really are. And, finally, the third is that those who feel a strong connection to God with a basic understanding of Jewish mysticism conclude that, "if God knows the future, He knows exactly what I am going to do. How then can I possibly change my behavior?"

The seeming predisposition to certain behaviors that are beyond human choice is contrary to a specific verse in the Torah. The verse reads, "Behold, I have placed before you today life and good and death and evil . . . You shall choose life." The Torah is impressing upon us that we are not preprogrammed, and we are able to make choices.

Rambam clearly writes that God's knowledge is different from our knowledge, and God's knowledge of our future does not in any way impact the choices we choose to make.[72]

Nature and nurture play a vital role in shaping and fashioning who we are. However, we must never forget that the greatest gift given to mankind is that we always have the ability to choose. And we should treasure that gift and choose right over wrong.

---

72. *Ahavat Yehonatan*

Do We Really Have Free Choice?

If you were brought up in a vegetarian home and were indoctrinated from a very young age on the ills of killing a living creature for your sustenance, did you freely choose to remain a vegetarian?

It is worth noting that we have absolutely no control over what defines our humanity. We didn't have a choice if we would be born male or female. We didn't decide who our parents would be. We did not decide *when* we would be born, whether in the Middle Ages or in the twenty-first century. We were also not given the option of *where* we would be born.

God has predestined whether we will be intelligent, how wealthy we will be, and how long we will live. The Talmud explains that our ability to choose freely is limited to those areas in life that relate to our service and relationship with God. We can choose to keep shabbat, and we can choose to keep kosher. We can also choose to steal or choose to take the life of a living creature.

That being the case, why would a person be punished if they robbed someone of their possessions or murdered someone? If it had not been preordained, then no matter how much you will strategize and attempt to execute your plan, you will fail. And if it was part of God's master plan that the person should be robbed or killed, why should you be held responsible when you are simply fulfilling God's wishes?

Reb Yehonatan writes that such a line of thinking stems from our evil inclination and outright foolishness. He explains that we are judged not only by what we do but also by why we do it. By way of analogy, the enemy of the king attempts to poison the king; what the person does not know is that while the poison he administered to the king would kill a healthy person, the king has a particular illness that the poison actually heals. Even though he has healed the king, this individual will be tried for murder since his intent was to murder the king.

God knows the thoughts of man, and when a person steals or commits the ultimate heinous crime of taking human life, the robber or murderer definitely doesn't view himself as a messenger of God, and he will be punished for the crime he has committed.[73]

Free choice and Divine Providence are from the deepest ideas in Jewish theology. One can spend a lifetime grappling with these concepts and still be none the wiser. We should not forget that God is infinite, and we are finite. And the finite can never begin to comprehend the infinite.

We don't have a say in our gender, our parents, our country of birth, or our moment of birth. However, we have the ultimate say in what kind of human being we will evolve into, and that is what truly defines us.

---

73. *Yaaroth Devash* 1,6

Friendship

Don't Forget Your Friends

Reb Yehonatan points out something we know only too well: Money doesn't just go into a person's pocket or bank account; it also goes to a person's head. He writes that we often see a person who becomes extremely wealthy forgetting his old friends and no longer wanting to associate with people of lesser means. He writes that the opposite of this was one of the great qualities of our forefather Yaakov. When Yaakov left his father-in-law's home, he had become extremely wealthy, yet he did not forget those he knew before he was wealthy.[74]

We often hear people say, "Now I know who my real friends are," after losing all their money. It is very sad for a person to discover that many of his friends were only there for the ride, and once the gravy train had crashed, he never heard from them again.

Something we should constantly remind ourselves is that it isn't by chance that for centuries money was in the form of round coins. The rabbis tell us that when speaking of wealth, it is never static; sometimes we can be on the top of the world, and then we could lose a fortune and hit rock bottom. It is like a round object that rolls, the top rolls to the bottom and hopefully it makes it back to the top.

Friendships should never be based solely on what we each have in the bank, as it is not necessarily a lifetime possession.

---

74. *Tiferet Yehonatan Chukat*

God

Love and Fear

We are obligated to love and fear God. What type of relationship should we strive for: one based on love or one founded on fear? Does God prefer that we love Him or that we have reverence for Him?

King Solomon in Proverbs writes, "Love conceals all transgressions." Reb Yehonatan explains it to mean that God is more forgiving when He sees that we are desiring to connect with Him because of our profound love for Him.[75]

There is a well-known saying that "Love conquers all." While this is debatable, we can all agree that love is an extremely powerful emotion. What does it mean to love God and how does one develop that love?

"Love at first sight" makes no sense. How can you love someone if the only thing you know about them is what they look like? You haven't even heard their voice let alone know anything about who they are. A more appropriate phrase would be "Lust at first sight" because you cannot love someone if you know nothing about them.

What distinguishes the human being from the animal kingdom is the intellectual capacity to increase or curb our emotions. The more we know someone and the more we are exposed to their virtues and refined qualities, the more we will appreciate them and want to be part of their lives. This is something an animal is incapable of doing.

This is equally true when we speak of our relationship with God. The more we learn and study about God, the more we will come to realize that every breath we take is a gift from the Almighty and that we owe our very

---

75. *Tiferet Yehonatan Eikev*

existence to God. *If we contemplate how God, the Master of the Universe, is concerned and intimately involved in every aspect of our lives, we realize that everything we have is a gift from Him. This will awaken within us a tremendous love for Him.*

True Love

In a very beautiful way, Reb Yehonatan describes what it means to truly love God. It is when we are willing to forsake all imaginable desires just to be given the chance and opportunity to give pleasure to God. If we love God with the very fiber of our body, there is nothing we could desire more than giving God pleasure.

Reb Yehonatan offers the following analogy to explain this profound sense of love between man and God: A servant is willing to live without food in the open without shelter during the bitter cold and relentless rain of winter and the scorching sun of summer in order to please the king.[76]

Rabbinic literature is replete with the analogy of a groom and a bride to reference God and the Jewish people—with God being the groom and the Jewish people being the bride. The giving of the Torah on Mount Sinai is described as being the marriage between God and the Jewish people. By extension, the love that is fostered between husband and wife is an indication what love between God and the Jewish people should look like.

Why We Serve

There are three different reasons we would want to serve God.

The first is purely self-centered. We serve God because we feel that this is the conduit to having a wonderful life. We believe if we do what God wants, we will be rewarded with good health, we will be blessed with long life, and we will have the financial success to enjoy it all. Such service is deemed as valueless. Why? What would our reaction be if we

---

76. *Ahavat Yehonatan Voetchanan*

did everything right, but we didn't become wealthy? We would think that we had simply wasted our time and will no longer want to serve God.

In a sense, it is similar to a student in the classroom. When the student behaves, he is rewarded, and when he misbehaves, he is punished. It is therefore advantageous for the student to behave. However, if the student sees that being good and doing everything right doesn't bring any rewards, he will simply not bother in the future.

The second reason is loftier. We don't focus on the rewards and punishments we will experience in this world since our time here is brief and fleeting. Therefore, any reward or punishment will be brief and short-lived. Our focus is on the eternal world—*Olam HaBa* (the world to come). We want to serve God because we know that the rewards in the world to come will be eternal.

While such service is superior, it still falls short. Ultimately, it is self-service. We are not just serving God; we are also serving ourselves. We want the prize that is on offer, and we will do whatever it takes to get it.

The third and ultimate reason for serving God is simply because of our desire to fulfill God's commandments. There is no personal interest or gain to be had that is influencing us in serving Him. To the extent that if we were told that by doing what is right, we would be sent to *gehenom* (hell) and, by transgressing God's will, we would be allowed to enter *Gan Eden* (the Garden of Eden), we would still do what is right and not even contemplate doing what is wrong.[77]

Relationships are tricky affairs; sometimes it is difficult to gauge if it is healthy or whether it needs attending to. One of the ways to measure the strength of one's marriage is to ask ourselves one simple question, do we keep a checklist? Is the relationship tit for tat (that is, if you do something nice for me, I will do something nice for you)? Such a marriage needs fixing. We should want to be generous with our spouses and help them simply because they are our partners for life.

---

77. *Chidushei Reb Yehonatan*

Count Our Blessings

Reb Yehonatan laments the precarious position the Jewish people were in during his lifetime, how the lengthy exile had taken such a severe toll on the Jewish nation and how we had very little strength and energy to continue. He therefore suggested that we should attempt to focus on what we can accomplish and not what we can't. He felt that we should recite the *Shema*, *Birchat Hamzon* (grace after meals), blessings on food and blessings on the *mitzvot* (commandments) with great concentration and imbued with great joy.[78]

When we are feeling depressed or just down in the dumps, we are told that we should focus on three things in our lives that we can be proud of and that will help us in lifting our mood.

It is interesting that Reb Yehonatan emphasizes the importance of saying the blessings with great attentiveness. Reb Yehonatan lived in a time that was very challenging for the Jew. There was widespread anti-Semitism. The Jew was a second-class citizen at best. We were restricted where we could live and what we could do in terms of making a living. The average Jew was extremely poor, barely making ends meet.

Reb Yehonatan wanted the Jew to focus on the positive aspects of his life. He may not have had a lot of food, but he did have some food and he was healthy enough to eat it. We may have been persecuted, but we were still able to perform many of the mitzvot. And, therefore, we should bless and thank God for these gifts. Hopefully this would lift our spirits and give us the strength and fortitude to do more of God's commandments.

All Our Faculties

Tisha B'Av, the ninth day of the month of Av, is the darkest day on the Jewish calendar. It was on that day that both *Batei Mikdash* (Temples) were destroyed.

---

78. *Yaaroth Devash* 1,3

The three Shabbatot leading up to this date the haftorah is not reflective of the weekly reading; rather, it speaks about the destruction of the Temple and the exile of the Jewish people. The first begins with the phrase "The *words* of Jeremiah." The second begins with the words "*Hear* the words of God." And the third begins with the words "The *vision* of Isiah." The three sections speak of speech, hearing, and sight. The Jewish people at the time sinned by what they said, by what they heard, and by what they saw.

Likewise, we can serve God by what we say, hear, and see—for example, with our speech, when we say words of Torah and prayer; with what we hear by listening to a Torah class or hearing the blowing of the shofar; and with what we see by making a blessing when we see the new moon or a rainbow.[79]

We all have talents. We need to view them as gifts that God has given to each and every one of us. And these gifts can be and should be used in the service of God.

If we are an artist, we can make beautiful paintings or sculptures that depict a biblically or holy scene that can inspire people. If we are musically inclined, when we play an instrument or we sing beautifully, we can touch the souls of so many people. And even if we don't excel in the arts, perhaps we have great organizational skills or are computer savvy. There are so many ways to use our skills in advancing Jewish life in the twenty-first century.

Is God Holy?

In our liturgy, we often refer to God as *Atah Kadosh*, which is translated as "You are holy." This translation is not completely accurate. A more precise translation would be, "You are separate; You are removed."

God is completely removed and separate from anything physical. The human mind does not have the capacity to comprehend God in

---

79. *Ahavat Yehonatan Chazzan*

anyway at all. God is indescribable. The only thing we can say about God is that He is the cause of all that is caused.

God is infinite. By definition, *infinite* is indescribable. By defining something, you have automatically given it limitations. If you can define it, it is no longer infinite because it must have limitations and boundaries by which it can be defined.[80]

How can we refer to God both in the holy texts and in our prayers by specific names? As soon as you call something or someone by a name, it is defined by and limited to that name. For example, if someone's name is Moshe, then the person is Moshe and not Leah.

God's essence is simplistic and indescribable. However, when God relates and involves Himself in the world, He manifests Himself using different attributes. These distinct qualities are described by using different names of God. For example, when God manifests Himself with the attribute of strict justice, the word describing God is Elokim. When compassion and mercy are expressed, the name Hashem is used.

God's Gifts to the Jewish People

The Talmud states that God gave the Jewish people three gifts. He gave them the Torah, the Land of Israel, and the world to come. The three festivals we celebrate each year correspond to these gifts.

On Shavuot, we received the Torah.

On Pesach, we left Egypt and began our journey toward Israel.

On Sukkot, we enter the sukkah. The sukkah protects us as does the world to come.

To enter the world to come, we need to repent and receive God's forgiveness. Therefore, the festival of Sukkot is preceded by Rosh Hashanah and Yom Kippur. It is on these days that we repent and beseech God for His forgiveness.[81]

---

80. *Yaaroth Devash 1,1*

81. *Yaaroth Devash 1,1*

The Jewish understanding of hell, or in Hebrew gehenom, is very different from the understanding professed by other faiths. God does not punish for the sake of punishing. By way of analogy, if we are invited to a wedding, we want to make sure our attire is pristine. We would be embarrassed if we had to attend the wedding and there was a stain on our tie or our dress was ripped. Prior to the wedding, if need be, we would send our clothing to the drycleaners or to a tailor.

Likewise, gehenom is a cleansing station or a repair stop to ensure that when we enter the world to come, we have our dancing shoes on ready for the first dance.

Goodness

Try It

The ultimate question people ask is, "Why did God create the world?"

It definitely wasn't because God was lacking something or needed something. Rather, God is the ultimate source of all goodness and He wanted to bestow goodness upon His creations and He therefore created the world.[82]

We must never forget that the only reason we are here is because of God's desire to do acts of goodness. We need to emulate God by doing good for our fellow man. A great rabbi once said, "The reason why the soul descends to earth for 70 years is in order to do a favor for another person."

---

82. *Yaaroth Devash 1*

Gratitude

Thank God

Imagine the following scenario: You excelled in school and the school rewarded you for your achievements by giving you a laptop as a gift. It would be highly unlikely that you would use the laptop during class time when not authorized. The reason is obvious: How could you use something given to you by the school to break school rules? Most of us would be comfortable with this line of reasoning.

By extension the same should be true when we think about our relationship with God. Recognizing that our very lives are a gift from God should impact how we conduct ourselves. How could we use our tongues to speak slander, how could we use our hands to strike an innocent man, and how could we use our mind to plot a crime when they are all God's gifts to mankind.

A true sense of gratitude is the perfect formula to prevent a person from sinning.[83]

Gratitude is a wonderful quality. We teach our children from a very young age the importance of saying thank you. Perhaps we need to focus more on extending that sense of gratitude toward God. Human nature is that we take our health for granted. It is only when we are unwell that we begin to appreciate what it means to be healthy. We should never take our good health or financial success for granted.

The next time we say, "Thank God," let us really say, "Thank God."

---

83. *Yaaroth Devash* 1,15

True Comfort

After the destruction of the *Beit Hamikdash* (Temple) and the Jews went into exile, God asked our forefathers and Moshe to offer words of comfort to the Jewish people. God wanted these great Jewish leaders to encourage them to return to the Land of Israel and rebuild the Temple. Each attempted to find the appropriate language that would accomplish this; however, they were unsuccessful.

Why were the Jews unable and unwilling to hear their words of solace? They were waiting for our forefathers and Moshe to say the word "everlasting." They wanted to be told that their return to the Land of Israel and their rebuilding of the Temple would be everlasting. This promise was something our forefathers and Moshe were not in a position to convey because the Jews may once again revert to their evil practices, forcing God to destroy the Temple and banish them from the Holy Land.

It was only when God comforted the Jewish people and encouraged them to leave exile and rebuild the Temple did they listen. They heeded the word of God since God was in a position to tell them that there would come a time when the world would be filled with His glory and sin would be banished to the annals of history. And, at that time, the Temple would indeed be everlasting.[84]

The traditional blessing, we bestow upon mourners is, "May God comfort you amongst the mourners of Zion and of Jerusalem." Why do we mention God in our words of comfort?

Human nature is such that when we have experienced tragedy or misfortune, we will only find true comfort if somehow the tragedy can be reversed and we can be assured that it will never happen again. This is something only God can ensure; therefore, when we comfort the mourners, we need to mention God.

---

84. *Yaaroth Devash*

We need to be sensitive to those who have suffered misfortune and recognize that no matter what we say or do, our words and actions will never completely alleviate their heartache. And together with our words of comfort, we should offer a silent prayer to God on their behalf.

Happiness

Keep It Personal

We have always been concerned by the power and influence of the *ayin hara* (known as the evil eye in English). One of the ways we can negate the impact of the evil eye is by maintaining a low profile. We may ask someone how many grandchildren they have and very often the answer we receive is, "We don't count" or "Blessed is God, a few."

In Yiddish, there is an expression that loosely translates into English as "Don't throw it at the eyes." This means we should not conduct ourselves in a manner that will cause others to become jealous.

Reb Yehonatan writes that this is also true when we speak about expressing one's joy. He says there are two types of joy: the joy of the heart and the joy of the mouth. The joy of the heart describes our internal and personal sense of happiness—a happiness that I share with no one. The joy of the mouth is the happiness I express through my words and my behavior.

The joy of the mouth needs to be balanced. We do not want to arouse the envy of others who are curious and perhaps even somewhat envious of our happiness. However, the joy of the heart can be unbridled as only God will be aware of what we are feeling.[85]

On the one hand, every moment of happiness and every beautiful experience is a gift from God. To truly express our profound gratitude for God's abundance and kindness, we should want to demonstrate our thanks and gratitude to Him in the most public manner possible. However, by doing so, we may cause pain and anguish to our fellow Jews who are struggling to come to terms with why they are less fortunate and why they don't seem to have much to be joyful about. We therefore must rejoice in moderation.

---

85. *Ahavat Yehonatan Nitzavim*

Reb Yehonatan shows how we can accomplish both. Our unrestrained sense of happiness should be internalized. Man will not be privy to it and will not be envious. And God who knows what is in our hearts and in our minds will see our eternal sense of gratitude. Meanwhile, our outward expression of happiness will remain somewhat restrained.

The lesson taught is truly sublime; even when our intentions are noble, we must always be conscious how our actions may impact others.

God's Joy

Reb Yehonatan writes that God cannot experience true joy when there are people who are struggling to put food on their tables. And when we alleviate their suffering, this brings great joy to the Almighty.[86]

I have no doubt that, as children or even as we matured into adulthood, we were sometimes motivated to do something because we knew it would make our parents proud and happy. We may not always want to give charity and we may be able to find many sound reasons not to. However, who would not want to make our Father in heaven happy? Is there anything loftier than knowing that by feeding the poor and clothing the destitute, we bring great simcha to God Himself. That should be sufficient impetus to help someone in need.

True Joy

What makes you happy? I am sure this is a question that we have all been asked or we have asked ourselves. And without a doubt the answer to this question will cover the full spectrum of life's experiences. Reb Yehonatan writes that, as a Jew, our greatest sense of bliss should be when we are fulfilling God's commandments.[87]

---

86. *Yaaroth Devash* 2,12

87. *Yaaroth Devash* 2,12

Another question we need to ask ourselves is "What is my relationship with God, His Torah, and His mitzvot? Is it strong or does it need improvement?" How do we answer such a question? How could we possibly gauge an honest response?

The answer is fairly simple. By way of example, we have to carry a sack of rocks and a sack of precious stones, both weighing the same amount to a particular destination. And once we have reached it, the sack and its contents are ours. Which sack would we be happy carrying? The answer is obvious.

If we feel an affinity to something, if we feel a deep sense of closeness to someone, and if we are passionate about an idea, then we will be overjoyed and truly ecstatic to accomplish the task. If we view the study of Torah and the fulfillment of mitzvot as a sack of rocks, we will do them begrudgingly. If we see them as a sack of diamonds, we will fulfill them with great glee and joy.

How do we measure our relationship with God? Simple, are we happy, glad, and joyful or are we indifferent and apathetic in our service of God? And there is your answer.

Finding Joy

Who doesn't want to be happy? We all deserve to be happy. But at times it seems elusive and beyond our grasp. When things are going well and we don't have a worry in the world, it is very easy to be in a good mood. The challenge is when things are not going according to plan. How do we find happiness when we are struggling and feel weighed down by the many obstacles and impediments placed in our path?

Happiness is a serious business; you have to work hard to acquire it and even harder to retain it. Reb Yehonatan writes that there are two prerequisites for attaining happiness.

The first is recognizing that having a sense of happiness is directly correlated to a particular mindset. He says we need to internalize, in a very meaningful way, that everything and anything we experience comes directly from God, and God is the source of goodness. The second is distancing ourselves from any form of conflict or disagreement. We should pursue peace and harmony. If we are able to live a life with these two guiding principles, we will be experiencing aspects of the world to come in the here and now.[88]

We have all likely experienced or seen two children fighting and calling each other all sorts of names but then five minutes later they are playing together as if they are the best of friends. Meanwhile, adults can bare grudges for so long that they don't even remember why they are fighting. Why is this so?

Adults prefer being right over being happy, while children prefer being happy over being right. As adults, we have a choice to be happy or to be right—let's choose right by choosing to be happy.

It Is in the Giving

Milestones are moments of great joy and happiness—for example, the day we get married, holding our newborn for the first time, taking our children to the chuppah, and the list goes on and on. There are also experiences that bring us great *simcha* (happiness and joy). While different things bring different people pleasure, we would all likely agree that if the king, queen, president, or prime minister of our country were to call us on the phone to ask us to do them a personal favor, it would be one of the highlights of our lives. We wouldn't be able to wipe the grin off our face for a very long time.

Reb Yehonatan writes that we may not realize it, but we experience this every day of our lives. Every time we do a mitzvah, when we make a blessing on the lulav and etrog, and when we hear the sound of the shofar, we are doing the will of the King of Kings. How could we not feel a tremendous amount of joy and happiness?[89]

---

88. *Yaaroth Devash* 2,12

89. *Yaaroth Devash* 1,11

Mankind, in general, has never been as affluent as we are now. Yet, at the same time, as a society, we have never been as depressed or as anxious as we are now. Studies suggest that close to 15 percent of the U.S. population is on antidepressants.[90] Clearly, the accumulation of wealth and the procuring of fancy houses and cars have no impact on our mood and frame of mind.

It may seem counterintuitive, but we are happiest when we are giving to others. Logic would seem to suggest that the more we receive from others and the more presents we are given, the happier we are. The truth is to the contrary. The more we put ourselves out there and the more we are willing to help those less fortunate, the happier we will be.

---

90. Brody, M.P.H., Debra J., and Qiuping Gu, M.D., Ph.D. "Antidepressant Use Among Adults: United States, 2015-2018." NCHS Data Brief No. 377, September 2020. Accessed March 3, 2022. www.cdc.gov/nchs/products/databriefs/db377.htm.

Haughtiness

The Cure

The greater a scholar is and the more knowledgeable he is, the more likely he will feel a sense of grandeur and self-importance. He will aggressively pursue honor and glory, even at the expense of others. He will act as if there is no one else who has reached his stature of greatness.

It is for this reason that we extol Moshe's greatness. Moshe had received the Torah directly from God; he was the teacher of all the Jewish people. There was never a person who had reached his heights. Yet, the Torah writes that he was the humblest person who ever existed.

How can we deal with the terrible quality trait of arrogance? The answer in one word is perspective; one has to put things in perspective. Twice a day, we say the Shema where we declare the oneness of God. The oneness of God is understood to mean that there is nothing besides God. God is all encompassing. When a person realizes that wherever they are, they stand before God, the Creator of the Universe, and how he is fulfilling the will of God every moment of each day and thereby becomes attached to Him, this will automatically arouse within him a true sense of humility.

One can be the greatest Torah scholar of the generation and at the same time be extremely humble. It is all a question of perspective and recognizing that God is everywhere.[91]

The mystics offer another understanding. Moshe realized that everything he possessed, including his incredible intellect and his innate qualities, were all a gift from God. And if someone else would have been given the same

---

91. *Yaaroth Devash 1,1*

opportunities and abilities, they would have reached even greater heights then he did.

We too need to tell ourselves that, with all that God has bequeathed us, we haven't even accomplished half of what we are capable of so we have nothing to be arrogant about.

Our Choice

How do we define holiness? How would we describe a holy person?

More than likely, we would describe the person as having separated themselves from the rest of society, living life as a hermit, speaking very little if speaking at all, sustaining themselves on the bare minimum, and even desisting from entering the sanctity of marriage.

Reb Yehonatan shares from the writings of Josephus that, at the time of the Roman occupation of Israel during the second Temple period, many Israelites were living such a lifestyle. The vast majority of the Jewish people at the time frowned upon such behavior.

If we want to lead and live a life that is both holy and spiritual and we are struggling to discover the path we need to take, Reb Yehonatan suggests we ask ourselves two questions: The first is "Would the majority of mankind find it enjoyable living like a hermit and refraining from earthly pleasures?" The second is, "If all Jews would lead such a lifestyle, would we flourish as a nation?" To both questions the answer is obviously no. If that is the case, argues Reb Yehonatan, then such a life is neither holy nor spiritual.[92]

If God wanted us to separate ourselves from all that the world has to offer, he should have made us angelic, and we could have remained living in the spiritual realm. Our souls were placed in a physical body, and we inhabit a physical world for a purpose. Our role is to elevate the mundane and the ordinary. When we eat and make a blessing, we have elevated the food.

---

92. *Tiferet Yehonatan Kedoshim*

And when we enjoy the wonders of the world and recognize how it is part of God's creation, then we have experienced a spiritual moment.

Everything that exists falls into three categories: That which is prohibited (such as the prohibition of stealing or eating foods that are not kosher like bacon); that which is holy (such as a Torah or acts that we fulfill such as men putting on tefillin daily and women lighting candles prior to Shabbat); and that which is neither prohibited nor obligatory, the category in which we spend most of our lives.

Here is an example: roughly one-third of our lives is spent sleeping, when we are oblivious to the world around us. To which category does this belong? There is no mitzvah to sleep and there is no prohibition in staying awake. However, if we go to sleep to enable us to serve God refreshed and reinvigorated, then our sleep will be considered a consecrated and holy act.

Healing

Blink of an Eye

Reb Yehonatan was a world-renowned orator, and on numerous instances, he was called upon to debate the leaders of other faiths who sought to denigrate the Word of God and to attack the Jewish people. On one occasion, he was instructed to explain the blessing, "[God] heals His people the Jewish Nation."

Reb Yehonatan explained the blessing to mean that we should never abandon hope and that God can heal us in a blink of an eye. This understanding is supported by an incident that is recorded in the Talmud. The Talmud relates that when Moshe was a young man living in Pharaoh's palace, Pharaoh suspected that Moshe was a Jew and instructed his guards to behead him. As the guard was swinging the sword down onto Moshe's neck, a miracle occurred, and his neck turned into marble and Moshe's life was sparred.[93]

One of the worst things a person could ever hear from a doctor who is treating a loved one is, "If you believe in a God, now is the time to pray," or "We need a miracle."

In Yiddish there is a saying that translates into English, "A small doctor is accompanied by a small angel and a great doctor is joined by a great angel. Therefore, we should always seek out the best doctor as the doctor is being guided by a great angel.

We should not turn to God in prayer when the situation is dire and all other avenues seem to lead to a dead end. Rather, we must believe that it is God who heals His people, the Jewish nation, and the medical fraternity are God's angels of cure.

---

93. *Hameor Hagadol*

Spiritual Medicine

Reb Yehonatan was a *maggid* (preacher) of great fame. The role of the maggid was to inspire the congregation in the adherence of Torah and mitzvot. He lamented the fact that, in his times, many were lax in their religious duties, and he would encourage them to accept higher levels of observance and adherences. The response he would receive was, "Our parents and grandparents never practiced these stringencies. Why should we?"

To this, Reb Yehonatan would respond, "We have no problem introducing into our lives foods that our forebearers never dreamed of. For example, tea and coffee. For many, it is a morning ritual; something we can't live without. Yet both beverages were introduced in Europe in the early 1700s. And at the time, no one wondered, "If our parents and grandparents never drank tea or coffee, should we be drinking it?'"[94]

When we look in the mirror. Most of us are happy with what we see. I am not talking about our physical appearance. I am talking about who we really are. We all think we are good, moral individuals; we contribute to society, and we are comfortable with our level of religious observance. We therefore feel very comfortable with the notion that our children should follow in our footsteps. We then map out a course of action for them to follow. Basically, it will be a carbon copy of the life we led in our formative years.

What we fail to realize is that the world we grew up in, that we were exposed to in our adolescence and in our formative years, is light-years away from the world our children are part of. It is illogical then to imagine that having our children walk in the path we walked will lead them to the same destination.

---

94. *Yaaroth Devash 1*

Honesty

What You See Is What You Get

The Holy Ark, which contained the two tablets, was housed in the Tabernacle in the section called the Holy of Holies. The ark was comprised of three boxes, each without a lid and placed one within the other. The outer and inner boxes were made of gold, while the middle box was made of cedar wood. Reb Yehonatan would often draw imagery and symbolism from events or objects as they are recorded in the Torah. He asks, "If the middle box was not visible, why was it necessary for it to be made from expensive wood?"

There are people who present as fine, upstanding human beings; however, if you could see below the surface, you would discover that they are rotten to the core. The rabbis relate that a man of stature is someone whose words and actions reflect what is within his heart. The well-known saying, "What you see is what you get," is considered a badge of honor from a Jewish perspective.

The ark's construction reflected this. While the wooden middle box could not be seen by the naked eye, it still had to be from the finest wood that money could buy, thereby ensuring that the middle wooden box was in harmony with its two outer gold boxes.[95]

A great rabbi once remarked that while it is a virtue to have your inner and outer self in sync, there is an exception. When we are feeling down and despondent, feeling as if we are carrying the weight of the world on our shoulders, and we have no reason to be happy or smile, he says whether we like it or not and no matter how difficult and challenging it maybe, we need to put a smile on our face. We need to present to the outside world as if we are happy and content. The reason for behaving and acting as if we are happy is because it will influence our melancholic demeanor and help us overcome any negative feelings pulling us down.

---

95. *Tiferet Yehonatan Teruman*

Human Body

God's Gift

Without a doubt, of all the wonders of creation, the most awesome and incredible is the human body. The brain has around 86 billion neurons, all of which are in use at any given time. Even a superficial understanding of anatomy will leave us in awe of its complexity, how God has created us in the most perfect manner, how every organ and limb is in sync and in harmony with the rest of our body.

Appreciating that our very being is an incredible manifestation of God's handiwork motivates us to increase our love and reverence for Him. This will encourage us to focus our lives on what is truly important and not concern ourselves with the frivolous and the insignificant.[96]

Our rabbis elaborate at great length that our bodies are not ours and they are on loan from God. We need to respect the body, keep it as healthy as possible, and cannot cause it pain or disform it in any way.

More often than not, we take our health for granted. We consider it a given that all our faculties are functioning correctly. We should appreciate and value good health at all times, not only when we are sick.

To help us value our health, we can perform a simple, specific exercise at least once a day. It is not strenuous, and it won't increase your heart rate, but it can be life changing. You can do it anywhere and at any time. It should take you no more than six seconds. Stand still, close your eyes, and begin to slowly inhale and exhale. Focusing on your breathing, offer a short prayer of gratitude to God for the miracle we call life.

---

96. *Yaaroth Devash 1*

Humility

No One Knows Everything

"He is a know-it-all" is a phrase we use to describe a person who is arrogant and thinks they know everything. In truth, there is no one who knows it all; even Moshe didn't know everything. Moshe had spent time in heaven receiving the Torah, and he in turn taught the Torah to the Jewish people. Yet the Talmud states that during the forty years the Jewish people wandered in the desert, there were a number of situations that arose that Moshe did not know what the correct ruling should be. Now if Moshe needed to ask and seek clarification in certain halachic issues, can we ever even begin to think that we know it all?[97]

There is a rabbinic statement that reads, "The ultimate level of knowing is to know that you don't know." If we have never studied a particular subject, such as atomic energy, we can rightfully say we know nothing about it. On the other hand, if we read a very brief synopsis of the topic, more than likely we will conclude that atomic energy is such a vast and complex subject and the little we have read on the topic only reinforces our initial view that we really know nothing about it.

In both scenarios, we come to the same conclusion: that we know little about atomic energy. There is, of course, a clear distinction between the two understandings. In the first scenario, we know little about atomic energy based on pure ignorance. In the second situation, we recognize that we know very little of the topic; however, our conclusion is drawn from knowledge and not from lack of knowledge.

---

97. *Yaaroth Devash 1,6*

The Torah is God's wisdom; just as God is infinite, likewise His wisdom, the Torah, is infinite. That there are matters we don't understand is obvious. How could a finite mind, bound within the confines of time and space, fathom the infinite knowledge of its Creator?

The great wonder is that there are matters we can understand. Therefore, the more we learn God's Torah, the more we realize how little we know.

A great rabbi wished to bless his grandson with great Torah knowledge. The young man refused as he wished to acquire the knowledge through diligence and toil and not as a gift. Later in life, he said he regretted his decision; no matter how much Torah knowledge he would have received from his grandfather as a gift, the amount of knowledge he could have acquired from that point on through effort and toil was truly limitless.

Remember, we don't know it all. No one does, not even Moshe. But let us devote our lives to its study and be in a position to say, "I really don't know it all."

False Humility

Arrogance is a terrible character trait to possess—to the extent that God says, "I cannot be in close proximity to an arrogant person." Humility is considered one of the most wonderful qualities to have. Of all the great qualities and attributes that Moshe had, the Torah singles out only one, that he was the humblest person who ever lived.

While this is true, we need to be extremely wary of a sense of false humility. The evil inclination that drives us to be conceited is the same evil inclination that pushes us into believing that we are not capable of succeeding and that we could never contribute to society.

It was this concern that led Moshe to add the letter *yud* to the name of Yehoshua (Joshua, previously known as Hoshua) before he embarked with the other eleven spies to spy out the land of Canaan. Moshe knew that his student Yehoshua was extremely humble. And he was concerned that the evil inclination would feed on this and lead

Yehoshua to believe that he didn't have the ability to stand up to the spies if they would return with a negative report about the land.[98]

There is an old saying, "Humility is not thinking less of yourself; it's thinking about yourself less." How can we discern if what we are sensing is a true sense of humility or is false humility?

If what you are feeling leads you to action, then you know the humility is real and true. As was true by Moshe. Moshe was the humblest human being, yet he stood up to Pharoah, the most powerful leader at the time, and he stood up to the revolt of Korach. If, however, the humility is preventing you from taking a stand or stepping up to the task, you should know that the humility you are sensing stems from your evil inclination and is a negative feeling that needs to be eradicated.

The Shepherd

We find something interesting concerning the life of King David. Prior to becoming the King of Israel, he spent his days shepherding his father's flock. Likewise, Moshe was a shepherd prior to God instructing him to return to Egypt and redeem the Jewish people.

Is there any significance in their chosen profession?

Who is more important: the head of state or the bodyguard protecting him? Of course, it is the head of state since he is the one being guarded; he is the one being protected. However, when one is shepherding sheep that would not be the case, as a human is far superior to an animal. Yet the very fact that a person is guarding something that is inferior to him creates a certain sense of humility. And that is why many of our great Biblical leaders were shepherds as this would help them in their journey toward true humility.[99]

Most of our day is spent at our jobs trying to make a living—whether it is sitting behind a desk, on the road, or out in the field. Spending most of our

---

98. *Magen Ha'eleph*

99. *Ahavat Yehonatan Ha'azinu*

time in a particular surrounding has to affect us. We need to ask ourselves before beginning a new job, will this job change me? Will it impact me negatively? As important as it is that we support our family, this should not come at the expense of our spiritual growth.

Moshe and King David are prime examples of this.

Where Do We Begin?

Is one character trait more important than another? When we are trying to become a better person, is there a particular characteristic we should focus on more?

Reb Yehonatan takes a cue from God's first interaction with Moshe. God appeared to Moshe from the burning bush. The bush is very short in stature. By appearing to Moshe by a bush, God was impressing upon him that the most important character trait we need to focus on and refine is humility. We can only reach a level of perfection if we are truly humble.[100]

The story is told of a rabbi on Yom Kippur who prostrates himself before the Holy Ark and cries out to God, "Before You I am a nothing." The president, the wealthiest man in the community, follows the rabbi. He too falls to the ground and in a somber tone shouts out to God, "Before You I am a nothing." Then the town beggar decides to get in on the act, and he lies on the ground and yells at the top of his lungs, "Before You God I am a nothing." The president turns to the rabbi and whispers, "Who gave him the right to be a nothing?"

How can we become truly humble?

It isn't as difficult as it sounds. If we recognize that every talent we have is a gift from God and that all our successes are attributed to God's blessings, then we have nothing to be haughty about. We can actually take it a step further by saying to ourselves, "If God had given someone else the same

---

100. *Yaaroth Devash 2,2*

abilities and opportunities he gave me, they would have reached far greater heights than I did." This will put things in perspective and help us ensure that our successes will not allow us to become conceited.

Do What It Takes

Rabbi Yehonatan refused to seek approbations on his scholarly works. He felt that people writing letters of recommendation overindulge in praising the author. He writes that he did not want any letters of endorsement as they will praise him without cause, since he knows that he isn't worthy of any form of praise and therefore silence is better than words.[101]

Rabbi Yehonatan was one of the greatest Torah giants of his era. His works are studied to this very day. Any acclaim he would receive for his books would be well deserved. Yet we see how careful he was in not doing anything that might have caused him to become somewhat arrogant. It is a lesson for us in how we need to be careful in distancing ourselves from any type of behavior that could cause us to become even somewhat arrogant.

God's Humility

As a prerequisite for receiving the Torah, the Jewish people needed to understand the importance of being truly humble in the eyes of God. It was for this reason that the Torah was given on the lowly mountain Mount Sinai. Likewise, when the Torah was given, Moshe taught the Jewish people the book of *Bereishit* (Genesis).

Why specifically *Bereishit*, the first of the Five Books?

In *Bereishit*, we read of God's humility. When discussing the creation of mankind, the Torah states, "Let us make man in our image." Who is the "us" referring to?

The rabbis explain that God sought the counsel of the heavenly court prior to creating man. We learn from this that just as God, the

---

101. *Introduction Kreisi U'Pleisi*

ultimate Judge, sought the input and advice of His court, likewise a judge no matter how scholarly he may be should seek counsel from judges who may be less learned than him.

At the time of the giving of the Torah, the Jewish people proclaimed, "We will do, and we will listen." This can be understood to mean, "We will do . . . we will become humble" and "we will listen . . . we will listen to the Torah."[102]

There is always the fear that striving to achieve humility will come at the expense of success. Of all the qualities that Moshe possessed, the Torah specifically highlights the attribute of humility. The Torah describes Moshe as the humblest person who ever lived.

If he was so humble, how was he able to confront Pharaoh and take the Jews out of Egypt? How was he able to crush the rebellion of Korach? And how was he able to challenge and question God?

Moshe was very well aware of his capabilities, and he acted on them. Yet Moshe understood that it was a gift and blessing from God, and if someone was given the same gifts, they would have accomplished a lot more than he did. Moshe was able to be, on the one hand, the greatest leader who ever lived and, at the same time, the humblest person who ever walked the face of the earth because he knew it was all a gift from God.

As long as we keep in the forefront of our mind that it is all a gift from God, we too should strive to accomplish great things and not be worried that it may impact our need to be humble.

Spiritual Leprosy

Tzoraas, or spiritual leprosy, can afflict a person's body, his clothing, or the walls of his house. One of the reasons for this affliction is a result of a person being extremely haughty. This will explain why even a great

---

102. *Ahavat Yehonatan Yitro*

Torah scholar who knows that he has been afflicted with this malady must still be examined by a cohen. This procedure will go a long way in diminishing the Torah scholar's sense of pride.[103]

How does one overcome a sense of self-importance? The answer is obvious: by removing "self" from the equation. We remove self by not having any personal ambitions, by recognizing that it is not about us and what we can accomplish. Rather, it is about fulfilling the will of God and bringing into fruition God's plan.

---

103. *Tiferet Yehonatan Taazria*

Illness

As Long as the Mind Is Working

While we need to show due respect to every human being, we need to be even more respectful to someone who is ill. Why is this so?

The Talmud explains that God's presence is found hovering above the head of the person who is bedridden.

This is considered a great act of kindness by God. When a healthy person has sinned, he is in a position to do teshuvah (repent) by doing acts of goodness and kindness. If someone cannot leave their bed and cannot perform any mitzvot, how can they do teshuvah? God does not expect the person to do mitzvot in his present situation. God, however, offers the sick another path to teshuvah and that is by simply thinking of repenting.

That is what the Talmud means when it says that God hovers above the head of those lying in bed sick. God is waiting for the sick to simply think of doing teshuvah.[104]

It's a terrible feeling to be sick in bed even if we only have a common cold. We feel helpless; we feel we can't do anything. We spend our days looking at the four walls or watching the arms of the wall clock slowly move.

What a profound insight from Reb Yehonatan. Our minds and our thoughts are not incapacitated due to having a cold. We can accomplish great things with our thoughts. Imagine how uplifting it is to know that God is by my bedside, and with my thoughts, I can connect with Him.

---

104. *Tiferet Yehonatan Vayechi*

Inclinations

It Is All Good

Every human being possesses two inclinations, or two driving forces: a good inclination and an evil inclination. In Torah literature, they are called the *Yetzer Tov* (the good inclination) and the *Yetzer Hara* (the evil inclination).

The Yetzer Tov only wants us to do good things, such as doing the will of God. The Yetzer Hara, even though it is the evil inclination, does not necessarily want us to sin. Its purpose and interest are for our physical self to indulge in and enjoy the pleasures of this world. And the more we indulge in the physical pleasures that the world has to offer, the less we will be sensitive and open to spirituality and Godliness. If we can convince the Yetzer Hara that true and eternal pleasure is to be found in the word of God and the physical pleasures are foolish and fleeting, our Yetzer Hara will become a driving force in the pursuit of spirituality.[105]

Self-gratification is what the evil inclination seeks for us. We have the choice in choosing what we find enjoyable and pleasurable. By participating and experiencing moments of spirituality and holiness, hopefully we will experience bliss and happiness and we will want to continue pursuing. It is our choice in choosing. Hopefully, we will choose wisely.

Fresh Daily

The saying goes, "Familiarity breeds contempt." This means the longer you know someone or something, the more likely you will discover negative things about the person. While this might be debatable,

---

105. *Yaaroth Devash 9*

human behavior has shown that the more we get used to something or someone, the less excited we are.

Our children can drive us crazy for a new toy. Eventually, we relent and purchase it for them. How long do they actually play with it before they start playing with the box the toy came in? This behavior is true by adults as well. We purchase a new car, and we give everyone strict rules such as no eating in the car. How long does that last?

There is one exception to this human character trait and that is when a person does something wrong: when his *Yetzer Harah* (evil inclination) has seduced him into transgressing the word of God. When he has gotten the taste of stealing and robbing others, his desire to steal never wanes. On the contrary, the more he steals, the more he is driven to steal.

Why is this so? The rabbis explain that the Yetzer Harah is rejuvenated every day. Every day the Yetzer Harah is starting afresh. In its eyes, it is never the tenth or twentieth time you have robbed someone; each time is the first time.[106]

We may find ourselves in a difficult situation, one we can't seem to step away from. We seem to be consumed and preoccupied with inappropriate behavior. What we might say to ourselves is that it is only a fad and it will pass. And we justify that line of thinking by recalling all the times we were excited about something, and it wasn't that long until we lost interest.

Unfortunately, the comparison will not stick. Thinking the problem will go away or it will die a slow death is not true. We never seem to tire in pursuing what we shouldn't. What we will need to do is take proactive steps in dealing with the issue. Sitting back and doing nothing will accomplish absolutely nothing.

---

106. *Yaaroth Devash* 5

Indulging

Root of All Evil

As long as the food is kosher, we can eat whatever we want and how much we want. As long as the clothing is not revealing and does not contain *shatnez* (mixture of wool and linen), we can wear whatever we want no matter how outrageous and outlandish the attire is.

Is this an acceptable school of thought? The answer is a resounding no. While we don't actually transgress any specific commandment by living such a lifestyle, by overindulging in physical desires and pleasures, it becomes extremely challenging to grow spiritually.

Reb Yehonatan laments his own predicament that, being a rabbi of great stature, he needed to dress accordingly. On the Shabbat, he would wear a silk garment and, during the week, a garment made from camel hair. He writes that he was able to accept wearing a silk garment on Shabbat since by doing so he was honoring the Shabbat. However, he was uncomfortable wearing a camel-haired garment during the week.[107]

Mankind and for that matter the Jewish people have never lived such an affluent lifestyle. There are individuals who have more wealth than some countries. It is hard for us to imagine that little less than a hundred years ago people got through life with very little.

We should be thankful for the world we live in and the financial security and comfort it affords us. However, at the same time, let us be conscious of the fact that animals spend their lives indulging in earthly pleasures. If we are happy being like an animal, then enjoy it all to an extreme. But I think most of us value our humanity, and if that is the case, there is nothing wrong in curtailing somewhat the pursuit of self-gratification.

---

107. *Yaaroth Devash 1,7*

Interest

It Doesn't Pay in the Afterlife

It is prohibited for a Jew to charge another Jew interest. All loans must be interest free. The rabbis speak in disparaging terms about someone who charges interest. They write that a person who charges interest will not merit the resurrection of the dead in the Messianic era.

With his brilliance, Reb Yehonatan offers a number of explanations for why charging interest could lead to such a severe punishment.

Tradition has it that after a person passes away, over time, the body decomposes, and eventually all that remains is a tiny bone called the *luz* bone. And at the time of the resurrection, the body is formed from this bone.

When a person transgresses the will of God and lends money with interest, what may have started off as a small loan accrues interest if it is not repaid, causing the loan to continuously grow. Therefore, the person is punished; at the time of the Resurrection of the Dead, they will not merit their remaining tiny bone growing to become the person they once were.

The second insight he suggests is that we are rewarded for fulfilling the word of God in the world to come. Lending money to someone in need is one of the highest forms of charity. By charging interest, the person is taking his reward in the "here and now." Therefore, he forfeits his right to enjoy the "there and then."[108]

Sir Moses Montefiore was once asked how much he was worth. He responded by mentioning a certain amount of money. The questioner then asked, "Sir Moses, I know you are worth a lot more than that." To this, Sir

---

108. *Tiferet Yehonatan, Ahavat Yehonatan Vayera*

Moses responded, "That is how much charity I gave this year. That money is truly mine because it can never be taken away from me."

God created the world with kindness and bestows kindness on every living creature. It becomes our solemn task to emulate God and walk in his footsteps. If God blessed us with wealth, we have to understand that God is entrusting us with His money. We become His banker, and it becomes our solemn task to distribute it wisely. Charging interest with God's money can never be a recipe for blessing and growth.

Israel

Gift or Inheritance

God promised Abraham that his descendants would receive the Land of Israel as their perpetual homeland. It is interesting to note that, in one verse, we are informed that we will receive the land as an eternal inheritance, while in another verse, we are told that the land will be given to us as an everlasting gift.

Are we to understand that there is an obvious discrepancy in how we came to be considered the rightful owners of the land?

Reb Yehonatan suggests that there is no contradiction. Rather, we are being taught that we acquired the land via two modes of acquisitions. We received it as an inheritance and as a gift. We inherited the land as we are the children of Abraham. The land possesses extraordinary properties, and that was a gift given to us by God. What was miraculous about the Land of Israel was that it seemed to be able to extend its boundaries. And no matter how many Jews would settle the land, there was always enough room for a few more.[109]

In the Talmud, the rabbis relate that every Jew, whether they reside in Israel or in the diaspora, own part of the land. No matter where they may live, a Jew is an offspring of Abraham, and as Abraham's children, we are entitled to part of the land as an eternal inheritance.

On the lips of every Jew is the fervent prayer that we should merit the coming of the Messiah and the ingathering of the Jewish people to the Land of Israel, where we will live with peace and prosperity. May our prayers be answered speedily in our days.

---

109. *Tiferet Yehonatan Voetchanan*

The Conduit

The Land of Israel has always been central in the life of the Jew. The Talmud states that when we pray, we should focus on our prayers going to heaven via the Land of Israel. Likewise, when we perform one of God's commandments, we should imagine that we are fulfilling it while standing on the holy earth of Israel.[110]

When drawing up plans for a building, an architect must consider the position of the building as it relates to the movement of the sun. Likewise, when an architect is drawing up plans for a shul, one of the first questions he needs to ask is "Which direction is Israel?" This is because the congregation needs to be facing Israel when they daven (pray). The hemisphere you are determines which direction you need to face when davening.

Where Do You Want to Live?

At the most basic level, when performing a mitzvah in the diaspora, one should imagine that they are fulfilling the word of God while standing in the Land of Israel. On a deeper level, while performing the mitzvah, one needs to hope that they will merit to actually live in Israel and perform God's commandments in the Holy Land.[111]

The Land of Israel has always been at the forefront of Jewish experience. Three times a day in our prayers we beseech Hashem to send the Messiah so that we can return to Israel and build the third Beit Hamikdash.

More Than Meets the Eye

The Land of Israel is unique both from a physical and spiritual perspective. The Talmud relates that there were certain cities in Israel that had an extremely large population. The rabbis question this by

---

110. *Tiferet Yehonatan*

111. *Yaaroth Devash*

pointing out that the size of these cities was fairly small, and how could they accommodate such large numbers?

The Talmud answers, the Land of Israel is referred to as the Land of the Deer. What is special about a deer that it is compared to the Land of Israel?

Just as the skin of the deer stretches to larger than its actual size to accommodate the body of the deer, so too the Land of Israel. When Jews lived there, it was spacious and could accommodate vast numbers, and when we were exiled, it contracted and its new size could only house a much smaller population. Physically, the Land of Israel is exceptional in that it is able to expand and contract.

From a spiritual perspective, the uniqueness of the Land of Israel is that besides the physical land, there is a spiritual, heavenly Land of Israel. And when the Talmud speaks of vast numbers of people living in a very confined area, it is referring to the otherworldly heavenly Land of Israel.

When we speak of the Land of Israel, we are really speaking of two lands: a physical land and a spiritual one.[112]

The Land of Israel is definitely more than meets the eye.

Aliya

Every human being strives for perfection and a sense of wholeness. Many people feel they are extremely accomplished and are living a complete life. What one needs to realize is that while living in the diaspora, they are lacking. Only when one lives in the Holy Land can an individual become truly whole. It is in the merit of living in Israel that our forefathers were able to reach the spiritual heights that they did.

One of the great rabbis of the seventeenth century, Rabbi Yeshayahu Horowitz (known as the Shelah Hakadosh) quotes a verse in the Book of Kings that speaks of the Land of Israel. The verse states,

---

112. *Tiferet Yehonatan*

"My eyes and My heart shall be there at all times." He writes that one should constantly be yearning for the Land of Israel.

This longing to live in Israel was seen by Yoseph, the son of Yaakov. Yoseph had been imprisoned in Egypt. His sole desire to be freed from prison was to enable him to return to the Holy Land; living in Israel would assist him in reaching the spiritual heights of his forefathers.[113]

Every mitzvah is performed with a different limb of the body. We wear tefillin on our left arm and on our head. We love God with our heart. We pray with our mouth and we hear the shofar with our ears. One of only two mitzvot that the whole-body experiences as one is the mitzvah of living in Israel. The whole person from his toes to the hair on his head fulfills this mitzvah.

And unlike many mitzvot that can only be performed at a specific time such as eating matzah or shaking the lulav. Every minute day in day out we fulfill the mitzvah of living in Israel. And even when we are sleeping as long as we are sleeping in Israel we are performing a mitzvah.

Is it any wonder then that the Jewish people have always had a burning desire to live in the Holy land?

Desolate or Fertile

Ramban lived in the 13th century and he shares what he encountered when visiting the Land of Israel. He writes that it was a desolate and barren land.

Why was this so?

Every country has a unique constellation or spiritual flow of energy via which it receives its specific character. The Land of Israel's spiritual flow of energy was such that it should have been a barren land unfit for human settlement.

God gave this Land to the Jewish people, and through our study of the Torah, the desert turned into a land flowing with milk and honey.

---

113. *Yaaroth Devash 1,15*

As a result of our sins, we were exiled from the land, and it returned to its natural state of being a desert. Our behavior and conduct directly impacts whether the land will blossom or will be bare.[114]

Some 600 years later, Mark Twain made the same observation. He recorded what he experienced when he traveled to the Holy Land in 1867. He writes that he encountered a "desolate country whose soil is rich enough, but is given over wholly to weeds-a silent mournful expanse . . . A desolation is here that not even imagination can grace with the pomp of life and action . . . We never saw a human being on the whole route . . . There was hardly a tree or a shrub anywhere. Even the olive and the cactus, those fast friends of the worthless soil, had almost deserted the country."

Flowing with Milk and Honey

Every country has its own spiritual energy known as its mazal. The mazal is the conduit through which God transfers His spiritual energy to the physical world. Israel's mazal was such that it had been designated to be an uninhabitable desert. However, when the Jewish people keep the Torah, this causes God's blessing to override the pre-ordained status of the land, and it becomes a land flowing with milk and honey.

Hence, when the Jewish people transgress, God doesn't need to punish the land. He simply removes His blessings, and the land returns to its natural state of a barren desert.[115]

Human nature is such that we take for granted when things are going well, when we are healthy, when we are making a living, and we are surrounded by a loving family. It is when we are confronted by difficulties and challenges that we begin to question and try and make sense of things.

The Land of Israel teaches us that we should take nothing for granted. The fact that Israel was blessed, that it flows with milk and honey was

---

114. *Tiferet Yehonatan Ha'azinu*

115. *Tiferet Yehonatan Ha'azinu*

miraculous. It received this blessing as a reward for our observance of Torah and the fulfillments of its commandments. Likewise, we should not see all the good things in our lives as a given. We should understand that it is all a gift and blessing from God. And the more we heed the word of God, the greater our blessings will be.

Jewish People

God Dwells Among Us

We have been a nation for more than 3,300 years. The pages of our history are soaked in blood. Yet, while other nations and empires such as the Greeks and the Romans have come and gone, we still exist. And the study of God's Torah continues to this very day.

The only rational explanation we can give for this anomaly is that God is always with us and protecting us.[116]

A great rabbi, living some three hundred years ago, once said, "Every morning when I wake up and I look in the mirror and I see a Jew, I know that I have seen a miracle far greater than the splitting of the sea." That we have survived and flourished against constant oppression is nothing short of miraculous. Bear in mind that the rabbi made this observation before the Holocaust.

When we look at the Jewish world today and how Judaism continues to flourish and grow, even in countries such as the former Soviet Union, where only a few years back Jews were prohibited from practicing their faith, and when we see how the Land of Israel, a tiny nation surrounded by its enemies, as the prophet writes, "like a lamb surrounded by 70 wolves," has evolved beyond anyone's wildest imagination, we should stop and ask ourselves, "How? How could this happen?"

The only plausible answer is that what we see before our very eyes is nothing short of being miraculous, and it is the hand of God that continues to guide us and protects us.

---

116. *Yaaroth Devash 1*

Supernatural Strength

Our forefather Yaakov is described in the Torah as a man who sat in his tent and devoted his life to study and prayer. By contrast, his twin brother, Esau, is described as a man of the field who would spend his days hunting. We, the descendants of Yaakov, are known as the people of the book, as people who extol the virtues of study and education. We have never been known as a bloodthirsty, all-conquering nation.

If we look back at our history, we see that it has been littered with pogroms, crusades, death, and destruction. How have the descendants of the man who preferred the tent over the field survived? How have the people who would rather spend their days in the house of study learning are still doing so while the nations that lived their lives on the battlefield are nothing more than chapters in the history books?

It has not been luck or being at the right place at the right time. We all know that eventually your luck runs out. And we can't always be right where we are meant to be. Rather, God blessed and continues to bless the Jewish people that we should have the strength and the courage to withstand all the pain and suffering we experience at the hands of our enemies.[117]

It is important for each and every one of us to occasionally pause and take note of the following: The mighty Greek, Roman, Assyrian, and Babylonian empires that sought our destruction no longer exist. In more recent times, the "Final Solution" was meant to rid the world of us. Stalin and his successors tried to eradicate Jewish life from Russia. Not only did they fail in their attempt. But we have flourished since those very dark days in a manner that is beyond human comprehension.

There is only one logical explanation to understand what is truly illogical. And that is God has never forsaken us. God has blessed us with the strength and ability to bear all of life's challenges.

And for that we need to be eternally grateful.

---

117. *Alon Bachut*

We All Count

There is a very powerful and profound statement recorded in the Talmud. The Talmud states, "Whoever sustains the life of a Jew, it is as if he has sustained an entire world." At the most basic level, the statement is impressing upon us the intrinsic value we put on life and how we need to do whatever we can to save life. By extension, the opposite is also true. As the Talmud states, "Whoever takes the life of a Jew. It is as if he has destroyed an entire world." There can be no greater criminal act than taking the life of another human being.

Reb Yehonatan offers the following very enlightening insight. He says that the Talmud is impressing upon us that every Jew is like the whole world and that the whole world needs every single Jew.[118]

One of the many reasons we may at times feel down and despondent is because we get a sense that we are insignificant, we don't make a difference. We may say to ourselves, "Does anyone really care if I am here or not?" Even if we feel we have lived a rich and rewarding life, as we get older and especially if we have retired from the workforce, we may start to get nagging thoughts that we are no longer needed and are no longer contributing to society; we have become a burden that needs to be packed up and shipped out.

Reb Yehonatan is impressing upon us that not only are these thoughts debilitating but also they are profoundly untrue. If we are here, if we are alive, we need to sense in our very core that we are needed. We need to appreciate that we make a difference and we contribute. We must never forget that the lives we live not only impact our family, friends, and our community but can also influence and change the whole world.

Like Stars

There is nothing more exquisite than being outside at night under a clear sky and seeing the twinkling stars in heaven. God told Abraham, "Your children will be like the stars in heaven."

---

118. *Yaaroth Devash 2,7*

What a beautiful metaphor. How are we to understand it?

Reb Yehonatan explains: Stars come in all sizes; there are large stars and smaller stars. The larger the star, the brighter it shines. Likewise, we are not all equal. It is the responsibility of the great Torah scholars who are the larger and brighter stars to teach and impart knowledge to the smaller stars, the less knowledgeable, with the hope that they will grow and become great in their own right.

Every star follows a specific path, never straying from its designated route. Likewise, we too should never leave our designated pathway of life. It comes with clear and straightforward directions—that being the Torah as the blueprint of existence.

It's impossible to know how many stars exist, but astronomers estimate that in the Milky Way galaxy alone, there are about 300 billion stars. However, every single star serves a unique purpose, and the world would be incomplete without it. Likewise, each and every one of us has our unique role to play in God's grand scheme of things.[119]

Everything that exists is an expression of Godliness. By examining the world and all of its intricacies, we can learn profound lessons in what it means to be a Jew and what is expected from us.

The Talmud relates that even if the Torah had not been given, we would nonetheless have learned modesty from the cat, which covers its excrement, and that stealing is objectionable from the ant, which does not take grain from another ant, and forbidden relations from the dove, which is faithful to its partner, and proper relations from the rooster, which first appeases the hen and then mates with it.

Once in a while, it would be a good idea to stop in our tracks, stop whatever we are doing, and observe God's beautiful world, pausing and viewing nature in its true glory. We may even surprise ourselves in what important messages we can glean from what we observe.

---

119. *Ahavat Yehonatan Lech Lecha*

Miracles of Miracles

What is the secret of Jewish survival? Throughout our history, we have lived through pogroms, the Crusades, the Inquisition, and the Holocaust, and somehow, we have survived. And not only have we survived but we have also flourished.

There is only one explanation we can offer, and that is Divine intervention. Our existence is truly miraculous. In truth, our very beginning was miraculous. The first Jew to be born was Yitzchak, the son of Abraham and Sarah. Both were of an age where they could no longer bare children. God performed a miracle, and they were blessed with the first Jewish child. From that moment on, our survival has been nothing short of miraculous.

In 1898, Mark Twain wrote an article in Harper's Magazine *titled "Concerning The Jews." He wrote:*

"If the statistics are right, the Jews constitute but one percent of the human race. It suggests a nebulous dim puff of star dust lost in the blaze of the Milky Way. Properly, the Jew ought hardly to be heard of, but he is heard of, has always been heard of. He is as prominent on the planet as any other people, and his commercial importance is extravagantly out of proportion to the smallness of his bulk. His contributions to the world's list of great names in literature, science, art, music, finance, medicine, and abstruse learning are also way out of proportion to the weakness of his numbers.

"He has made a marvelous fight in this world, in all the ages; and has done it with his hands tied behind him. He could be vain of himself, and be excused for it. The Egyptian, the Babylonian, and the Persian rose, filled the planet with sound and splendor, then faded to dream stuff and passed away. The Greek and the Roman followed, and made a vast noise, and they are gone. Other peoples have sprung up and held their torch high for a time, but it burned out, and they sit in twilight now, or have vanished.

"The Jew saw them all, beat them all, and is now what he always was, exhibiting no decadence, no infirmities of age, no weakening of his parts, no slowing of his energies, no dulling of his alert and aggressive mind. All things are mortal but the Jew; all other forces pass, but he remains.

"What is the secret of his immortality?"

Mark Twain asked the question and Reb Yehonatan answered it some 150 years before: Divine intervention. There is no other logical and rational explanation that can be given.

Second Nature

Human nature is such that there are certain foods that a person finds repugnant to eat even without being taught that it is not fit for human consumption, such as eating insects. Likewise, the nature of the Jew is that they instinctively want to serve God and find idol worship repulsive.[120]

Throughout our history, there have been countless numbers of Jews who were nonobservant and estranged from their faith, yet when they were commanded to bow down to an idol or face certain death, they chose death. The reason being is that every Jew possess a Godly soul that does not want to be separated from God. And idol worship is the ultimate expression of severing ties with our Father in heaven.

Living with Pain

Certain factors can contribute to a person having a higher threshold for pain, including genetics, age, and gender, to name a few. The Jewish people, since they possess a spark of Godliness, are able to endure a higher level of pain over a longer period of time than the rest of humanity.[121]

---

120. *Ahavat Yehonatan*

121. *Ahavat Yehonatan Vayishlach*

We have always been described as "people of the book." We consider excelling in education and a thirst for knowledge worthy goals for ourselves and our children. Physical prowess and dominance in sports have never been high on our agenda. Yet what we, as a nation, have endured and survived and then ultimately flourished is beyond the capacity of any human being.

This has never been more pronounced than in our own recent history. We heard living testimony and read firsthand accounts of the brutal, cruel, and sadistic manner in which the Jews were treated in the concentration camps during the Holocaust. The work was backbreaking in the freezing cold with thin, bare rags called clothing and ill-fitting so-called shoes on their feet. And they were sustained on a meager ration that wasn't fit for human consumption. How was it humanely possible for anyone who had lived through hell on earth to start life again? Many who had lost their husbands or wives and all their children remarried and had more children. The only rational explanation is that we possess something that is irrational, and that is a Godly soul, a spark of God.

Jews in the Diaspora

At the time of the destruction of the second Beit Hamikdash, there were twice as many Jews living in Egypt and in other parts of the diaspora as there were Jews living in Israel. Why was this so? At that time, *lashon hara* (negative speech) about a fellow Jew and unwanted hate between Jews were rampant. Many Jews could not bear living in such an environment, so they fled the Holy Land.[122]

One of the most stressful experiences we can go through is having to relocate, especially if it means to another country. If it is stressful in today's world where we have all the conveniences one could ever imagine, including white-glove movers, how much more so in the times of old? Yet many Jews were willing to forgo and endure the hardship of relocation in order to avoid being dragged into a world of baseless hatred of one Jew for another.

---

122. *Yaaroth Devash 1*

We may not be in a position to uproot ourselves and our families like our forbearers did. However, we should be inspired by what they did and do whatever we can to ensure that we don't succumb to unwanted hate of our brothers and sisters.

The Mighty Empires

Even a cursory understanding of Jewish history will reveal something rather astonishing. Every single nation from the beginning of time that attempted to conquer the Land of Israel or annihilate the Jewish people were the world's superpower at that time—starting with the Egyptians, the Greeks, the Romans, and the Babylonians. Through God's intervention, they were ultimately unsuccessful and soon thereafter they ceased to exist.[123]

If we study world history, we will find that many nations were defeated in battle, yet they were able to regroup and continue to exist and at times flourish. The exception to this was a nation that had attempted to annihilate the Jewish people; not only were they defeated, they also ceased to exist in any shape or form. Today, there is no longer a Roman Empire or Greek Empire, but the Jewish people continue to thrive. We have the same Torah, we practice the same faith, and we speak the same language.

The only explanation we can give is that God is the Master of History and He is our loving Father. By reflecting on this historical enigma, it will undoubtedly cause us to have a deeper connection with Him.

One Entity

How should we view the Jewish people? We need to the view the Jewish people as if collectively they are like one person. Just as a human being is comprised of many organs and many different limbs, so too the Jewish people. Each organ and limb has a unique role to play, though certain organs and limbs are more important than others. For example,

---

123. *Yaaroth Devash 1*

you can't live without a brain or a heart, but you can live with only one kidney. And obviously missing a leg is a lot more challenging than missing a finger. However, a person is considered whole when he is not missing any organ or limb.

The same is true for the Jewish people. Each person has a unique role to play. Certain individuals have the status of being the head or the heart, while others are like the finger. Yet the Jewish people would be incomplete without the presence and participation of every single Jew.[124]

Have you ever experienced the following? You are in the middle of nowhere and you meet someone for the first time, and you discover they are Jewish. The excitement is palpable; you feel like you have met a long-lost relative.

Why is this so? The answer is because it is true. In fact, not only have you met a relative for the first time, but you have actually met part of your extended self.

When we bang our thumb with a hammer, our whole body hurts, not just our thumb. When we win a running race, our whole body feels excited, not just our legs. Likewise, when we hear of another Jew's misfortune, we need to try to feel the pain as if it is our own misfortune. When we hear of another Jew's accomplishment, we need to be happy as if it is our own success.

Never Forsaken

One of the most important conversations that took place between God and man was the conversation between God and King Solomon. God assures King Solomon that even though the Jewish people may sin, resulting in the destruction of the Temple, He will always remain among the Jewish people and will never forsake His nation.[125]

---

124. *Yaaroth Devash*

125. *Yaaroth Devash 1*

In the Torah and in our prayers, we refer to God as our father and we the Jewish people as His children. Just as a parent cannot and will not abandon their child, so to God will never abandon the Jewish people, as we are His children. No matter how distant we have wandered from God, what a beautiful idea to think about. No matter to what extent we no longer live the life He would like us to, He is always waiting with outstretched hands to embrace us once again.

We Are One

What should our reaction be if we see someone doing something wrong? Should we pretend we didn't see what happened or should we, in an appropriate manner, influence the person to mend his ways?

Imagine your business partner takes money from the cash register and throws it out the window. How would you respond? You would rightfully become extremely angry. And more than likely, you would tell your partner, "If it was only your money, do whatever you want with it. However, it is also my hard-earned money. What right do you have in throwing my money away?"

Similarly, we need to view our fellow Jew as our partner. And if they do something wrong, we are affected, and we can be punished for the sins of others. Is there any room for doubt how we should respond?[126]

A group of people are in a rowboat, and one person takes out a hand drill and starts drilling a hole under his seat into the hull of the boat. One of the other passengers screams out, "What are you doing?!" To which he responds, "It is my seat. I paid for it, and I'll do whatever I want." To which the first person responds, "But don't you realize, when you drill a hole under your seat, you will cause all of us to drown."

We are in this together. We are a team, and we each play a vital role. No one can do it alone. When we see someone floundering, let us extend a

---

126. *Yaaroth Devash 1,15*

welcoming hand to bring them closer to God and His teachings. If altruistic reasons are not enough motivation to concern ourselves with someone else's life choices, then for purely selfish reasons, we should want to influence and change someone's inappropriate behavior.

Judging

The Power of One

Reb Yehonatan makes a very empowering and inspiring statement when he writes that even if there is only one righteous Jew alive, the holiness of that single Jew can protect and safeguard the whole Jewish world.[127]

There are approximately 7.9 billion people in the world. And if we want to know how many people have lived on planet earth since God created Adam and Chava, the jury is still out. But suffice to say, we are talking in the tens of billions to over a hundred billion people. Now, that is a lot of people. This may lead some of us to question our very existence. Do we think we matter?

The knee-jerk reaction is, of course, we matter. Everyone has their source of pride, their source of affirmation. Let us then rephrase the question: If we were never born, would it make a difference to anyone? This is not an easy question to tackle. If a person is honest with himself, this question can make him uncomfortable and queasy. Because if the answer is no, that it wouldn't make a difference or he doesn't know if it would make a difference, how invested can he be in his choices in life if his choices don't really make a difference anyway?

The next time we feel inadequate and unworthy, we must remember the stirring words of Reb Yehonatan, who is telling us that we should never underestimate ourselves and what we can accomplish and that through our actions and behavior we can literally save the entire world.

---

127. *Yaaroth Devash* 2,19

To Judge a Fellow Jew

Human nature is that we are quick to judge. We very often become judge and jury and pronounce innocence and guilt based on nothing more than hearsay or a fleeting view of a scene unfolding before our eyes.

Reb Yehonatan correctly dismisses such an approach. He writes that God alone is the true Judge, as only He knows the workings of man since God is able to penetrate the depths of man's heart. This is something we mere mortals are unable to do.[128]

No one has the right to judge another Jew and label them as being a good Jew or a bad Jew. God is the one who gives out the grades. We live in a results-based world. If you produce and if you complete the task, you are a success. However, if you put in the effort and you tried but you were unsuccessful, you are deemed a failure. Judaism sees man as living in an effort-based society. God looks to our effort and perseverance rather than to our accomplishments.

To fully appreciate the distinction between a success and effort-based worldview, let us visualize a ladder. Someone was born on the sixth rung of the financial ladder because he inherited $50 million, and when he retired, he had only reached the seventh rung because his wealth had increased to only $55 million. Another person was born on the first rung because he had no inheritance, and when he retired, he had reached the fifth rung because he had amassed $20 million.

Who is wealthier? The person with $55 million, of course; however, who put in more effort? Who tried harder? The other person, of course.

So is it true when it comes to religious observance. A person can be born on the sixth rung of the spiritual ladder by receiving a spiritual inheritance that included being born to an observant family and going to a religious school and only having pious friends. And at the end of his life, he had reached the

---

128. *Ahavat Yehonatan Bechukotei*

eighth rung of the ladder. Meanwhile, another person was born on the first rung of the ladder having grown up in a home and in an environment with no exposure to authentic Jewish life and observance. And at his passing, he had grown in his Judaism and had reached the fifth rung of the ladder.

Who is greater? Who is the better Jew? If you ask man, the answer is obvious. The Jew on the eighth rung because he is more observant and more pious. However, if the litmus test of defining who is a good Jew is our effort, the second person wins hands down. Even though at the end of his life he didn't even reach the level the first person was born at, the first person had only climbed two levels, while he had climbed four levels.

Who is greater? Who is the better Jew? These are not questions that we should attempt to answer. In our eyes, every Jew should be considered a good Jew. Let's leave the judging to the Judge of all judges.

Favorably

A person enters a room and sees a man lying on a bed. Another individual is hovering over the bed with a knife in his hand that he is about to plunge into the person's chest. Our immediate reaction would be to imagine that a murder is about to take place. In truth, that is not what is unfolding. The room is an operating theater, the man is a surgeon who is about to perform open heart surgery, and he is holding a scalpel.

If we saw this scene, 99.9 percent of us would know what was happening. However, much of life's experiences are not so clear cut. Life is not two dimensional, either black or white; there is a lot of gray area in between. We need to be very conscious of this when passing judgment. Very often we act as judge and jury to find the person guilty without knowing the whole picture. We need to train ourselves to always view a person favorably until we have all the facts.[129]

---

129. *Yaaroth Devash 1,8*

In 1894, one of the most revered principles in the American legal system, "innocent until proven guilty," was established. A bedrock principle of the American criminal justice system is that a defendant accused of a crime is presumed innocent until proven guilty beyond a reasonable doubt. This protection comes from the due process guaranteed in the Fifth and Fourteenth Amendments of the U.S. Constitution.

As a Jew it is important for us to know that this basic human right has been part of Jewish law since when we stood at Mount Sinai and received the Torah over 3,300 years ago.

Why is it so important to be aware of this? We need to appreciate that much of Western civilization, its laws and moral compass, are rooted in the Torah. Our constitution, however, extends this revered principle beyond the hallowed chambers of the courthouse. We need to live by this principle at all times and in all places.

Judgment

The Boomerang Effect

One of King David's great virtues was his ability to forgive anyone who had mistreated him and had done him ill. God took a leaf out of King David's approach, and He too forgave King David.[130]

We have either experienced the following scenario ourselves or we have seen other people act in such a manner: We see someone doing something inappropriate. How quick are we to denounce such behavior? Someone then points out that we did exactly the same thing. How do we respond? More than likely, we would answer, "Oh no, you cannot compare me to the other person. My circumstance was completely different. There are mitigating reasons why I acted like I that."

A great rabbi once remarked that God allows us to judge ourselves. He explained this rather cryptic statement in the following manner: There is a person who always judges other people harshly and never gives them the benefit of the doubt and doesn't attempt to try to find extenuating circumstances to explain that person's seemingly inexplicable behavior. God will follow the person's modus operandi and will also not attempt to justify his behavior when he does the same inappropriate act. However, if the person tries to find a path that will help him defend a person's conduct, God will follow this person's lead and God will find reasons to absolve the person if he does the very same thing.

It is in our own self-interest to judge others favorably, because if we don't, it is like a boomerang; it may come and hit us on the head.

---

130. *Ahavat Yehonatan Ha'azinu*

Lashon Hara/Derogatory Speech

It's Only Words

Lashon hara means that it is forbidden to speak negatively about someone else, even if it is true. Lashon hara differs from defamation in that
lashon hara is truthful speech rather than lies. As children, we either
said or were told, "Sticks and stones may break my bones, but names
will never hurt me." This is a funny saying, but there is little to no truth
to it. King Solomon in Proverbs (18:21) strongly disagrees with it, as
he writes, "Death and life are in the power of the tongue."

When discussing the severity of lashon hara, the Talmud states
that from a certain viewpoint, it is even more severe than idol worship.
It comes to this conclusion by comparing the monarchy of King Saul
and King Achav.

During the reign of King Saul, the Jewish people were defeated in
battle, while during the reign of King Acahv, the Jewish people were
victorious in battle. The Talmud explains why this was so: During the
reign of King Saul, the people were righteous. They weren't idol worshippers; however, they were prone to speaking lashon hara. On the
other hand, during the reign of King Achav, the people were wicked.
They were idol worshippers; however, they had one saving grace: they
didn't speak lashon hara.

It was as if King Saul's army carried a banner saying, "We don't
serve idols, but we do speak lashon hara." While King Achav's army
carried a banner that read, "We serve idols, but we don't speak lashon
hara." And we know whose banner shone brighter.

Reb Yehonatan offers his own understanding of the severity of
lashon hara. He asks which is worse: striking someone and causing
grave bodily harm or speaking lashon hara venomously about someone?
He feels, as King Solomon does, that the tongue can be more harmful
than the sword. If we hit someone, they can seek medical attention and

they can be healed. When we speak lashon hara about someone, the damage caused by our words can never be rectified.[131]

Dieting is a billion-dollar industry. We live in a time when we are very aware of the health risks of obesity. We have become calorie counters, making sure that what we put in our mouths is good for us. There are certain illnesses, such as diabetes, that eating the wrong type of food may not only be harmful but also may even be deadly. And, of course, people who are allergic to certain food types need to be extremely vigilant when it comes to food intake.

Unfortunately, as a society, we have sunk to a new low when it comes to what comes out of our mouths—not only in the prevalence of foul language but, more important, in the manner we speak about others. We feel no sense of compulsion to measure our speech or to understand the impact our words may have.

It may be right, but it can still be wrong. Remember the information you are sharing may be right, but you may be wrong in sharing it. We need to be concerned about what goes out as much as what goes in our mouths.

Like a Bullet

The first Beit Hamikdash (Temple) was destroyed by the Greek Assyrian Empire, and the second Beit Hamikdash was destroyed by the Roman Empire. The Greek Assyrian Empire neighbored the Land of Israel, while the Roman Empire was a fair distance away.

Reb Yehonatan explains that it was not by chance that it was the Romans who destroyed the second Beit Hamikdash. The Talmud states that the second Temple was destroyed due to unwanted hatred among the Jewish people and the prevalence of lashon hara.

He points out that when one speaks lashon hara about someone, that person could be living on the other side of the globe and your words could be as harmful and as devastating as if the person was

---

131. *Yaaroth Devash 1,16*

living next door. Therefore, the second Beit Hamikdash was destroyed by a nation that lived a great distance away and not by a neighboring country.[132]

"If a tree falls in a forest and no one is around to hear it, does it make a sound?" is a philosophical thought experiment that raises questions regarding observation and perception. We can debate the question until the cows come home. What is not debatable is that the sounds that come out of our mouths and form words are like bullets, and they travel great distances.

We can be sitting in the comfort of our home talking to a friend and our words could be destroying the life of someone living thousands of miles away. Remember, if you have nothing nice to say, don't say it.

---

132. *Yaaroth Devash 1,7*

Love

Am I in Love?

It's the million-dollar question, posed by man from the beginning of time: Am I in love? Is this love, or is it nothing more than a fleeting infatuation?

Reb Yehonatan writes that to answer this question, you will need to ask yourself, "Why do I think I love this person?" If the reasons you give are rational logical and can stand the test of time, then your question has been answered. If, after reflection, the reasons you come up with are silly and likely fade into the sunset, then more than likely what you are experiencing is nothing more than a fleeting infatuation.[133]

The Hebrew word for love is ahavah; it comes from the word hav, which means to give. It may seem counterintuitive, but the more you give to someone, the more you will come to love them. Try it. You may be pleasantly surprised.

Love Is One

How does true love express itself? Ahavah has a numerical value of thirteen. The Hebrew word for one is *echod*, which also has a numerical value of thirteen. Words with the same numerical value are considered to have an intrinsic connection. True love evokes a feeling of oneness and bonding between the two individuals.

This is seen in the book of Samuel 1 18:1 where it describes the love between David and Jonathan, the son of King Saul. The verse reads, "Jonathan's soul had become *attached* to David's soul, and Jonathan loved him as *himself*."[134]

---

133. *Tiferet Yehonatan Voetchanan*
134. *Ahavat Yehonatan Voetchanan*

This is illustrated by the story told of a great rabbi who accompanied his wife to the doctor and informed the doctor, "My wife's leg is hurting us."

How to Respond?

How should we respond when a person we love has done something that has made us extremely upset? The knee-jerk reaction would be to become angry and perhaps even question their love for us.

What we need to do is pause, take a deep breath, and say to ourselves in a calming and soothing voice, "I know this person truly loves me and would never hurt me and more than likely it has been one big misunderstanding."[135]

We need to do whatever we can to ensure that we don't reach a point where our loved one begins to question our relationship. There is one word that will define the success or otherwise of any type of connection between two people, and that is communication. What we say and how we convey it will either enhance our connection and bond, or it will challenge it and may even destroy it.

We may not have been taught healthy communication skills in school; however, it is never too late to learn. Our most precious possessions, our relationships, may be at stake.

---

135. Ahavat Yehonatan Voetchanan

Love of God

Physical Pleasure for a Higher Cause

Our love of God is strengthened by our understanding of the interplay between spiritual growth and earthly pleasures. Most faiths see abstinence as the key to spiritual growth—where one refrains from eating, abstains from speech, lives in solitude, and remains celibate.

God, however, says to channel your physical desires in the service of God and don't see them as being evil that needs to be crushed and shunned. Eat to have the strength to fulfill the mitzvot. Speak words that bring hope and comfort to others.[136]

Realizing that God has given us an easier path to spiritual growth—one that allows us to embrace and channel our physical desires appropriately—and not the more arduous path that would demand we despise our physical needs will lead us to increase our love of God.

---

136. *Ahavat Yehonatan Voetchanan*

Lying

Steppingstone to Arrogance

We all know about the boy who cried wolf once too often. There are many drawbacks to being a liar. That is why parents become very concerned if they witness their children not telling the truth. The parental statement "Whatever you do, don't lie to me; tell me the truth" rings loud and clear in many a household.

What is interesting is Reb Yehonatan's take on the perils of being a liar. He writes that if we feed ourselves falsehoods about our own standing, if we tell ourselves how smart, how benevolent, and how kind we are, we may start believing it. We will let it go to our head, and we will become extremely arrogant. We will have totally forgotten that the accolades and praises have nothing to do with reality as they are all self-induced, and in reality, we have nothing to blow our own horn for.[137]

The perils of arrogance are well documented in Jewish literature. The Talmud writes that God needs to distance Himself from an arrogant individual. In fact, the rabbis equate arrogance with idol worship. The prohibition of idol worship and the recognition and belief in God are the very first two commandments of the Ten Commandments.

Why is arrogance considered sinful to the extent that the arrogant person is considered an idol worshipper? The Hebrew word for "idol worship" is avodah zarah. The literal translation of avodah zarah is foreign worship. When a person serves anything or anyone besides God, they are considered to be an idol worshipper.

---

137. *Yaaroth Devash* 1,15

Idols come in all shapes and sizes. It may even be the spitting image of ourselves. An arrogant person believes that he is a self-made man and all his successes in life are his own doing. Such a belief is self-worship, which is another form of idol worship. Imagine every time an arrogant person would look at the mirror and instead of seeing his reflection, he would see the image of an idol. More than likely it would help the person deal with his arrogance.

How Do I Stop?

Most people appreciate and recognize that one should not lie. There are many people where lying has become second nature. The more a person lies, the more comfortable they become with lying, until it reaches a point when they can't distinguish between what is true and what is a lie.

What can a person do to stop lying? The person should contemplate the following: At least twice a day, we say the Shema prayer. In the Shema, we declare and affirm the oneness of God. We also declare the eternal truth of God's Torah, both fundamental principles of Jewish faith. If a person is a habitual liar, why would anyone believe him when he makes such lofty proclamations?[138]

It is like the boy who cried wolf. Remember, if a person wants his statements that are near and dear to him believed, then he must ensure that everything else he utters is also the truth.

---

138. *Yaaroth Devash 1*

Mankind

Being Holy

The Hebrew word *kadosh* is commonly translated to mean "holy," such as *ish kadosh* (holy man). The Torah obligates us to be kadosh. What is the understanding of this command? What does it mean to be holy?

The literal translation of the word *kadosh* is not "holy"; rather, it means to be removed from or to be separated from. God is instructing us that we should not overindulge in the trappings of the material and the mundane; rather, we should focus on the spiritual and sublime.[139]

One of the reasons God gave us the commandments was to refine us and to make us better human beings.

It is feasible that a person doesn't transgress any of God's commandments, yet he is a crude, unrefined individual, who indulges in worldly pleasures. There is no sin in driving a nice car or owning a boat or having your own private plane. But if you focus only in acquiring more adult toys, how holy can you possibly be and how righteous could you possibly become?

There must be more to life than being able to purchase a very expensive luxury item. Remember, we take nothing with us after 120.

Lead by Example

Somebody who is in the world of academia or finance or is a successful businessperson can have a greater impact on his fellow Jew more than a rabbi can ever have. Why?

In a sense, you could argue a rabbi is paid to look the part, to study and to take the time to come to the daily *minyanim* (services). People

---

139. *Yaaroth Devash 1,1*

may therefore reason that since the world they live in is so different than the rabbi's world, there is nothing they can garner and learn from the life of the rabbi.

However, if we are successful in the outside world, and at the same time, we remain very visibly Jewish, this can have a great impact on the vast majority of Jews who live in that same space.[140]

For a great period of our history, we were forced to live in ghettos and were very restricted in how we could earn a living. Over time, those barriers were removed, and a Jew was granted the same privileges and opportunities as everyone else. However, to get ahead, you had to hide your Jewishness and blend in with everyone else. And you definitely couldn't portray yourself as an observant Jew.

I will never forget the occasion when I was accompanying a world-renowned psychiatrist, specializing in addiction therapy, on his way to give a lecture at the psychiatric department of a large hospital. One of the nurses we passed in the hallway stopped us and told us that we must be lost. She explained that we were in the teaching section of the hospital. With a wry smile, the doctor responded that he was there to give the lecture. The nurse's surprised reaction was worth a million dollars. You see, the doctor had a long white beard with payot (side curls) and was wearing a long black coat and a Chasidic hat.

We live in a completely different world. It is not uncommon to see doctors in hospitals wearing a kippah or women wearing a wig or head covering presenting at trial. Being observant is not a handicap any longer; on the contrary, it is a plus on a person's résumé. It portrays the individual as being an upright, moral person, a person of principle, someone who can be trusted, a man of his word.

A famous celebrity wanted to hire a religious Jew as his lawyer on the condition that he would have to be available 24/7. The lawyer said he couldn't take him up on his offer because he does not answer his phone on

---

140. *Yaaroth Devash* 1,6

the Shabbat. The following Shabbat, the lawyer's phone rang incessantly. The lawyer had no idea who could be calling him every half hour. Of course, he didn't answer the call.

When it became dark on Saturday night, the phone rang again, and it was the same celebrity on the line. He said that he had been the one calling the whole day because he didn't believe him when he said he wouldn't answer the phone and thereby miss out on such a lucrative opportunity. Now that he saw that the lawyer really didn't answer the phone and is a man with principles, he wanted him to be his in-house lawyer.

The golden rule is people respect those who respect themselves.

Human Interaction

Many people are familiar with the phrase "broken heart" and associate it with sadness. It is a metaphor for the intense emotional stress one feels at experiencing great and deep longing. It is a phrase usually associated with a breakup with someone who was very special in one's life.

Rabbinic literature speaks of a *lev nishbar* (a broken heart) in somewhat different terms. One great rabbi said, "There is nothing as wholesome and complete as a broken heart."

When discussing a lev nishbar, Reb Yehonatan puts a positive spin on it. He understands the phrase in the following manner: The heart represents and is the source of a person's desires. It is where the *Yetzer Hara* (evil inclination) resides. When one breaks the heart, so to speak, what we are really saying is that we have weakened our want for physical pleasure. And, at the same time, our yearning for the spiritual, the eternal, comes to the fore.[141]

The rabbis teach us that it is not by chance that there are no two people on planet earth who are truly identical. Even identical twins have slightly different features. The reason for this is to impress upon us that no two people think alike.

---

141. *Yaaroth Devash 1*

We need to be very mindful of that when we interact with others. This is especially so when we deal with people from other cultures and upbringing. Even when it comes to language, we may both speak the same language, but that doesn't mean we understand each other. Take, for example, the word "football." If your English friend asks you to play a game of football, you will be playing with a round ball, using your feet. If he is American, you will be playing with an oval ball, using your hands.

If someone tells you they have a broken heart, make sure you understand what they are really saying before you either pat them on the back and congratulate them for their spiritual growth or put an arm around their shoulder and tell them you are here for them.

Nature versus Nurture

There is great debate whether human behavior is determined by external factors, such as our exposure and experiences during our lifetime (referred to as nurture), or by the way we are wired, our genetic inheritance, and other biological factors (referred to as nature). A third approach is that we are a product of both nature and nurture.

Reb Yehonatan speaks of two drives or forces that cause us to behave badly. They are known as the internal and external *Yetzer Hara* (evil inclination).

The first is an internal drive based on our temperament. Some people are hotheaded and have a difficult time controlling their anger, while others are easygoing, and they aren't challenged when it comes to controlling their anger. This would be defined as nature.

The second drive or motivational force is external. Where the Yetzer Hara plants ideas in your head and encourages you to transgress the word of God.

Concerning our internal drive, or nature, we possess the ability to prevent ourselves from transgressing. However, when we are confronted by our external Yetzer Hara, we could not defeat it on our own and need God's help in dealing with it. However, God will only help us defeat the external Yetzer Hara if He sees that we have put in the effort and defeated our internal Yetzer Hara, and we have attempted to defeat our external Yetzer Hara.[142]

Very often we hear people say, "It's not my fault; I was born like that." While it is true that we are all born with some good qualities and perhaps some challenging qualities, that does not mean that they are a life sentence. What it means is that we may struggle in certain areas that others don't. At the same time, there may be situations we don't find difficult, while others do. However, it is important to recognize that we were given the tools and ability to deal with our challenging and negative qualities.

We are familiar with the phrase, "God helps those who help themselves." Even if we feel the challenge is too great, that the mountain is too high, God wants to see if we are willing to try to give it our best shot, and if we do, He will take care of the rest.

Remember, "I was born like that" is no excuse; it just means you have to work harder. Remember, God is waiting in the wings to help. However, he is waiting for us to take the first step.

Walking the Same Path

Very often a person will say, "If it is good enough for so-and-so, it is good enough for me. If he can do it, so can I."

Would this be considered an approach worth living by? The answer is a categorical no.

The rationale can be understood by contrasting the behavior of two great rabbis who happened to be brothers-in-law: Rabbi Yochanan and Rabbi Shimon ben Lakish.

Rabbi Shimon ben Lakish was very careful with whom he would communicate—to the extent that if you saw someone speaking with Rabbi Shimon, you knew the person was of upstanding character, and one could extend the person a loan without taking any security. On the other hand, Rabbi Yochanan would greet anyone and everyone

---

142. *Tiferet Yehonatan Ha'azinu*

he came in contact with to the point that there was never an occasion when someone greeted him first.

Why such dissimilar behavior in their interactions with others? Rabbi Shimon did not have your typical great rabbi upbringing. Prior to becoming a great rabbi, he had a career as a thief. He therefore felt that because of his past, he needed to distance himself from people of susceptible character. On the other hand, Rabbi Yochanan had your typical great rabbi upbringing and he therefore felt that he would not be compromising himself by interacting with all segments of society.[143]

If you can't swim, you don't dive into the deep end of the pool. The fact that everyone else in your class are diving in is irrelevant, since more than likely they have all learned to swim.

No two people should walk the same path. The path we need to take in the future is very much dependent on the well-worn path we have traversed in the past. We need to focus on our own needs and recognize our own strengths and weaknesses and not be constantly looking over our shoulder to see what everyone else is doing.

Our Purpose

A human being is unique in the sense that he has the capacity to question, to ask, to challenge. Perhaps the most fundamental and important question a person can ask is, "Why am I here? Why did God create me?"

If a person in unable to answer this, they will go through life like a ship without a rudder. The answer to this question is alluded to in our very name. The Hebrew word for "person" is *adam*. That is why the first human being was called Adam. The Hebrew word for "earth" is *adamah*. Both words are linked as they have the same root letters ADM.

---

143. *Yaaroth Devash 1*

The Torah relates that Adam was a composite of the physical and the spiritual. God gathered dust of the earth and formed a body. He then imbued it with a living spirit. Why is man called adam, referencing his physical component, the dust of the earth, and not a name that reflects the greatness of man, that being his soul his spirit?

The very name the Torah gives to mankind, Adam, answers the ultimate question, "Why am I here? Why did God create me?"

Man's/Adam's purpose for existing is to take the physical, the mundane, the earthly (Adamah) and turn it into the spiritual, the holy, and the heavenly.[144]

If a person ever queries why he is here, just remember that your name is Adam, and you will have your answer.

What Should a Person Wish For?

If a person could wish for one thing and their wish would be answered, what should they wish for? The list is endless: good health, financial success, children, and long life, to name just a few.

Three times a day, we pray to God, and we recite the Shemoneh Esrei, the Amidah that contains nineteen blessings. We ask God for nineteen different things, such as health and wealth. However, the very first blessing and request we ask God for is the intellectual capacity of understanding. For unless a person can understand and appreciate life and all that it encompasses, he can never truly value his blessings.[145]

What sets a human being apart from the animal kingdom is his intellectual capacity—his ability to discern, contemplate, evaluate, and so on. If offered a choice between being blessed with eternal health and a $50 toy with flashy lights that makes noise, a child will more than likely choose the toy. The child's mind has not fully developed to recognize how badly he has chosen. To know what to ask God for and to reap the benefits of His blessings,

---

144. *Yaaroth Devash 11*

145. *Yaaroth Devash 1,1*

we first need to possess a certain level of maturity and insight. May we be blessed with the foresight to know what to ask for from the source of all blessings, God Himself.

Long Life

At a house of mourning, it is quite common to wish the mourners long life. During the High Holiday period, a person asks God to remember them and bless them with life. What type of life are they asking God for?

There are those who see a life worth living as one that is intrinsically bound with the accumulation of wealth and honor. That is not the kind life one should be beseeching God for. There is a more sublime and spiritual type of life that one should strive for, where one sees his life as an opportunity to fulfill the will of God.

This is seen in Psalms were King David writes, "The departed cannot praise God." Likewise, in Ethics of the Fathers, it says, "A moment in this world devoted to the study of Torah and performing God's commandments is worth more than all of the world to come."

This is the type of life a person requests from God in their prayers. The prayer reads "(God) remember us for life . . . for Your sake, O living God." A person requests life for God's sake—to be able to fulfill the will of God and not for personal pleasure.[146]

At a house of mourning or on any occasion when one blesses someone with long life, bless them that their long life be imbued with purpose and meaning.

Our Ancestors Were No Dummies

One of the fascinating stories depicted in the book of Bereishit (Genesis) is the episode of the Tower of Babel. Mankind was worried that God would bring another flood and destroy the world and

---

146. *Yaaroth Devash* 14

decided to build a tower that would make its way up to heaven. And if God brought a flood, they would be saved because they would be in heaven.

Building a tower that would reach heaven is an impossible task. What were these people thinking?

The people of the time were extremely intelligent. They knew that rain doesn't come from the heavens. Rather, the sun causes water to evaporate and become gas that disappears into the air. This vapor rises and cools and turns into water droplets, which form clouds. When the droplets become too heavy, they fall as rain. Therefore, as long as the people could build a tower that reached above the clouds, they would be safe. They had the engineering and building skills to accomplish this.[147]

Each generation thinks that it's the smartest generation that ever lived and that no one from a previous generation can teach them anything. We view our parents and definitely our grandparents and great-grandparents as being somewhat intellectually inferior. The episode of the Tower of Babel clearly shows that mankind, from the beginning of time, was extremely well educated and knowledgeable. When it comes to previous generations' intellectual ability and insight, we should not look at them with disdain. Rather, we should say to ourselves that perhaps they were a lot smarter than we give them credit for.

My Thoughts Count

Ask yourself which is worse: thinking about stealing something or actually stealing it. Of course, your response would be that actually stealing something is a lot worse. If this is so, how then do we understand the Talmudic statement, "Thinking about sinning is far worse than actually committing the sin itself"?

Jewish law distinguishes between a thief and a robber. A thief is someone who steals at night, hoping that there are no witnesses to the

---

147. *Tiferet Yehonatan Noach*

crime, and a robber steals during the day and doesn't care if he will be caught.

The punishment for a thief is more severe than for a robber. The reason is because the thief by his actions fears being seen by another human being but is not concerned that God will see him. The robber, on the other hand, makes no distinction and fears neither God nor man. The thief who fears man more than God is punished more severely.

From a similar perspective, thinking of sinning is worse than actually sinning. Why does the person only think of sinning but will not sin? Because he is scared people will find out. And, at the same time, he has no qualms thinking of sinning because no one else knows his thoughts and he is not concerned that God knows what he is thinking.[148]

We are all familiar with the saying, "Action speaks louder than words." However, we also understand and appreciate the power of the spoken word and the impact it can have. What we don't spend enough time reflecting on is the place our thoughts have in the larger scheme of things. We always tell people, "Think before you speak."

Perhaps we need to think about what we are thinking—since, from the Talmud's perspective, our thoughts can have a greater impact than our actions.

Someone Is Watching

Very often we hear people say, "It's my life; I will live it as I please." We may even cloak it in religious belief by saying, "I am answerable to no one besides God."

Do we really need to worry what other people think?

The Talmud states that one of the worst transgressions is when we cause others to sin. This does not just mean when we encourage or force someone to sin. It can also be understood to mean that if my behavior or actions will encourage someone to sin, it will be considered

---

148. *Yaaroth Devash 14*

as if I have aided and abetted the sinner, and I will bear a certain level of responsibility.

We hear it all the time, when a righteous person does something noble and profound, we respond by saying, "Of course he did it; he is a very special person. I could never do that." If, however, the righteous person does something that is not all that kosher, we immediately say, "If it's good enough for him, it's good enough for me." A righteous person needs to realize that if people copy any of his bad behaviors, he will be somewhat responsible.

It isn't just the holy who need to be watchful of their conduct and how it will be perceived by others. This is true for everyone. For example, if our financial success is gained through illegal means, this may lead others to act in a similar fashion, believing this is the only way to become wealthy. Without even realizing it, we have encouraged others to sin, and we will be held somewhat responsible.[149]

The Torah is replete with laws that impress upon us the importance we need to place on how our conduct is viewed by others. Each and every one of us needs to be aware that our actions, good and bad, are being viewed by others. And many may be inspired to replicate the good and unfortunately find justification in copying the bad.

Do we really need to worry what other people think? We certainly do. We must never forget that life is like a stage, and we are all actors, and the audience is watching and learning how to play the part.

Innocent until Proven Guilty

In Hebrew, there is a saying that translates into English as "A disease known is half the cure." Similarly, we can say that if we realize we have committed a sin, then there is every chance we will mend our ways and seek forgiveness from God. However, if we don't believe we have done anything wrong, why would we think we need to seek forgiveness?

---

149. *Yaaroth Devash 1*

Rambam gives a prime example: Most people wouldn't consider it a sin if we suspect an innocent person of committing a crime, as all we did was assume something about someone. Yet, the Torah deems it as a transgression, and we need to seek atonement—and his punishment will be quite severe.

If a person thinks that he is squeaky clean and things are not turning out as he planned, he won't attribute it to any shortcomings on his part. Therefore, he is punished in a way that will get him thinking that perhaps what he is going through is a result of his behavior. By examining his actions, he will hopefully work out what he has been doing wrong.[150]

Very often, without our even realizing it, we fill the roles of judge and jury over our friends, neighbors, and even total strangers. More often than not, we find the person guilty of a crime even before we have heard any particulars of the case.

One of the most revered principles in the Western democratic legal system is the theory of "innocent until proven guilty"—a phrase coined during the late eighteenth century. The presumption of innocence is crucial to ensuring a fair trial in individual cases and to respecting the human dignity of people who are accused of committing crime.

From a Jewish perspective, "innocent until proven guilty" is not simply a mechanism to ensure everyone receives a fair trial. It is a beautiful mindset that we need to nurture: that being everyone is born holy and pure. Everyone is good. It is in our hands whether we remain as such.

There was a high school teacher who entered the classroom on the first day of the new school year and wrote every student's name on the board. And next to each name she put an A. She told them as of today, you each will receive an A grade at the end of the year. It is up to you to retain it. You guessed it—at the end of the year every student received an A grade.

---

150. *Yaaroth Devash 1*

Manna/Bread from Heaven

All Tastes

Throughout the Jewish people's sojourn in the desert, they were sustained by the manna that fell from heaven on a daily basis. One of the many miracles associated with this food was its taste. Whatever a person wanted the food to taste like it did. If he wanted it to taste like chicken, it did, or like potatoes, it did. You could never become tired of having the same menu day in and day out.[151]

We no longer have food falling from heaven. However, that shouldn't stop us from marveling at the tremendous acts of kindness that God bestowed on our forebearers, the generation that left Egypt. We didn't have to work to earn a livelihood to provide food for our family. We didn't have to worry where our next meal would come from. We could eat to our heart's desire as we created our own menu on a daily basis.

---

151. *Tiferet Yehonatan Shoftim*

Marriage

He Is One

Reb Yehonatan explains that a male and a female are both incomplete since each contain half a soul, and when we marry, our souls unite to form one complete soul.

He further writes that the male, prior to marriage, is considered physically incomplete. When discussing the creation of Adam and Chava, the Torah states that God took a piece of one of Adam's sides and used it to form Chava. When a male and a female marry, they are physically reunited, and the male once again becomes physically complete.[152]

We live in a world where we speak of rights, our rights. As citizens of any given country, we feel that we have certain rights that need to be met. This is true not just in terms of our expectations from government; this is also true in our everyday interactions. We feel a sense of entitlement. We are constantly asking ourselves, "What is in it for me?"

The words "duty," "responsibility," and "service" have somehow disappeared from our vocabulary; our rights trump any sense of obligation. This attitude has unfortunately caused grave harm to the institution of marriage. We no longer ask, "What are my obligations toward my spouse?" Rather, we couch the marriage contract in terms of rights and benefits. And if our needs are not being met, then we see no reason in remaining.

Such an approach to life and to the sanctity of marriage is the antithesis to what Judaism is all about, and it resonates from our animal soul and evil inclination. The Hebrew word for "love" is ahavah, which comes from the root word "hav," which means to give. If you love someone, your focus should be on the giving and not on the receiving.

---

152. *Tiferet Yehonatan Shoftim*

Marrying the Family

Very often we hear people say, "When you marry someone, you marry their entire family." This is because you will inevitably have to interact with your spouse's family.

It is a given that children will look like their parents or grandparents. Reb Yehonatan suggests that the link between parent and child is not only true in their physical appearance; it is also correct in terms of character and nature. There is a Yiddish expression that translates, "An apple doesn't fall far from the tree." Or, in English, we very often refer to someone as a "chip off the old block." This means that the child's character and nature are very similar to the parent's character and nature. There is a great likelihood if the parents are quiet and reserved, the children will be as well. And if the parents a very giving and caring people, there is a very good chance the children will be as well.

According to Reb Yehonatan, "When you marry someone, you marry their entire family" may not be entirely accurate; however, it is fair to say that when you marry someone, you marry some of your spouse's parents' character traits, both the good and the bad.[153]

We go to school and learn reading, writing, arithmetic, and many other subjects. However, we are not taught some of the most important subjects and life skills. We are not taught how to be a good, loving spouse. We do not learn how to raise healthy, well-rounded children. Where then do we know how to behave in the important roles of partner and parent?

We learn it from our life experiences, from our own upbringing, and whether or not we like it, it becomes part of our DNA. How often did we say when we were children, "I will never do or say what my parent just did or said" and many years later when we are married and have children, we do exactly what our parents did and we remind ourselves how we said we would never do it. We learn how to be a spouse from observing our parents. Our parenting skills are fashioned on how our parents raised us.

---

153. *Tiferet Yehonatan Pinchas*

We must always remember that we cannot hide behind the walls of our homes since, as parents, we are constantly actors on a stage and the audience is our offspring.

We Are One

Even though spouses comes from a different set of parents, maybe from different parts of the world, and perhaps from totally different backgrounds and upbringings, they very often discover upon getting married how much they have in common and how their dispositions are very similar.

This is true because the true essence of a person is their soul. And the souls of husband and wife come from the same source. And since their essence is hewn from the same spiritual receptacle, it would stand to reason that the couple would have a lot in common.[154]

Jewish mysticism explains that each partner has half a soul, and when they unite in marriage, each of their souls become complete via the other.

Western society views marriage as two individuals, where each is considered complete prior to their marriage. Using mathematics as an analogy, it is one plus one that gives us two,. while according to Kabbalah, it is a half plus a half that gives us one.

If our mindset is that we are complete before we get married, it becomes challenging to be receptive to our spouses' point of view or their desires. However, if our approach is that we are incomplete without my other, then it is in my best interest to be attuned and sensitive to the wants and needs of my spouse.

It is not by chance that, when we speak of our spouses, we refer to them as our better half.

---

154. *Tiferet Yehonatan Bereishit*

Peace in the Home

During the time of the Beit Hamikdash, the citizens of Jerusalem had a very strong love for each other and rarely became angry with one another. This was seen in the fact that none of the inhabitants of Jerusalem ever complained that they didn't have enough space to live or that their neighbors were infringing on their property. As the saying goes, "Where there is room in the heart, there is room in the home."

Why were the citizens of Jerusalem so predisposed?

There is a strong correlation between sanctity and holiness on the one hand and friendship and love on the other. Jerusalem was the holiest city in Israel; therefore, the friendship and love among its inhabitants was far greater than in other parts of Israel.[155]

In Hebrew, this is called shalom bayit (peace in the home). Every marriage should be blessed with peace and harmony. The million-dollar question is, how does a couple achieve this? By increasing the holiness and sanctity in the home, the flow-on effect will be a peaceful and tranquil home.

Why?

Perhaps we can suggest that the more we are exposed to spiritual things, the more it puts things in perspective, and we are able to properly prioritize what is important and what is trivial. This then becomes a very strong foundation in building a healthy marriage.

They Are so Similar

How often are people amazed by how similar a young married couple is to each other? The reason for their surprise is because the young man and young woman were raised in different homes by different parents with different experiences yet are still so alike.

Most people are of the understanding that there are two partners in the birth of a child: the father and the mother. If that were the case,

---

155. *Yaaroth Devash* 1,1

then the similarity between the young husband and wife would be truly surprising. However, there is a third partner in the birth of a child: God. God is the major provider as He contributes the soul, the life force, while the parents are responsible for the body and the physicality of the child.

How do we define a person? It isn't by their external appearance since that evolves and is constantly changing from the moment of birth until they reach a ripe old age. Rather, it is their spirit, their soul, that defines them. The souls of mankind all stem from the same spiritual realm, hewn from the same rock.

The young couple are not total strangers who share no common bond. Their souls emanate from the same spiritual source. We therefore shouldn't be surprised when a young married couple seem to be so much alike—because, in truth, spiritually they are indeed one.[156]

When a person loses a loved one, they tear a garment. Why is this so? If we go scuba diving and then go into a space capsule, we obviously dress differently. When we are on dry land, we wear different clothing once again. We may be dressed differently, but we are the same person. We simply change our clothing depending on the circumstance.

The soul is the essence of the person, and the soul is eternal. While the soul is here on earth, it needs a unique set of clothing: the body. The mourner tears his garment to remind himself that his loved one has moved to another location, and it was necessary to change its clothing.

Honeymoon Period

After their marriage ceremony, many couples go on a honeymoon before they return to the workforce. One could argue that this is counterintuitive. When a couple gets married, their collective financial responsibilities increase exponentially. Shouldn't they return to work the very next day?

---

156. *Tiferet Yehonatan Bereishit*

The answer is obvious. The pleasure the couple will experience while enjoying their honeymoon is of more value to them than the financial impact of lost wages.

Rabbi Yehonatan also had a dim view of the husband immediately returning to the workforce. He also felt there needed to be a honeymoon period. He, however, had a different type of honeymoon in mind. He was concerned that if the husband immediately returned to work, then the study of Torah would greatly diminish, and the knowledge of Torah would be lessened.

He therefore felt that the heads of the various Jewish communities should establish a guideline stating that for the first five years of marriage, the husband should devote himself completely to the study of Torah. The couple should not worry about how they will manage money-wise. They should have complete trust in God that He will look after their financial needs.[157]

When we bless a couple about to get married, we refer to marriage as a building, a structure. The foundations of a building need to be strong, unwavering, and secure. The same is true when we speak of marriage. The beginning of the marriage needs to be based on a strong commitment to Torah and mitzvot. It has therefore been encouraged that, at the outset, the young man should devote his day to full-time Torah study. Such learning takes place in an institution called a kollel.

---

157. *Yaaroth Devash* 1,2

Medicine

Preventive Medicine

It is fascinating to note that Reb Yehonatan, who lived in the early eighteenth century, had a keen understanding of the importance of preventive medicine.

He writes that it would be advantageous for a person to be conscious of what he eats and to take certain natural supplements to enhance his health rather than waiting until he falls ill. This is because, once a person becomes unwell, he would need to be on a regimen of medication, and most medicines have harmful side effects.[158]

What many people don't realize is that many of the great sages of the generations were not only giants in Torah learning, but they also had a vast knowledge and a deep understanding of secular knowledge. Rambam (Maimonides), who lived in the twelfth century, was a preeminent astronomer and physician, and served as the personal physician of Saladin. The first medical textbook printed had been written many years earlier by Maimonides.

Likewise, Rabbi Eliyahu of Vilna, known as the Vilna Gaon, who lived during the eighteenth century, was one of the greatest rabbis of the last 400 years. Besides writing many books encompassing all aspects of Jewish study, he also authored books on grammar and mathematics.

What is truly fascinating is the answer to the following question: Who was the first person to discover that the world was not flat, and we couldn't fall off?

---

158. *Yaaroth Devash* 1,5

Most attribute it to Pythagoras in the sixth century BCE and Parmenides in the fifth century, who both stated that the earth is spherical. What is not that well known is that Isiah the Prophet, who lived in the eighth century BCE, writes in the Book of Isiah some 100 years before Pythagoras that the world is round and not flat.

Meditation

What Should I Meditate On?

When you ask someone who enjoys meditation what they meditate about, more often than not, they will tell you that they try to recall a childhood memory that makes them feel safe and happy, or picture a scene that makes them feel relaxed.

Reb Yehonatan suggests that we should meditate on the greatness of God—His strength and His awesomeness—and that God has given us His Torah. We also need to meditate that God is infinite and we are finite, and God has chosen us to serve Him. How could we then not feel a sense of inner happiness and joy?[159]

It seems that a twenty-four hour day is never near enough time for us to accomplish all that we need to. We barely have enough time to catch our breath. It would be extremely healthy if, every so often, we would pause and get off the treadmill of life and meditate and reflect on how we have been handpicked by God to serve Him.

---

159. *Yaaroth Devash 1*

Miracles

Never Alone

Three times a day in the Amidah (18 Blessings), we offer praise to God for all of the miracles He has done for us. We may be under the impression that we are thanking God for all the miracles we, the Jewish people, have experienced throughout our history. While this is true, we need to understand that it is also referring to our own daily lives. We may go through a day and feel that we haven't experienced anything life shattering or anything out of the ordinary. We definitely don't think we have experienced any miracles.

This prayer is a reminder that every single day, unbeknown to us, we have experienced personal miracles and for that we need to thank God for.[160]

What a wonderful perspective to have on life, were we see every day as a gift given to us by God, and God is protecting and sheltering us. At times, we may feel down and alone. We may feel no one really cares about us. If we ever have these negative thoughts, we need to realize and sense that, on a daily basis, God is performing miracles to protect and safeguard us. What could be more uplifting and heartening than that?

---

160. *Yaaroth Devash 1,1*

Mitzvot/Commandments

"We Can" Attitude

We have been given 613 commandments. Our lives are governed and defined by God's laws. From the moment we wake till the moment we go to sleep, God has something to say about how we need to behave. And, in fact, even while we are sleeping, we are bound by rules and regulations.

These laws dictate what we can eat, when we can work, and who we can marry, just to name a few. This may, at times, seem extremely daunting, and we may fall into the trap of believing that leading an observant lifestyle is beyond the reach of a mere man.

Reb Yehonatan writes that it is all a question of perspective. We need to be of the firm belief that God has no intention of making life difficult for us and that God's mitzvot are not overbearing or difficult to fulfill; rather, they are pleasant and enjoyable to fulfill.[161]

If we are at the early stages of our spiritual journey, the first thing we need to be very conscious of is that Rome was not built in a day. We need to walk before we can run. Each time we take on a new commitment, we need to make sure we are comfortable with what we have been doing till now. If we feel overwhelmed with what we are doing to date, it makes absolutely no sense to add to the burden. The only thing we will accomplish is crashing under the weight of responsibility and expectations.

As long as we have a "we can" attitude, we will forever be drawn closer to God.

---

161. *Yaaroth Devash 1,11*

Rewards Unknown

At Mount Sinai, God gave the Jewish people the Torah and its commandments. There are in total 613 mitzvot. The commandments are subdivided into two categories: positive commandments and negative commandments. There are 365 negative commandments and 248 positive commandments.

From a tender age, we remember receiving candies or toys as a reward for behaving at home or at school. As we grew older, we were enticed to perform and extend ourselves in the workforce with the promise of bonuses and dividends. Why then does God not inform us the rewards we will receive for fulfilling His commandments? Wouldn't that knowledge be a very strong motivator to heed the word of God?

The concern may be that, if we have that information, we may start weighing the mitzvot, one against the other. And we would relegate those mitzvot whose reward is minimal and focus our attention on the mitzvot that will give us the most brownie points.[162]

In Ethics of the Fathers, we are taught that we should serve God and fulfill his commandments without viewing or contemplating the reward waiting for us at its conclusion.

The rationale behind this understanding is self-understood. If we are in a relationship that is based on tit for tat (that is, I will do this for you if you will do that for me), that relationship cannot be considered a deep and meaningful one. Because the reason I am stepping out of my comfort zone to do something for you is because the gift or barter I will receive in return far outweighs any level of discomfort I am now experiencing.

If you truly love someone and you care about them, you want to answer their call and do as they desire simply because of who they are and not because of any incentive that may be offered.

---

162. *Yaaroth Devash 1*

While it is true that we are not told the rewards for the commandments in order that we don't pick and choose, a higher level of service would be to reach a place where our commitment to God and His mitzvot is such that it would make no difference what the reward may be.

What Comes First?

There are two types of mitzvot: mitzvot between man and God (such as eating kosher and keeping the Shabbat) and the mitzvot between man and his fellow man (such as visiting the sick and comforting the mourner). Reb Yehonatan writes something extremely profound: He says that before we fulfill a mitzvah that falls under the category between man and God, we should first do a mitzvah between man and his fellow man.[163]

Jewish law mandates that we should give charity to our fellow man before we pray to God. There are those who customarily declare, "I am fulfilling the mitzvah of loving your fellow Jew" prior to beginning to pray.

Someone once asked his teacher, "We are obligated to love God and to love our fellow Jew. I cannot do both. Which one should I choose?" The rabbi answered, "Love that which the one you love loves." God loves our fellow Jew. By loving our fellow Jew, we are expressing our true love for God.

Why 613

We have 248 positive commandments and 365 negative commandments. The 613 commandments define our lives from the moment we are born till we pass away. And then there are laws that apply to a fetus and to a corpse.

Why do we have so many commandments? To answer this question, we first need to understand the unique relationship we have with God. Our connection with God is similar to a soldier who is always on duty even when they are sleeping. And our duties as a faithful soldier is

---

163. *Yaaroth Devash 2,16*

to recognize that we are constantly in God's presence and that we are obligated to present God with gifts; those gifts are the commandments we fulfill.

By giving us so many commandments, God is giving us opportunities to present Him with gifts at every moment of our lives.[164]

Many of us are challenged by the enormity of obligations and duties we are presented with. This is especially true when a person is beginning their journey in becoming more observant. We can view all the laws as being very restrictive, as we have 365 rules that dictate what we can't do and 248 directives that we must do. They are like a heavy load placed on our shoulders that weighs us down.

Reb Yehonatan gives us a most beautiful way of viewing the many laws God gave us. He explains that the laws—both what we must do and what we may not do—are to be understood as being 613 different ways to give God a gift.

We are given 613 opportunities to present God with a gift. What greater gift could we have been given?

Blowing Your Own Horn

The Hebrew word *tzniut* means "modesty." We usually understand it as it relates to the way we dress, that we need to dress modestly. *Tzniut*, however, is much more than just the way we clothe ourselves. Our very demeanor, the way we conduct ourselves should be in a way of *tzniut*, in a modest fashion. We shouldn't flaunt our wealth or our successes. There is no need to let people know how brilliant we are and how much knowledge we possess.

Reb Yehonatan extends this mindset as it relates to our service of God. Our relationship with God is a very personal one, and that is how it should remain. We shouldn't blow our own horn by telling people how righteous we are and how many commandments we have fulfilled.

---

164. *Tiferet Yehonatan*

He takes it even a step further and says not only should we not boast this to our friends; we should also not feel haughty and proud when thinking of all the commandments we have fulfilled as this will diminish our reward.[165]

One of the many reasons given for why God gave us the commandments is that performing the mitzvot regularly will impact our very core. Being exposed to spiritual activity on a daily basis will help us become more refined and develop noble character traits. There is nothing more obnoxious than being in the company of someone who thinks they are God's gift to creation. In fact, the rabbis write that God has declared that He cannot remain in the presence of an arrogant and conceited individual.

Many view the performance of the commandments as nothing more than going through the motions and performing rituals, and, as a result, they feel that God's laws don't speak to them. We all want to improve, and we all want to become a better person. By studying and delving into the meaning of the laws, we will discover that God has presented us with a clear guide and instructions on how to become a better and more refined human being.

The commandments are there to refine us and not to make us obnoxious.

The Reward

Esau would present himself to his father, Yitzchak, as being a righteous individual. He would ask his father questions pertaining to Jewish law. One of the questions he would ask is whether we need to give tithe from salt. Why did he single out a question concerning tithe and not one of the hundreds of other commandments?

One of the fundamental principles of our faith is the belief in *Olam HaBa* (the world to come). The world to come comprises two time periods. The first period occurs after a person passes away. At that time, the soul will make its way to *Gan Eden* (the Garden of Eden). The second period commences after the Messianic era, when we will

---

165. *Tiferet Yehonatan Voetchanan*

experience and witness the resurrection of the dead. During both of these periods, a person will be rewarded for all the commandments they fulfilled during their lifetime.

The only commandment we will be rewarded for during our sojourn in this world is for the charity we give. Logic dictates that if we give away our money, it will decrease our wealth and make us poorer. The rabbis write that this is not the case; the reward for giving charity is that God will bless us during our lifetime with an abundance of wealth, even more than what we had given to charity. And we are permitted to test God to see if this is, in fact, the case.

Esau did not believe in the world to come; hence, there could be no rewards given in a nonexistent world. In Esau's eyes, the only world he could believe in was one he could see and touch. The only reward given in this world is for the giving of tithe and charity. Therefore, Esau asked his father about tithing salt.[166]

One of the greatest challenges we face as God-fearing individuals is how do we answer the question, "Why do the righteous suffer and the wicked prosper?"

This question was asked by Moshe, our teacher who received the Torah from God, and the Book of Job (Iyov) is devoted to this issue. It is a subject that has challenged the great theologians of every generation.

The above thought of Reb Yehonatan will help us unravel one of the great mysteries of the ages.

If there was no world to come, we could question God's implementation of reward and punishment. However, this world is not the end of the story. It continues to unfold in the eternal world, a world we are not privy to. And it is there where reward and punishment fully play out. With the arrival of the Messianic era, when we will be able to see the full story, we will no longer be baffled and confused by our life experiences.

---

166. *Tiferet Yehonatan Toldot*

A great rabbi once remarked that when he was a young boy, he anxiously waited for the arrival of Moshiach so he could understand the reason for Jewish suffering.

Power of Thought

You hire someone to do a job and you inform them that it needs to be completed in seven days. At the end of the seven days, they tell you, "We really wanted to do it, but we were sick in bed the whole time and we didn't have the strength to do the work." Would you pay the person because they had good intentions and they would have done the work if they didn't get sick? Without a doubt you would answer no.

What would be your response if after the seven days, they tell you, "We wanted to do the job and we spent many hours working on the project; however, everything began to unravel beyond our control and we were unable to do it."

Would you pay the person because they had put in time and effort even though the task was not completed? More than likely, you would answer no. You may feel sorry for the person since he spent so much time and effort. However, at the end of the day, he was unable to produce the finished product.

This is not the approach of God. God knows what we are thinking and what we desire. And He judges us accordingly. By way of example, a person has a tremendous desire to give charity. He would love to help the downtrodden and the unfortunate. He wishes he could help as many people as possible. The only problem is he has been extremely unsuccessful when it comes to making money. Every venture he enters and every business he starts have all failed. His sole drive and motivation in trying different avenues to make money was not to line his pockets but rather to give it to charity. In such a situation, God rewards the person as if he had indeed given all that money to the poor.[167]

---

167. *Yaaroth Devash 2,10*

Our history has been plagued by expulsion, the Crusades, the Inquisition, the pogroms, and the Holocaust. During these tragic times of upheaval, many hundreds of thousands of Jews were unable to perform God's commandments. Does that mean all these Jews would not be rewarded for the mitzvot they were unable to perform through no fault of their own?

The answer is, it really depends on how they reacted and felt at the time. If they were very upset and heartbroken that they couldn't put on tefillin because there weren't any available or they would be putting their lives at risk, then of course they would be rewarded. In God's eyes, they had put on tefillin.

If, however, they were indifferent to their inability to put on tefillin, then it stands to reason that they would not be entitled to a reward.

If we ever want to know how significant God and His Torah is in our lives, we should see how we react and feel if, God forbid, a situation arises in which we are unable to fulfill one of God's commandments.

No Reason

Why do we do a particular mitzvah? Why do we put on tefillin? There are two schools of thought regarding whether we should attempt to answer these questions.

One approach is that we should try, to the best of our intellectual capacity, to understand the reasons for the commandments. Imagine you do the same thing every day of your life but don't really know why you are doing it. It would be very challenging not to lose some of the excitement and fervor over time. However, being able to contemplate the meaning and purpose of each commandment inspires us to do the mitzvah with greater desire and with more enthusiasm.

The other approach is that there is a certain level of risk if we are privy to the why. Take, for example, the mitzvah of putting on *tefillin* on a daily basis. *Tefillin* comprises of two small leather boxes, one placed on the head and the other on the forearm facing the heart. The rabbis offer the following explanation for this mitzvah: The tefillin teaches us that both our intellect corresponding to the tefillin worn on the head and our emotions that correspond to the tefillin placed near the heart need to constantly remember God.

A person could argue that they remember God even without putting on tefillin; therefore, they don't need to wear tefillin. As the saying goes, a little knowledge is dangerous. While it is true that the reason we put on tefillin is to remind us of God, this is not the *only* reason. There are many other reasons given why we wear tefillin and then there are the many reasons we simply are unaware of. And the fact that we are constantly feeling attached to God does not negate the mitzvah of wearing tefillin.[168]

Is it one or the other? Are these two schools of thought mutually exclusive? The answer is no and, in fact, we need to live our lives drawing on both approaches.

What is the distinguishing feature between man and beast? Man's intellectual capacity. We are able to think, to rationalize, to explore, to use our knowledge as a tool of personal advancement. If we don't tap into what makes us different, then we have reduced ourselves to be no better than an animal.

We wouldn't buy a used car without doing proper research and investigation to make sure we are not buying a lemon. In the grand scheme of things, a car is a trivial possession; it is nothing more than a means of transportation to take you from point A to point B. Yet we engage our mind to help us decide which car to purchase. When we speak of our religion, when we speak about being Jewish, that speaks to the very core of who we are. Then, without question, we must draw on our intellectual aptitude in exploring our faith.

While this is all true. There is a very important caveat we need to be aware of. God and by extension His Torah are infinite; we on the other hand are finite. A finite creature cannot understand an infinite existence.

---

168. *Ahavat Yehonatan Yitro*

What school do we go to? We go to both. In one school, we explore, we question, we challenge, and we seek understanding and insight into God's laws. And, at the same time, we are attending the other school, which teaches us to appreciate that the finite can never and will never understand the infinite. These two schools of thought have ensured that G-d's commandments remain vibrant and meaningful to this very day.

Good or Bad

A doctor tells you that you are allergic to peanuts and, if you eat even a single peanut, you could become extremely unwell. You would be forever grateful to your doctor for making you aware of the dangers of eating peanuts.

When the Torah says we cannot eat bacon or prawns, how are we to understand this precept? Is it because nonkosher foods are unhealthy and they would be detrimental to our health? Or perhaps God decreed that we cannot eat them for reasons we cannot comprehend?

God refers to us as His servants. This implies that we are obligated in following His instructions whether or not we want to do them. If eating bacon is unhealthy, even if we were not God's servant, we wouldn't eat the bacon. By God equating our relationship with Him as a servant serving His master, we can conclude that bacon is healthy, and the reason we don't eat it is because our Master said not to.

The rabbis echo this thought when they write that we should not explain the reason we are not eating pig is because it is unhealthy and revolting; rather, it is because God commanded us not to.[169]

Those of us who are old enough have experienced what we could call food cycles. For many years, we were told and led to believe that certain foods are bad for us, such as egg yolks. The yolks are high in cholesterol, which means eating them will raise your cholesterol levels, putting you at risk for heart disease. New research has found that cholesterol levels in our bodies are impacted by the types of fats in our food, not as much from the dietary

---

169. *Tiferet Yehonatan Voetchanan*

cholesterol content. In fact, the yolk contains nutrients that may help lower the risk of heart disease.

We were also led to believe that certain foods were good for us, such as margarine. This is another holdover from the eighties when everything fat-free was considered the way to go. We are now told that spreads like margarine are full of unhealthy trans fats that can contribute to heart disease, cancer, bone problems, and hormonal imbalance.

Many of us rationalize that we keep kosher because nonkosher foods are unhealthy. What would happen if science proves beyond a shadow of a doubt that a particular nonkosher food is extremely heathy? Would we start eating that food? Of course not.

Good or bad is not the decider whether we do or don't. We do because God said to, and we don't because God said not to.

Question of Perspective

Parenting is a juggling act. We constantly ask ourselves, "Is this in the best interest of my child?"

At times the parent will need to be strict with their child and may even need to punish the child to ensure the child does what they are supposed to do. While being disciplined, the child only senses that their parent is reprimanding them. They are unable to see the broader picture. The parent, on the other hand, sees beyond the moment and knows how beneficial it will be if their child accomplishes this specific task. Realizing the minor and temporary discomfort the child will have to endure will be far outweighed by the benefits the child will reap at the end.

Likewise, God, who sees the grand scheme of things, knows that by fulfilling His commandments we will benefit greatly. There may be times when we don't appreciate this, and God has no choice but to be strict with us to ensure we carry through with the task. God's perceived discipline is really an expression of God's love for us as His ultimate desire is to reward us and bless us for fulfilling His commandments.[170]

Everything is a question of perspective—how we perceive things, how we understand things. Our relationship with God is such that we are called God's children, and God is called our father. As a parent or as a child, we know of the unbreakable bond and the everlasting love that exists between a parent and their child and between a child and their parent. We can surmise then what it means when we are told that God sees Himself as our father and we are His children.

When our parents take us to the doctor to be vaccinated, it hurts and we may not know at that age why they did so. But as we grow older and mature, we realize how thankful we need to be for what they did. While we may not always see it and appreciate it, God has only our best interest at heart. Understanding that God is our loving parent puts everything we experience and endure in a totally new perspective.

All or Nothing

How often do we hear people say, "It's all or nothing"? Either I am going to be completely observant or not at all. And more often than not, they use this line of reasoning to justify why they are going down the path of "nothing at all."

Or people will say, "I don't want to be a hypocrite." They say to themselves, "How can I put on tefillin if, ten minutes later, I am going to eat nonkosher?" And, as a result, they don't put on the tefillin.

Reb Yehonatan shares with us a very profound understanding of our relationship with God and the role the commandments have in forging that connection. He writes that the phrase "all or nothing" should not be part of our lexicon. We need to view each and every commandment independently. And, in God's eyes, we have reached a level of perfection when we fulfill even one commandment properly.[171]

---

170. *Yaaroth Devash 1,1*

171. *Yaaroth Devash 1,1*

Though, as the saying goes, Rome wasn't built in a day, at a certain point, we do have to start building. No one dives into the deep end of a pool if they don't know how to swim. However, if you want to be able to dive into the deep end, you have to start off in the shallow end, and by learning and practicing how to swim, you build up your confidence and you slowly venture into the deep end.

Likewise, if a person decides one bright and sunny day, "From now on, I will become completely observant and keep all of the commandments," he will never succeed. We need to start somewhere. We need to take one commandment at a time, practice it, fulfill it until it becomes second nature, and then begin practicing another commandment. And always being conscious that each commandment is a world to itself and with each commandment we reach a level of perfection in our bond with God.

Effort versus Result

We live in a result-based society. If our employer gives us a task to do and we spend most of the night working on it, but we didn't complete the task, our boss won't care how much time and effort we put into it. He only cares about the bottom line: Was the project completed or not?

A straight-A student will be placed on a pedestal and lauded for his achievement. It could very well be the student who received a C grade is a very weak student and had to study and work very hard to achieve his grade, while the A-grade student is very gifted and didn't overexert himself at all. The A-grade student gets all the praise because society values results over effort.

This is not the case from a Torah perspective. From a Jewish perspective, we rate effort as being far more significant than results. We are rewarded based on our effort, not on our achievements. A student who spent many hours trying to understand a section of Talmud is to be rewarded and applauded more than the brilliant student who exerted very little effort in studying the same section.

This idea is reflected in a Yiddish saying, "A Jew just needs to do; his task in life is not necessarily to accomplish."[172]

Educators often remark that teaching extremely gifted students is, at times, more challenging than teaching a below-average student. The reason being, the brilliant student need not exert himself to achieve a perfect score on his exam. He can simply coast along and remain top of his class. The teacher is frustrated because the teacher knows that this student should and could achieve so much more than simply getting a 100% on the exam.

The student needs to be told that when he is studying God's Torah, the only person he needs to compete against is himself. The mere fact that he topped the class is unimportant. He needs to exert himself to the best of his ability.

Being top of the class tops nothing if it didn't take blood, sweat, and tears.

With Joy

Fulfilling God's commandments with *simcha* (joy) is imperative. When we are happy in doing something, we will do it with a lot more enthusiasm and commitment. This is also true when we speak about serving God. When we are excited and when we are happy serving God, this impacts our relationship with Him. It increases our awe and reverence, and at the same time, it intensifies our love for Him.

If we are honest with ourselves, there are times when we would rather be having a good time and enjoying ourselves then being cooped up in the synagogue or having to fulfill one of the many commandments. How do we increase our joy and excitement in fulfilling the commandments?

We can all recall how proud and responsible we felt when sitting in the classroom the teacher called upon us to take an important message to the principal. That out of the whole class the teacher thought we were the most capable and trustworthy to get the job done.

---

172. *Yaaroth Devash 1,1*

In a sense, that is how we need to view our relationship with God when it comes to observing all of His commandments. We need to think of how fortunate we are and what an incredible gift we have been given that each and every one of us mere mortals of flesh and blood have been asked by God to carry out His requests. Wouldn't that bring a smile to your face and make you very happy?[173]

What makes you happy? Answering this question will go a long way in helping you ascertain what you value and what is important in your life. What we may not realize is that we can acquire happiness. Experiences that we once thought were boring and perhaps even burdensome can become some of our most treasured moments. How? The more we learn about something and comprehend its deeper and sublime meaning, the more we recognize the benefits it brings us. This in turn will cause us to feel happy and excited about doing it.

Beyond the Commandments

To paraphrase a Yiddish proverb, "Just because we can doesn't mean we must." This proverb sheds light on how we need to view the wonderful world we inhabit.

God gave us 365 negative commandments—things we are not allowed to do. For example, we are not allowed to eat nonkosher. As long as the food is kosher, the Torah permits us to eat it. There is no law that limits how much we can eat, only what we can eat. While this is true, an important ethos of the Jewish faith is the need for mankind to grow spiritually to become a more refined human being. The more we indulge in the pleasures of the world and the more we seek physical self-gratification, the less likely we will be attuned to any semblance of Godliness and holiness.[174]

---

173. *Yaaroth Devash 1,1*
174. *Tiferet Yehonatan Ha'azinu*

Is the following scenario good or bad? Every night for dinner, you are served a five-course kosher meal that includes a hundred-dollar steak and a five-hundred-dollar bottle of red wine. The food is kosher, so that is good. However, this scenario is not 100 percent kosher. Why? The real question we need to be asking is whether such eating habits are conducive to spiritual growth—and the answer is a resounding no.

Money

Kosher Money

The Torah relates a fascinating story about our forefather Yaakov. When he was returning with his family to his parents' home, he inadvertently left some of his possessions at their last encampment. Yaakov went alone at night to retrieve his small jugs. He remained there the whole night, and during the night, he battled Esau's angel.

The Talmud comments that the items he left behind were not of any significant value. Why then did Yaakov put himself in harm's way to retrieve them? The Talmud responds, "The righteous do not accumulate their wealth by illegal means." Therefore, Yaakov saw everything he owned as being holy and to be valued. However, a person whose money is accrued by thievery and the like will not give much value and significance to his possessions and losing something will have little impact on him.[175]

After reading how Yaakov went back to get his small jugs, how should we view our worldly belongings? Yaakov is not teaching us that we should become hoarders. It also doesn't mean we should be stingy with what is ours.

Rather, it is impressing upon us that the way we make our money should impact the significance we give it. Money made honorably should be valued. It is something we should be proud of. Illegal wealth is something we should shun and distance ourselves from. We definitely should not bestow it with any value.

---

175. *Tiferet Yehonatan Metzorah*

False Service

It isn't sufficient to simply follow God's instructions. Equally important is to follow them for the correct reasons. If a person serves God
because he sees this as opportunity to become wealthy, while he may
have fulfilled God's instruction, he cannot be considered as a servant of God. Rather, he would be considered a servant or a slave of
money.[176]

*Anyone with any intelligence knows the futility and the absurdity of serving
an idol that is nothing more than an inanimate object. While this may be
true, how many of us serve the all-powerful dollar bill? It too is a lifeless
object.*

*We may even play intellectual gymnastics to justify our behavior by
explaining how we are really serving God and the accumulation of wealth
is nothing more than a wonderful byproduct. We need to be honest with
ourselves and ask one simple question: If I would not become wealthy as
a result of following God's laws, would I still be interested in doing them?
Would I still do them with the same joy and enthusiasm? Serve God for
God's sake!*

The Greatest Challenge

Reb Yehonatan makes an interesting observation. He writes that we all
face life challenges where we have to choose between right and wrong.
Some tests are harder than others. However, the most difficult trials
are those that involve money.

When confronted with a situation that may cause them pain, suffering, or embarrassment, many people rise to the occasion and choose
what is right, even though such a decision may ultimately affect their
health. Yet these same individuals will not be able to overcome a financial challenge, and they will choose wrong over right.

---

176. *Tiferet Yehonatan Balak*

If a person is able to overcome financial challenges, such as not stealing or taking that which isn't theirs, he should be confident in the fact that he has the strength and commitment to deal with all of life's challenges. Reb Yehonatan concludes this idea by stating that human experience shows that the pursuit of wealth is life's greatest challenge, and it is so self-evident that we don't have to bring any proof to prove this point.[177]

While Reb Yehonatan lived many hundreds of years ago, human nature has not changed. The challenges he speaks of are the same challenges we face today. We could argue that the challenges have only increased. The opportunity to make a lot of money in a very short time is unique to our times. The fine line between "kosher" money and money earned in a somewhat nonkosher fashion has never been so blurred.

We need to be extra vigilant in our business affairs to ensure that we remain squeaky clean. It is not by chance that after 120 years, the very first question we will be asked by the heavenly court is, "Were you honest in your business transactions?"

---

177. *Yaaroth Devash* 1,7

Moral Behavior

Learn It, Live It

We have all heard of the three Rs; it was the basic elements of an elementary school curriculum. They were *reading*, *'riting* (writing), and *'rithmetic* (arithmetic). These three basics were the mainstay of education. However, as technology progresses, more and more schools are undermining these basic principles because students need to know more and be able to work with computers, software, and other pieces of technology.

Unfortunately, what is lacking in our educational system is a failure to teach our students how to become moral and upstanding members of society. Little or no effort is expended in instilling a sense in the students that they need to work on their personal growth, that they need to recognize the flaws in their own character and find ways to correct them.

Reb Yehonatan was of the strong opinion that this is true not only of the young but for adults as well. He felt that we must dedicate time during the course of the day in studying Jewish texts that focus on self-development. He writes that we need to study those texts that will help us in refining our character.[178]

Do we focus on the "what" or on the "who"?

"What we do." Is education simply the vehicle to enable us to have the skills and knowledge to be able to accomplish what we want to do with our lives. We want to be a doctor, so we study biology. We want to be an engineer, so we study physics?

---

178. *Yaaroth Devash* 1,5

"Who we are." Or does education also encompass the need to study and learn who we are and what it means to be human—with emphasis on self-improvement?

There was a fascinating study done in contrasting the issues teachers faced in the 1950s and the present day. In the fifties, teachers were concerned that students were talking out of turn, were leaving their seats without permission, and chewing gum in class, to name just a few. Today, due to concerns of safety and student well-being, many schools have metal detectors that the students need to pass through before entering the school building. There are random sweeps for contraband and the tragic rise of students taking the lives of fellow students and staff.

If this study doesn't elicit a wakeup call, I am not sure what will. Evidently something is broken and needs fixing. Over 250 years ago, Reb Yehonatan shared with us good news and bad news. The bad news is you don't automatically grow into a law-abiding, moral citizen. The good news is you can learn it, and you can be taught it.

We need to remember that "who we are" is far more important than "what we do." And if it isn't taught in school, then we need to teach it at home.

Moshe Rabbeinu/Moshe Our Leader

Once a Leader Always a Leader

We find a rather remarkable statement in the Talmud concerning Moshe. The Talmud says that Moshe did not pass away. How are we meant to understand this statement?

Moshe is the faithful shepherd of the Jewish people, and even though he physically passed away, his role has not changed. Moshe continues to feel our pain. He continues to implore God to forgive the Jewish people for their iniquities as he did when he was physically alive. That is how we are to understand the Talmudic statement that Moshe did not pass away.[179]

None of us could ever imagine of aspiring to be like Moshe and lead the life he did. However, Rabbi Shneur Zalman of Liadi, in his magnus opus the Tanya, writes that every Jew has within them a spark of Moshe. This means that each and every one of us can, to a degree, emulate Moshe. This should be viewed as a duty and responsibility. We all can and must feel the pain of our fellow Jew. And when we pray, we need to pray not only for our own needs but also for the needs of our brothers and sisters.

---

179. *Yaaroth Devash 1*

Moshiach/Messianic Era

The Time Line

Reb Yehonatan offers a time line as it relates to the Messianic era. The ingathering of the Jewish people and their return to the Land of Israel will not coincide with God's return to the Holy Land. God will return prior to the Jewish people's return. This will explain why in the Talmud it states that many great rabbis were concerned of the time period just prior to the Messianic era. The apprehension was based on the understanding that, at that time, God will have already returned to Israel. And, in a sense, we would be left to our own resources in the diaspora.[180]

One of Rambam's thirteen principles of faith is the belief in the coming of the Messiah and the Messianic period. We are to anxiously await his arrival every day of our lives. Our prayers are replete with us beseeching God that we should merit his arrival. The final prayer we say in a loud voice at the conclusion of Yom Kippur, the holiest day of the year, is, "Next year in Jerusalem." Similarly, at the seder on the first two nights of Pesach (Passover), where we acknowledge, thank, and praise God for taking us out of slavery, we conclude by emphatically stating, "Next year in Jerusalem."

Let us pray and let us hope that each and every one of us will merit the experience of the ultimate purpose of creation: the Messianic era—when the world will be filled with the knowledge of God, and we will live in peace and tranquility.

---

180. *Ahavat Yehonatan Nitzavim*

Peek into the Unknown

Much has been written about the Messianic era, *Olam HaBa* (the world to come). Throughout his writings, Reb Yehonatan shares his understanding of what will unfold. The following are snippets of those thoughts:

There will be a sense of true brotherhood among the Jewish people. The Jewish people will reach levels of spirituality that will elevate them above the Ministering Angels.[181]

At that time all the nonkosher animals will be permitted to be eaten.[182]

We will have no need to involve ourselves in procuring a livelihood. All our needs will be taken care of. We will devote our time entirely to the study of Torah, and we will be exempt from fulfilling all the other positive commandments.[183]

In the Messianic era, the Torah and its commandments will remain unchanged. However, God will reveal to us the deepest secrets that are found there.[184]

At present, God judges the Jewish people with the attributes of justice and compassion. However, in the Messianic era, God will judge the Jewish people only with the attribute of mercy and compassion.[185]

We will all do *teshuvah* (repent), and there will be no remnant of our sins.[186]

We will be loved and blessed by God, and we will serve God with love and fear.[187]

---

181. *Ahavat Yehonatan Korach*

182. *Ahavat Yehonatan Ha'azinu*

183. *Ahavat Yehonatan Nitzavim*

184. *Ahavat Yehonatan Nitzavim*

185. *Ahavat Yehonatan Shoftim*

186. *Ahavat Yehonatan Vayigash*

187. *Ahavat Yehonatan Maasei*

All negative qualities will be removed from us, such as anger.[188]

There will be no *Yetzer Hara* (evil inclination), and we will not be tempted to sin. Hence, there will not be the notion of reward and punishment. The righteous will miss the times when they were able to do battle with their evil inclination and come out victorious.[189]

While there will be no Yetzer Hara and we will not have any desire for physical pleasure, there will still be the concept of sinning. We will strive for spiritual levels that we are not properly prepared for, and such behavior is considered a sin.[190]

The elderly will be rejuvenated and have the energy and vitality as when they were young.[191]

The Talmud links sleep to death, and since in the time of Olam HaBa, there will be no death, there will be no need for man to sleep.[192]

People will live for eternity, as there won't be death.[193]

Why? Why are we here? Is this a legitimate question that we should ask ourselves?

Even a young child who builds something out of bricks will have a reason why he made what he did. It stands to reason then that God, the Creator of the Universe, has a plan and purpose for man and the world He created.

Our rabbis explain that God wanted His presence to be revealed in the world. This physical world, seemingly so distant from anything Godly and spiritual, is really an expression of Godliness, and it is our mission to reveal that. The ultimate revelation will occur at the time of the Messianic era and Olam HaBa when God in His full glory will be revealed.

---

188. *Ahavat Yehonatan Balak*

189. *Ahavat Yehonatan Voetchanan*

190. *Ahavat Yehonatan*

191. *Tiferet Yehonatan Toldot*

192. *Tiferet Yehonatan Chayei Sarah*

193. *Yaaroth Devash 1,5*

Our journey and purpose during our lifetime is to begin this process. It is a cumulative one. Throughout our history, we have been placing the bricks necessary in constructing God's home here on earth.

We don't know how many bricks are still missing. There may be only one brick lacking, and it could be you who will place that final brick and usher in the Messianic era.

No Jew Will Be Left Behind

Part of the Messianic process is the ingathering of the exiles. After the destruction of the first and second Temple, the Jewish people were scattered to the four corners of the globe. You can find Jews living in the most unexpected places. Sadly, as a result of assimilation and other factors, there is a countless number of Jews who are Jewish but don't even know it. One of the great tragedies of our recent past occurred after the Shoah. Many Jewish parents gave their children to gentile families to care for until they would return at the conclusion of the war. Most were murdered, never to return, and these children were brought up not knowing that they were Jewish and part of the Jewish nation.

Reb Yehonatan writes, when Moshiach will arrive and return the Jewish people to the Land of Israel, even those individuals who never knew they were Jewish will also be part of the ingathering.

He quotes from the writings of the Abarbanel, who says that the Jews who were forced to abandon Judaism and embrace Christianity at the time of the Spanish Inquisition will also be part of the ingathering of the exiles.[194]

You may be better, but you can't be more. This means we can speak in terms of one Jew being better than another Jew. Of course, God is the ultimate arbitrator when it comes to who will be considered a better Jew. However, the notion of someone being more Jewish than another has no basis in

---

194. *Ahavat Yehonatan Tzav, Balak*

Jewish theology. Either you are or you are not. Either you are Jewish or you are not Jewish. There is no in-between, and there is no gradation in how much Jewishness we may possess.

Therefore, if someone goes through life never knowing that they are Jewish, they are as a Jewish as a person who is aware of their Jewishness from day one. We are Jewish because we possess a spiritual soul; it is part of our DNA whether or not we know it or act upon it.

Unlike the Exodus from Egypt where not every Jew left Egypt due to their wickedness, at the time of the final redemption, every Jew will return—even those who don't even know of their Jewishness. Truly, no Jew will be left behind.

Olam HaBa/World to Come

Experience It Today

One of the questions we often ask is, "What will it be like in the world to come?"

Reb Yehonatan shares the following: in the world to come, we will always be in a state of joy and bliss; we will not be sad or feel unhappy. There will also be no conflict or strife. He writes that if we want to experience the world to come in the present, we should do our utmost to always be happy and never feel down. We should remember that everything we experience is from God, and only good emanates from Him. We should also not become embroiled in disagreement and conflict; rather, we should seek peace and harmony.

If we always have a positive attitude toward life and we distance ourselves from conflicts, we will be experiencing in this world the beauties of the world to come.[195]

We have little to no control over what happens in our lives. We are driving the speed limit, being careful, and obeying the rules of the road and someone jumps a red light and badly damages our car. There is nothing we could have done to prevent the accident. The only thing we can control is how we will react to what has just happened. We could focus on the damage to our car and how inconvenient it will be while our car is being repaired or we could reflect on the fact that we came out of the accident unscathed, and we don't need to seek medical attention.

You can have two people experiencing the same thing, but one person is smiling and happy while the other is miserable and sad. The difference is in their attitude.

---

195. *Yaaroth Devash 1,4*

Surrounded by his students, a great rabbi called over an elderly person and asked him how his day was going. The man replied, "Miserably, I am eighty years old. I am no spring chicken, and I still have to work to make a living. And the work isn't easy. I have to carry these heavy buckets to the well to be filled and then carry them to people's homes."

A few days later, the group saw the same man again, and the rabbi asked the same question. This time, he responded, "Wonderfully! Look, I am already eighty. I am no youngster, but I am still healthy enough to work. And not just any work, hard work, because I am fit and strong. I bring water to people's homes. They couldn't manage without me. I am needed. People love me because of what I do."

Same man, same question, different perspective. Enjoy the bliss of the world to come in this world; it is all a question of attitude.

Godly Understanding

Crows in the air, elephants on land, and dolphins in the sea are among the smartest creatures on earth. Imagine if you could communicate to these animals that there are creatures on earth that can make a vessel to travel the mighty seas and that these creatures also made a machine that marks the exact time of the day. And, without any outside input, at a certain time every day or even every hour, the machine plays musical notes—and this can continue uninterrupted for many years.

Take note here that Rabbi Yehonatan gave these examples of great human innovations during his lifetime. In today's world, we can speak of man landing on the moon or our ability to send information from one side of the globe to the other in less than a second.[196]

As smart as these animals are, they could never comprehend or believe that creating such inventions could ever be accomplished. Likewise, we can never fathom and understand the wisdom and the workings of God.

---

196. *Yaaroth Devash 1*

As smart as we are and the great strides we have made in all areas of human endeavor, we need to always be conscious of the fact that we are finite creatures created by God. That we are finite creatures created by God is something we have in common with the animal kingdom. If the elephant could never grasp the accomplishments and mental capacity of the human species, it stands to reason that the finite human who was created can never ever understand the infinite creator, God.

Orphan and Widow

The Father of All Orphans, the Judge of All Widows

God proclaims that He is the Father of all orphans and the Judge of all widows. When we lose a loved one, it creates a vacuum, an emptiness that can never really be filled. A child who loses a parent will undoubtedly feel abandoned. They will wonder who will care for them, who will look after them. We say to the bereaved child, God has assumed the role of your father.

Similarly, a woman who has suffered the loss of her husband will worry how she will fend for herself. Will she be taken advantage of since she is a woman? We inform the distraught widow that God will be judging those who will interact with her to make sure she is treated properly with respect and dignity.[197]

Loneliness is a terrible feeling. We all need to know that there are people who care about us, that there is someone who will worry about us and be there in our time of need. If we realize this to be a truth and a basic human need, we must assume this role as well. We need to seek out those less fortunate than us—the orphan, the widow, the person down on his luck. It may be as simple as making a phone call or inviting them to our home. Let them know that they are truly not alone.

Let us partner with God in the most noble of tasks by helping those who feel helpless.

---

197. *Alon Bachut*

Parenting

Hitting versus Cursing

One of the Ten Commandments is the obligation of honoring one's parents. A great rabbi once remarked that a child needs to remember if it wasn't for his parents he wouldn't be here. Therefore, he owes them a tremendous amount of gratitude and by extension respect and honor.

The Torah states that a child is prohibited from striking or cursing a parent. What is somewhat puzzling is the punishment given for these two hideous crimes. You would think that hitting a parent is far worse than cursing a parent. However, the punishment for cursing is more severe than hitting. Why is this so?

You are punished for cursing a parent if you curse them using God's name. When a person hits their parent, as terrible and inexcusable as it is, we can always say that they lost control, they weren't thinking, and they struck out like an animal. If someone curses his parent by using the name of God, at that moment, he is being rational. He is using his unique human faculty and that is why his punishment is more stringent.[198]

What distinguishes us from an animal is our ability to discern and to comprehend that our actions have consequences—both for the good and the bad. When we act without thinking, we have entered the realm of the animal kingdom. Is there anything worse than that? Yes, there is: when we use our Divine gift of intelligence to behave and act in an inappropriate manner.

---

198. *Tiferet Yehonatan Mishpatim*

You Can't Pick and Choose

Reb Yehonatan laments the fact that there has been a general decrease in how children are honoring their parents. He attributes part of this to the lack of honor that siblings need to give to their eldest brother. And, secondly, to the lack of honor shown to God. He argues that God is the Father of all existence; if we cannot honor God appropriately, it stands to reason that we wouldn't be honoring our parents either.

Reb Yehonatan is suggesting that if we don't have the proper reverence for someone we should be respecting, this will impact how we will treat others who are also deserving of our respect.[199]

Respect is a noun: a deep feeling of profound admiration for someone or something elicited by their abilities, qualities, or achievements.

Respect is a verb: to admire someone or something deeply, as a result of their abilities, qualities, or achievements.

Whether it is a noun or a verb, it is a word that is slowly disappearing from our vocabulary. Respecting our elders and respecting authority are not a given. We need to educate our children from a very early age about the importance of being respectful. Part of the education process is impressing upon them that we can't pick and choose. We need to respect everyone, whether or not we like them and whether or not we know them.

If you have ever had the opportunity to spend time with a very righteous individual, one thing that stands out is how they treat their fellow human being. It makes no difference if it is a bellhop carrying their luggage or the clerk behind the cash register, they are courteous, thankful, and respectful. They are well aware that if you are disrespectful to one segment of society, it will impact how you relate and treat other members of society. What a wonderful world we would live in if we would treat anyone and everyone with equal respect.

---

199. *Yaaroth Devash 2,12*

Protecting the Jewish People

One of the most powerful statements you can say to a person is, "You make a difference." Your actions not only impact your life but also impact the lives of all the Jewish people. A case in point is the commandment of honoring your parents. By honoring your parents, you are protecting the Jewish people as a whole.

How is this so?

Esau, the brother of Yaakov, was the forebearer of the Amalekites, the nation that attacked the Jewish people when they left Egypt. Haman, who tried to annihilate the Jewish people in the times of Queen Esther and Mordechai (miracle of *Purim*), was a descendent of Esau. The Roman Empire that destroyed the second *Beit Hamikdash* (Temple) descended from Esau.

As evil as Esau was, he had one redeeming factor and that was he excelled in the commandment of honoring one's parents. If we want to protect ourselves from our adversaries, we need to emulate the one positive quality Esau had by equally excelling in the commandment of honoring our parents. By honoring and respecting our parents, the flow-on effect is that we are safeguarding our people.[200]

"Scientia potential est" is a Latin aphorism meaning, "Knowledge is power."

What does this mean? It means that knowledge is more powerful than physical strength, and no great work can be done without knowledge. Knowledge is a powerful factor that empowers people to achieve great results. The more knowledge a person gains, the more powerful he becomes.

This is certainly true when it comes to performing God's commandments. The basis and the starting point for fulfilling God's instructions is because He said to. In Hebrew, it is referred to as serving God with "Kabbalat Ol," by accepting the yoke of heaven. Once that is understood, we are encouraged

---

200. *Yaaroth Devash 2,2*

and, in fact, instructed to explore the depths of the commandment—to discover its beauty and far-reaching affect.

A case in point is the commandment of honoring our parents. Won't we put in more effort, try harder, and fulfill it with greater resolve and enthusiasm even when it comes to making our parents a cup of tea, knowing with that cup of tea, we are safeguarding the whole Jewish world?

Pleasure

At a Price

There is always room for ice cream. Somehow, no matter how much we have eaten, we manage to find room for at least one scoop of ice cream—because, in all honesty, who doesn't like ice cream? Imagine, however, if you were to eat tub after tub of your favorite flavor, you would more than likely suffer from a terrible stomachache.

This is true when it comes to any pleasure. No matter how much we enjoy it and want it, there will reach a point when we will say or even cry out, "Enough!" In this world, there is no such thing as pure pleasure; at a certain moment, the pleasure is no longer pleasurable and what we enjoy is no longer enjoyable. As the saying goes, "It is too much of a good thing."

Reb Yehonatan writes that, in the Messianic era, we will experience unbridled pleasure and no negativity as a result.[201]

A great rabbi once reflected on the rabbinic inference that when the Torah says, "What God had created was very good," it is to teach us that God, at that moment, had created the evil inclination and the angel of death. He asked, "How does the word 'very' in the phrase 'very good' have such a negative connotation?" He replied that life should be lived in moderation; we should not desire for anything that we could describe as being "very," such as very wealthy or very beautiful, as anything in the extreme is not healthy.

In this world, there is no such thing as a free lunch; everything comes at a price and too much of a good thing also has a price attached to it.

---

201. Yaaroth Devash 1,4

Praise

Unwanted Praise

Who doesn't like to be praised? We all like to get our egos massaged.

Reb Yehonatan writes that there are times when being praised is counterproductive and can have a negative effect on us. He speaks about the spiritual energies in heaven that seek ill for the Jewish people or for the Jewish individual.

One of the ways the forces of evil seek to harm the Jewish people is by lauding them with praise—by telling God how wonderful the Jewish people are and how God had created the world for the sake of the Jewish people and that we were the nation to receive the Torah on Mount Sinai. And after being praised extensively and elevated to great heights, the forces of evil then attempt to cut us down at our knees.

By impressing upon God that if the Jewish people are such an exalted nation, then they should not act and behave in the manner that they do, and more needs to be expected and demanded from them. And if they do not live up to their expectations, then they need to be, God forbid, punished accordingly.[202]

A famed psychiatrist once explained in simplistic terms why someone would take drugs. He said, "If we feel worthless, if we view ourselves as being garbage, then we will have no problem in consuming garbage."

There are two ways we can discipline a child: 1) We can rebuke the child and tell them how terrible and naughty they are and what they did was very bad. The downside of this approach is that the more we tell a child how bad and ill disciplined they are, the more they begin to believe it about themselves and will behave accordingly. Or 2) We can impress upon the

---

202. *Alon Bachut*

child how special they are and how much potential they possess, and it is really below their dignity and self-respect to act in the manner they are.

Every child and, for that matter, every one of us wants to feel good about ourselves. We want people to value us and recognize our worth. When we build up the child, we have a greater chance at ensuring that our children will reflect the values we hold so near and dear.

The forces of evil heap praise to create destruction; we need to heap praise to create growth.

Prayer

Gateway to Understanding

How is it humanely possible for a finite creature to grasp and comprehend the wisdom of an infinite being? How can we be sure that we have properly understood what message God is trying to convey in the Torah verses?

Reb Yehonatan understood this dilemma, and he therefore writes that we cannot do it alone. We need to pray from the depths of our heart to God and shed tears in beseeching God that we merit to uncover the deeper meaning of the Torah and be able to comprehend His holy words.[203]

There are many reasons why we pray. At the most basic level, we pray to God for all our needs as the saying goes, "There are no atheists in foxholes."

On a deeper level, prayer is not just about what we need. Doesn't God know what we need and want, just as a parent knows the needs of their child? Why then pray to inform God what He knows already?

To pray is to afford us the opportunity to self-judge and introspect. God is impressing upon us that three times a day we need to pause and take stock of our lives and to appreciate all the blessings we have received from our Father in heaven, even though we may not be deserving of them.

True Prayer

Prayer is God's gift to mankind. Prayer is giving us the opportunity to have a private audience with the King of Kings. We may be under the impression that access is afforded to us when our mind is focused and

---

203. Yaaroth Devash 1,4

our thoughts and requests are organized and coherent. And we need to ensure that we can fully concentrate when we speak to God.

Reb Yehonatan says this is not necessarily the case. He writes that when a person is facing a crisis and is in the depths of despair and his pain is so intense that he can't think straight and he cries out to God, God will certainly hear his prayers. [204]

Many of us find prayer challenging. There is the language barrier, as synagogue services are conducted in Hebrew. And there seemingly is no opportunity for personal expression and reflection, as we all say the same prayers day in and day out.

Soon after the Six-Day War, a blind person went every day to the Wailing Wall. When he reached the wall, he would gently caress the stones with his fingers, feeling 2,000 years of Jewish history and then he would begin to pray. On one occasion, he was overheard saying, "Sorry, God. I told you that yesterday." This person could see more than many who have 20/20 vision could. He could, in a sense, see God, and he knew that He was listening and there was no need to repeat what had already been conveyed.

While the words are the same and the language may be foreign, every day is a new opportunity to connect with God. We need to view the structure of the prayers as a springboard for personal expression. There are only 88 keys on a piano, and every song has specific notes, yet you can express yourself in so many different ways as you play the very same notes.

Pray for Others

Reb Yehonatan offers a very insightful understanding into the power of prayer. Being part of the Jewish people means that when another Jew is in pain and suffering, we need to feel their pain. And it isn't sufficient to simply feel someone else's pain; we need to pray on their behalf. It is not by chance that the focal point of our daily prayers, the

---

204. *Yaaroth Devash* 1,15

Amidah, where we make our bequests of God for health and financial security is written in the plural.

He adds that we need to recognize that, if we were up to par, our fellow Jew would not be experiencing so much sorrow and grief. And, therefore, it is incumbent on us to pray for them, as to some extent we may be responsible for their misfortune.[205]

When a non-Jew wants to convert to Judaism, they must accept upon themselves all of God's commandments. A great rabbi added that they must also feel and sense the pain of our suffering throughout the ages and up to the present day. To become part of the Jewish people, it is not sufficient to identify with and acknowledge our tragedies. The convert must imagine that it was his parents, his ancestors, who lived through the Crusades, the Inquisition, the pogroms, and the Holocaust.

Join a Club

Prayer has always played a significant role in Jewish life. We are obligated to pray three times a day. And on Yom Kippur, the holiest day of the year, we pray no less than five times in a twenty-five-hour period. While prayer is a very personal experience, it is an opportunity for each and every one of us to connect and unite with God. We are instructed to pray with a quorum, as this will help our prayers be elevated to God.

Why is praying with a quorum considered more advantageous than praying alone? Reb Yehonatan explains by way of analogy. If a retailer purchases goods and he isn't sure of the wholesaler's reputation, he will examine the products prior to payment. However, if the wholesaler has a very reputable reputation, the purchaser will take him at his word and accept the goods without examining them first.

Likewise, when we pray as an individual, God carefully examines our prayers. However, when we pray as a group, God does not examine the group to such an extent.[206]

---

205. *Yaaroth Devash* 2,9

206. *Yaaroth Devash* 2,12

Here is another way of understanding the distinction between communal and individual prayer: Imagine you have to sing a solo in front of a very large audience but you don't have a great voice; you would probably be mortified, as every note sung out of key would be heard by the audience. However, if you are part of a choir of ten voices, then your singing inability will be drowned out by the other nine voices.

It's a Two-Way Street

One of the many reasons we pray is the realization that everything comes from God and we need to ask Him for what we need. At times, our prayers may not seem to be answered. One of the reasons given is that the person is under the rubric of strict justice and his prayers may not be accepted in heaven.

What are his options? He will have to implore others to pray on his behalf.[207]

While this insight may seem challenging in the sense that, no matter how much we pray, it may not make much of a difference. On the other hand, what Reb Yehonatan is sharing with us is extremely uplifting and inspiring, and that is we can make a difference. God listens when we pray for someone whose prayers are not being answered. The Amidah (the 18 blessings) is in the plural since we are never just praying for ourselves.

What a beautiful thought to have when we begin to pray, to know that our prayers can impact and change someone else's life. When we pray, we should not just pray for our needs; let us pray for the needs of our fellow Jew. We never know whose prayers will be accepted.

Remember it's a two-way street; we may need someone else's prayers one day too.

---

207. *Yaaroth Devash* 2,9

Don't Lie

If you have ever gone on a job interview, you know how stressful it can be. More than likely, you would have sought out what qualities and abilities were necessary to fill this position. And you would have prepared the necessary answers that highlight your strengths in these areas. Or, if you have an appointment with your bank manager because you want him to approve a home loan, you will come prepared with documentation showing income and expenditures that clearly shows you can repay the loan.

What is crucial in both scenarios and is true in any situation that you are interacting with another person is that you must be present. You can't be daydreaming and allowing your brain to be traveling to some distant land. By doing so, you would be giving the impression that you are really not interested in what is transpiring, and no matter how many answers you practiced or how many spreadsheets you prepared, you may walk out of the meeting empty-handed.

If this is vital when we seek something from our fellow man, how true it must be when we seek something from the King of Kings—God, to whom we owe our very lives. We must realize that, when we pray, we must be totally focused on the words we are saying and trying to the best of our ability to understand and comprehend the depths of what we are saying. If we simply mumble the words and miss out on every second one while our mind is floating in outer space, we may very well leave with our cap in hand with nothing to show for our prayers or time spent in the synagogue.

Reb Yehonatan suggests a more compelling reason we need to be very attentive in our prayers. He quotes from the writings of King David in Psalms where it is written that we need to guard our tongue from evil and our lips from speaking deceitfully. He suggests the verse is alluding to the frame of mind we need to be in before we begin to pray, that if we pray without the necessary concentration and awareness, our prayers will be considered as all lies.[208]

---

208. *Yaaroth Devash 1,5*

When it comes to prayer, we always say it is better to pray a little with intent than to pray a lot without intent. According to Reb Yehonatan's explanation, this makes a lot of sense. If prayer said with no intent is tantamount to lying, then the longer you pray, the more you are lying to God.

When we pray without the necessary intent, it is feasible that our prayer will not be answered. We may think, "OK, they won't be answered. It is my loss, and I will have to live with that." Reb Yehonatan is impressing upon us that it is more serious than that and every word said flippantly is as if you were lying before God.

Prison

Punishment Fits the Crime

There are various schools of thought when it comes to the purpose and function of punishment or incarceration. From a Jewish perspective, the purpose of any form of penalty or prison time is to rehabilitate the person. Therefore, one needs to ensure that the individual, when faced with the consequences for his actions, does not see it as a mountain too high to traverse, resulting in having no interest in mending his ways.[209]

What is interesting is that unlike Western civilization where upward of 70 percent of all criminal behavior will result in a prison sentence, according to the Torah, prison is not considered a form of punishment.

Why is this so?

The purpose of man's existence is to reveal God's presence in the world. In all other forms of punishment, after the criminal is penalized, hopefully he will have learned from his errors and he can begin to lead a productive life, which will include serving God. However, when a person is imprisoned, he does not have the freedom to serve God, and, in a sense, we remove the very reason for his existence. And that is a punishment that is too heavy for a person to bear.

---

209. *Yaaroth Devash 1*

Prophecy

How to Become a Prophet?

I am sure we have all been asked the question, "What do you want to be when you grow up?" And more than likely our response evolved over time. At a certain age, we understood that simply wanting to become something doesn't mean we would automatically become that. If we wanted to become a doctor, it would take years of study and then a considerable amount of time interning in a hospital.

I am not sure if anyone ever responded, "When I grow up, I want to be a prophet." However, have you ever wondered what it takes to become a prophet? There are many prerequisites and requirements to become a prophet. One of them is being a teacher of Torah and, specifically, that you teach young children, who are considered sinless.[210]

What is the connection between a teacher of young children and becoming a prophet? And what does this say about such a teacher?

One of the important qualities a prophet needs to possess is humility since he needs to be truly receptive to the word of God. Without a doubt, one of the most important traits a teacher of young children needs to be is being humble. Imagine if you spend forty or fifty years teaching children the Hebrew alphabet. You really have to put your own self and intellectual pursuit to the side and focus solely on the needs of the children.

We may have no aspirations of becoming a prophet or, for that matter, becoming a kindergarten teacher. That shouldn't, however, prevent us from aspiring to becoming a little humbler and giving of ourselves to others without receiving anything in return.

---

210. *Yaaroth Devash 2,7*

Punishment

Pity the Poor

A person who is poverty stricken may feel he has no choice and needs to rob and steal for his survival. How should we view such a person?

The Talmud writes that there are three matters that cause a person to act against his own will and the will of his maker. One of them is the depths of extreme poverty. We could then argue that the pauper shouldn't be held responsible for his actions and that he has suffered enough, and by punishing him, we will only exacerbate his terrible predicament.

As tragic as the situation is, the person must be held accountable. This is the understanding of the verse, "You should not favor a poor person."[211]

We may find ourselves in a difficult situation, and there are two ways we can deal with it. We can take the law into our own hands and find excuses to allow us to bend the rules or break the law. Usually, this is the easy way out. Or we can recognize that we cannot play judge and jury, and we may need to take a path that is both long and arduous.

Quick and easy versus long and arduous shouldn't be the two sides of the coin that we choose from. Rather, right and wrong must be the basis of our choice. If that is the case, then the choice is easy.

Punishment That Fits the Crime

There is a great deal of discussion when it comes to sentencing someone for criminal behavior. Should we look at the severity of the crime and set the punishment accordingly without considering any

---

211. *Tiferet Yehonatan Kedoshim*

mitigating circumstances? Or should fair and appropriate sentencing include other factors besides the actual crime committed, no matter how heinous the crime may have been?

If we take a leaf out of the ultimate Judges code of sentencing, we see that God does not just view the crime and punish accordingly. God considers other factors as well.

Earlier generations were on a far higher spiritual level than the later generations. The more spiritual the generation or the holier a person may be, the higher the standard God will hold him accountable for. By way of analogy, if a general and a new army recruit both disobey an instruction, it stands to reason that the general will be punished more severely. The reason is obvious: the general should have known better.[212]

Growing up, we may have all experienced an occasion when we misbehaved and our younger sibling or a student in a lower class did the same thing, but we were reprimanded or punished more severely. When we would question why we were judged more harshly, the response would usually be, "You are older; you should have known better."

Hopefully, with maturity, we can look back on that experience and realize how right they were. Perhaps without even realizing it, they were following the sentencing guidelines formulated and implemented by the Judge of all judges.

---

212. *Alon Bachut*

Purim

Happiest Day of the Year

The festival of Purim marks the day when the Jewish people were saved from the evil decree of Haman, who had sought their annihilation. When we greet someone on the festival of Purim, we usually say *Simchat Purim* (Happy Purim).

What is the reason for our happiness and joy? The same God who causes the sun to rise every morning is the same God who split the sea when we left Egypt. Why then do we make such a big deal of the splitting of sea but take sunrises for granted?

The sea split at the exact moment the Jewish people needed to enter it to escape the mighty Egyptian army. We therefore mark that moment in time as it is a defining moment in our understanding of God's relationship with the world. God did not create the world and then move on to bigger and better things. The miracle occurred at the exact moment it was needed. This clearly demonstrated, beyond a shadow of a doubt, that God continues to run the world. It also clearly indicates how much God loves us.

The same is true when we reflect on the story of Purim. God was clearly pulling the strings that saw Esther become the Queen of Persia and the death of the wicked Haman. We therefore rejoice because we once again see how God is intimately involved in the running of the world and how much he loves us.[213]

We often hear people say, "If I was living at the time of the Exodus and saw the splitting of the sea, then I would believe." Or we may hear people ask, "Why don't we see miracles today similar to those recorded in the Torah?"

---

213. *Yaaroth Devash 1*

There are two types of miracles: the supernatural (such as the splitting of the sea) and the miracle that is seemingly nothing more than a random set of events coming together (such as the miracle of Purim). And both are as miraculous. The distinction is that one is blatantly obvious, while the other needs a level of self-reflection.

We don't need to experience overt miracles such as the splitting of the sea to prove God's existence in our own lifetime. We know such miracles occurred because our parents told us they did, and their parents told them they did, going all the way back to our forbearers, who experienced and witnessed the crossing of the sea.

Let us pause for a moment and reflect on something we witnessed in our own lifetime. For over seventy years, millions of Jews were persecuted in the former Soviet Union. Then miraculously over night, without a single bullet being shot, Jews were granted their freedom. More Jews were freed from the former Soviet Union than the Jews who left Egypt.

Miracles do happen; we just have to open our eyes to see them.

Rebuke

Giving and Receiving

For many years, Reb Yehonatan held the position as the *maggid* (preacher) of Prague. In that role, he would address the community and encourage them to desist from sinning and at the same time inspire his community to embrace God and His commandments. When reflecting on his life, he writes that the best moments of his lifetime were when he was able to influence people in returning to and embracing God. At times, this was accomplished by rebuking and chastising the individual. He also felt that a person should not shun and despise receiving words of rebuke if they will have a positive effect in bringing him closer to God.[214]

A great rabbi once said, that in our generation, we no longer have the capacity or ability to rebuke someone for their misdeeds. If anything, harsh words will only drive the person further away. We need to be concerned about other people's behavior, but it must be done with love and compassion. We need to find the appropriate words that will draw the person closer and not push them further away.

214. *Yaaroth Devash 1,11*

Redemption

Kindness through Strength

The two main attributes God uses when interacting with the world is *chesed* (kindness) and *gevurah* (strength or strict justice).

At face value, it would seem that when God is bestowing blessings and goodness upon the Jewish people, it emanates from the attribute of chesed. And when God seems to be punishing the Jewish people, it stems from the attribute of gevurah.

When we implore God to usher in the period of the final redemption, we refer to God as the mighty Redeemer. We ask God to express Himself with the attribute of gevurah. It would seem the attribute of chesed would be the more appropriate attribute to beseech God to use to usher in the Messianic era. God should shower us with kindness and bring this exile to an end.

Why do we refer to God as the mighty Redeemer?

There is the physical realm, and there is the spiritual realm. In the physical world, we speak about the laws of nature, such as the laws of gravity. These laws are part of God's creation. Likewise, in the spiritual realm, there are laws by which the spiritual world is governed. We understand that based on God's spiritual rules, we may not be worthy of redemption. Therefore, we beg of God that He demonstrate His great strength by not following His spiritual laws and redeem us even though we may not be worthy.[215]

We all interact with others. Our interactions will be driven by our desire to show kindness and compassion or the need to demonstrate a position of strength and severity. There may be times when we seek to be benevolent

---

215. *Yaaroth Devash 1,1*

and giving; however, our personality or circumstances make it extremely difficult.

We need to remember that, in our prayers, we refer to God as the mighty Redeemer. We need to realize there may be times in our lives when we will need to tap into our reservoir of inner strength to be able to extend the hand of kindness and compassion.

Reincarnation

Good or Bad?

Reincarnation, the return of the soul to this physical world, is part of Jewish belief. A soul that has not completed its purpose and mission on earth may need to return. Likewise, as a form of spiritual cleansing, the soul may need to leave its heavenly abode and return to this world.

There are instances when the soul's return to earth is not linked to any shortcoming of the soul. Rather, a particular generation needs the spiritual guidance and influence of the departed *tzaddik* (righteous individual). The soul of the tzaddik returns for the benefit of the generation.

There is one caveat for the soul of the tzaddik to return. That being, when the tzaddik passed away, he was eulogized and given the proper respect. If he was not eulogized, the tzaddik's soul will not return, as he sees that he wasn't honored correctly.

The Talmud asks why we give a eulogy at a funeral: Is it for the benefit of the departed or for the living? It would seem that it is for the benefit of the living. By eulogizing a righteous person, the person's soul will be willing to return to help the living.[216]

The phrase "No good deed goes unpunished" is a sardonic commentary on the frequency with which acts of kindness backfire on those who offer them, since very often, those who offer them are doomed to suffer as a result of being helpful. This, of course, is the antithesis of Jewish belief. One of the thirteen principles of faith is the principle of reward and punishment. We are rewarded and punished based on our actions.

There are times when we don't see or comprehend the reward for our behavior. As humans, we are limited in terms of vision and what we can grasp.

---

216. *Yaaroth Devash 1,1*

For example, you have delivered a very beautiful and meaningful eulogy, and this seemingly has had no positive impact on your life. We know this is not true. As a result of your eulogy, the departed soul will return if it is needed. Your eulogy may have saved a whole generation.

Don't be disheartened if you feel you are a pin-up boy for "no good deed goes unpunished." Remember, every good deed is rewarded at times beyond our wildest imagination; we just don't always see it.

Relationships

How to Mend Them

Unless a person lives their whole life on a deserted island, they will have to interact with other members of society. They will form relationships—some fleeting and superficial and others deep, strong, and everlasting. There will be times when they will feel badly done by. How should this person respond? Should he ignore the person in the future or perhaps act in kind?

The Talmud teaches us that both approaches are unacceptable. Giving a modern twist to the case brought in the Talmud, a person notices that two cars both have flat tires. He then discovers one car belongs to a dear friend, while the other is owned by the person who slighted him and now dislikes.

Whom should he help first? Based on a verse in the Torah, he must help the person who he despises. Showering your adversary with love and kindness is the surest method to reconciliation.

As the saying goes, "It takes two to tango." Very rarely is one person to be blamed when there is a conflict. Recognizing that is the first step we need to take in creating a more peaceful and pleasant relationship with our adversary.

Respect

Your Elders

A society is measured by how it treats its elderly. In certain societies, the elderly are viewed as a burden and a strain on society, as if "past the use by date" should be stamped on the forehead of every senior citizen. In other cultures, however, the elderly are respected and treated with the dignity they truly deserve.

Reb Yehonatan quotes a rabbinic dictum that states that when we greet an elderly individual, it is comparable to greeting the Almighty. Reb Yehonatan adds that while this comparison is a rabbinic statement, it is based on a Biblical verse.[217]

The fable is told of a man who had been lost in a vast forest for many years and was unable to find his way back to civilization. One day, he stumbles upon an old man with a long white beard. This is the first human he has encountered since entering the forest so many years before. The lost soul was delirious as finally he would be given directions out of the forest. You can imagine the dismay on the young man's face when the old man told him that when he entered the forest, he had a black beard just like him, and after all these years, he has still not found his way out.

The old man seeing his crestfallen demeanor told the young man that he shouldn't be upset because he will be able to tell him where he does not need to search as he has already tried and failed in those parts of the forest.

Our elders have lived and experienced life. We should tap into their reservoir of knowledge because life experience teaches a person something no amount of money in the world could buy.

---

217. *Tiferet Yehonatan Bereishit*

Sanctifying God's Name

How?

One of the most severe sins a person can transgress is when he makes a *chillul Hashem* (when he desecrates the Name of God). One of the ways to rectify this transgression is by increasing the study of Torah.

In the story of Purim, Achashverosh, the king of the Persian Empire, calculated that the time for the Jewish people to end their period of exile and return to Israel to rebuild the second Temple had arrived. And since the Jews were still in Persia, it meant that they would never return to the Holy Land; he therefore celebrated this milestone with a grand feast. The Jewish people joined and took part in the festivities. There could be no greater example of the desecration of the name of God than having Jews celebrating their exile. And they were therefore punished.

Mordechai, the savior of the Jewish people, knew the only way to remedy the situation would be through an increase in the study of the Torah, God's wisdom. And, therefore, the rabbis write that Mordechai encouraged the Jewish people and, in particular, the Jewish children to increase their study of Torah.[218]

The greatest accolade we could ever receive is when we are told that our conduct and behavior created a kiddush Hashem (a sanctification of the Name of God).

How do we sanctify the Name of God? Maimonides writes, "If a person has been scrupulous in his conduct, gentle in his conversation, pleasant toward his fellow creatures, . . . Not responding even when affronted, but showing courtesy to all, even to those who treat him with disdain, conducting his business affairs with integrity . . . and doing more than his duty in

---

218. *Yaaroth Devash 1,5*

all things, while avoiding extremes and exaggerations—such a person has sanctified Gd."

We must always be aware that we are viewed and judged, not just as an individual but as an ambassador of the Jewish people and as God's representative to earth. This is vividly portrayed in the following amusing story.

When the news came through to a cruise liner about the daring Israeli raid on Entebbe in 1976, the passengers wanted to pay tribute, in some way, to Israel and the Jewish people. A search was made to see if there was a Jewish member of the crew. Only one could be found, Mendel the waiter. So, at a solemn ceremony, on behalf of the passengers, the captain offered his congratulations to Mendel, who suddenly found himself elected de facto as the ambassador of the Jewish people. We are all, like it or not, ambassadors of the Jewish people, and how we live our lives reflects not only on us as individuals but on Jewry as a whole. Let us accept this awesome role with pride, honor, and great joy.

Sanhedrin/
The Jewish Court System

Law and Order

The highest court in the Land of Israel during the time of the Temple was called the Great Sanhedrin. It was comprised of seventy-one great Torah scholars of impeccable character. While the Great Sanhedrin was functioning, all Jews served God in the same manner. Whenever there was confusion or disagreement, the Sanhedrin was the final arbitrator, and its decisions were universally accepted.

Prior to the coming of the Messiah, the prophet Elijah will return and reinstitute the Sanhedrin. The Sanhedrin's initial task will be to resolve all questions pertaining to Jewish law and practice.[219]

Three times a day in our prayers, we beseech God to reestablish the Sanhedrin. One of the reasons for this request is based on a fascinating statement by the rabbis in the Talmud. The Talmud states that if a person is punished by a court adjudicated by mankind, he will not be punished for the same crime by the heavenly court. This means that if a person is liable to receive a heavenly punishment, it can be removed if he would be punished by the Sanhedrin. The reason it was preferable to stand in judgment before the Sanhedrin was because judgment and punishment via the heavenly court was more severe than the verdict and sentence given by the Sanhedrin.

It seems strange that three times a day we would ask God to reintroduce law and order in our lives. You would imagine that, if we could ask from God anything, we would ask for complete freedom that we should live in a world where there were no consequences for our actions.

---

219. *Yaaroth Devash 1,1*

It is well documented that children do better when there are restrictions and rules set in place. Students have fond memories of teachers who were both strict and at the same time caring. But very few students will recall a teacher who allowed the classroom to turn into a zoo. This is equally true for adults. As a society and as individuals, we can only thrive and grow when we are willing to abide by a code of rules and principles. It therefore stands to reason that we would ask God to reestablish the Sanhedrin.

Self-Examination

Fooling Oneself

Over the years, we may have heard or said, "I know you better than you know yourself." There is a copious amount of literature written on this claim. Reb Yehonatan weighs in on this discussion and suggests the following:

The easiest thing we are capable of doing is fooling ourselves. And we are constantly doing so. A very proud person may honestly believe they are a very humble individual. The most challenging thing for us is to be able to honestly appraise ourselves. While we are able to see all the flaws a friend possesses, we are unable to find even one flaw within ourselves.

According to Reb Yehonatan, making the claim, "I know you better than you know yourself," is nothing to be proud of, since most people don't have an honest understanding of who they really are anyway. Why is it that we are able to notice deficiencies in others, but we struggle at times to be aware of our own shortcomings?

There is a verse that reads, "Love covers all flaws." A similar English expression is, "Love is blind." When there is love, you do not see faults. Self-love is the strongest love of all. When a person is in love with himself, he finds it very difficult to really see his own shortcomings.[220]

If we really want to honestly appraise ourselves, we should keep in mind a pithy remark from a very great rabbi. He said, "You are certainly not fooling God, and you are not fooling anyone else either. The only one you are fooling is yourself, and is there anything impressive of a fool fooling himself?" None of us want to be labeled a fool.

---

220. *Yaaroth Devash 1,1*

Shabbat

Our Security

The well-known saying, "More than the Jew has kept the Shabbat, the Shabbat has kept the Jew," is said to have been coined in the late 1900s. Truth be told, many years prior, Reb Yehonatan had articulated the significance of the Shabbat by declaring that the observance of the Shabbat is a shield of protection surrounding the Jewish people.

No matter how learned and saintly you may be, you cannot proclaim catchy slogans without a source or basis. Reb Yehonatan draws on our history as the relevant source for this idea. The Jewish people, after leaving Egypt, were given a number of commandments prior to the giving of the Torah on Mount Sinai. One of the laws given was the obligation to observe the Shabbat. That very first Shabbat, a Jew desecrated it. Immediately after that, we read how the Amalekites waged war against the Jewish people. He infers that it was the lack of observing the Shabbat that enabled the Amalekites to wage war against the Jewish people.[221]

A great rabbi was once asked why was it that, in the 1920s and 1930s, many children of observant Jews did not remain Shabbat observant?

He responded that, at that time, people had to work on Saturday, and if they would not, they would be fired. Every Friday, when these God-fearing Jews informed their employers that they couldn't work the next day, they were immediately fired, and on Sunday morning, they would begin the arduous task of seeking new employment, knowing full well that they would relive the same experience the following Sunday.

---

221. *Yaaroth Devash 2,3*

Each Friday night, as the father sat at the head of the Shabbat table, he would agonizingly bemoan the difficulty of being a Shabbat observer and faithfully following in his parents' footsteps. The children would see their father's pain and made a simple decision; they would rather be happy than miserable. And by seeing the pain their father displayed every Friday night, it was abundantly clear that observing the Shabbat, no matter how meaningful it may be, is a sure path to a life of misery. And that is something they could not live with.

The Shabbat protects the Jewish people, but if we want it to be an integral part of our children's lives, we need to show them the true beauty and the joy that the Shabbat brings to our lives.

Shalom/Peace

Worth Praying For

The importance of shalom is so essential to the Jewish people that not only should we seek shalom and pursue it, but it is also something we need to pray for. Our rabbis write that God's blessings can only be found when there is peace among His children.

When we pray for shalom, we should beseech God that there shouldn't be conflict among the Jewish people. There shouldn't be jealousy and hatred between Jews. We should pray that the Jewish people should love one another and that we should be united as one.[222]

A simple way of discovering what we consider important in our lives is to ask ourselves, "Do I pray for it? Do I beseech God for it?"

Find me a human being who doesn't consider good health of paramount importance in our daily lives. Therefore, not only do we do whatever it takes to be healthy, each and every one of us in our own way will offer a prayer to God for our continued health.

Reb Yehonatan is impressing upon us that peace among the Jewish people is so vital that it is something we need to pray for. Ask any parent what gives them the greatest nachas (joy); more often than not, they will respond, "When our children have a loving, warm relationship with each other." This is true from God's perspective as well. God is our father, and we are His children. There is no greater joy for God than seeing his children loving and caring for one another.

We need to remember that the second Temple was destroyed because of unwanted hate among the Jewish people and that we will merit our ultimate redemption when there is true unity among us.

---

222. *Yaaroth Devash 1,1*

Shemitah/Sabbatical Year

While the Jewish people were sojourning in the desert for forty years, God sustained them in a miraculous manner. Once we entered the Land of Israel, we began to toil the ground to produce the food needed to feed a nation.

Since so much time would be spent in the fields, God instructed the farmers among the Jewish people to leave their fields barren every seventh year and devote their time to the study of Torah.

Reb Yehonatan writes that if we had not sinned by dancing around the golden calf, God's miracles would have continued even after we entered the Promised Land. As such, we would not have had to become farmers to provide for our families, and our days would have been wholly devoted to the service of God and the study of His Torah. Hence, there would have been no need to introduce the law of the sabbatical year, which was to compensate for the lack of learning incurred while working the land.

There have been great spiritual giants of our past who were on par with the Israelites prior to the sin of the golden calf. They therefore were able to devote themselves wholeheartedly to the study of Torah, and God miraculously sustained and provided them with all their needs.[223]

The rabbis tell us that these spiritual giants were few and far between. Very few ever reached such lofty heights. We more than likely will never even come close to reaching such a lofty level. Yet that does not mean there isn't something we can't learn from their actions and behavior.

Have you ever scratched your head and wondered why? You went to school with him; he wasn't one of the brightest in the class. He wasn't one of the more popular guys, and he definitely didn't give the impression that he would amount to much at all Yet, he proved everyone wrong, and he became mega wealthy. And we wonder why.

---

223. *Tiferet Yehonatan Behar*

There is a saying that success is 1 percent hard work and 99 percent luck. Let us simply substitute the word "luck" for "God." Our financial success is 1 percent hard work and 99 percent a gift from God.

It is simply a shift in attitude; we need to realign our thinking. Our attitude needs to be that our financial success is a gift from Above. Of course, we need to go to work; money doesn't grow on trees. We need to roll up our sleeves and create the necessary vessel to receive God's blessing. But how successful we are is not 99 percent luck; rather, it is 99% a gift from Above.

What Is Our Goal in Life?

If we stop to think for a moment, the obligation of shemitah is very taxing and challenging. Imagine if we were told that we need to close shop, not for one day out of the week but for a whole year.

Reb Yehonatan writes that we are being taught a crucial life lesson. And that is we should not spend our lives chasing the "god" called the green dollar. Rather, we should find contentment and satisfaction in having less rather than in having more.[224]

At the end of their life, no one says, "I wish I spent more time at the office." However, studies have shown that some of the regrets people over age fifty have include not doing more for others, not nurturing good relationships, and not spending more time with their children.[225]

We may not be farmers, and we don't need to put away our plow or hoe once every seven years, but that doesn't mean we can't learn one of life's most important messages: Richness is not an end in itself; it is a means to an end. If we devote our whole lives to the means and we don't allow time for the end, what have we then accomplished?

---

224. *Yaaroth Devash 1*

225. Khaleeli, Homa. "Writing Top Five Regrets of the Dying Has Brought Me to Tears." *The Guardian.* November 16, 2014. Accessed March 3, 2022. www.theguardian.com/lifeandstyle/shortcuts/2014/nov/16/writing-top-five-regrets-of-the-dying-has-brought-me-to-tears.

Shul/Synagogue

Live Longer

A study in 2007 of 1,811 Jewish men and women over the age of seventy concluded that "Synagogue attendance is seen to promote survival mainly through its function as a source of communal attachment and, perhaps, as a reflection of spirituality as well."[226]

Rabbis are constantly looking for ways to increase attendance in their synagogues. The Talmud states that when one arrives early for the service and leaves late, they will be blessed with long life. Why? The Torah writes that a person living in Israel lives longer. [227]

Why is this so?

Jewish tradition sees the *mazalot* (constellations) on high as directing the destiny of individuals and nations down below. This is true in the diaspora; however, in the Land of Israel, God Himself is directing the fate of the person and the country.

Living a long life in Israel is a direct result of the person not being influenced by the constellations. By living in Israel, the individual is living beyond the laws of nature and the typical running of the world. Likewise, the synagogue is a place where God's presence, the *Shechinah*, is more pronounced and evident—similar to what one experiences when living in Israel.

By spending time in the synagogue, a person is imbued with the sanctity that they would absorb by living in Israel and therefore will be blessed with a long life. Attending synagogue services and a long life go hand in hand.[228]

---

226. Or Hadash Synagogue. "New Study Suggests That People Who Attend Religious Services Live Longer." April 5, 2018. Accessed March 3, 2022. orhadash. org/2018/04/05/live-longer/.

227. *Devorim 11,21*

228. *Chidushei Rabbi Yehonatan*

A congregant walked past the rabbi to wish him a happy new year. The rabbi remarked that he hadn't seen him in a while. The congregant responded that he was part of the secret service.

After losing a loved one, one of the many things people say about going to shul three times a day for eleven months to say the mourner's kaddish is how much the comradery and friendship of the congregants helped them during this most trying time.

Making synagogue attendance a more frequent life endeavor can only benefit us.

Sin

One Big Accident

"Don't worry, accidents happen"—I am sure we have all been told this on numerous occasions. Perhaps we are a guest in someone's home and accidentally spill some of the red kiddush wine on the pristine white tablecloth. Or we accidentally drop a glass, and it shatters all over the kitchen floor. More than likely, the host will say, "It was an accident. Don't worry about it."

How does God view a person who accidentally transgresses one of His commandments? The Torah teaches us that a person who accidentally transgresses one of God's commandments must seek atonement

Why is this so?

We could perhaps argue that since the person did not willingly transgress, he should be forgiven and not held accountable for his actions because accidents happen.

The rabbis explain that doing something by accident indicates that the person has a connection with sin. And, for that, the person needs to seek God's forgiveness.[229]

By way of example: When was the last time you heard about someone who left his house without his pants on? Never? Walking out of your house without pants on is just so foreign and so beyond the pale that we could live five lifetimes, and it just would never happen.

Accidentally transgressing one of God's commandments should be a wakeup call that we are not completely immune to transgressing this particular sin and therefore we need to repent.

---

229. *Tiferet Yehonatan Kedoshim*

Slippery Slope

If you look at the rap sheet of somebody who has been convicted of armed robbery you will rarely find that this is the first crime they have committed. More than likely they started with misdemeanors and over time their crimes increased in severity.

Once a person has become a hardened criminal, it becomes extremely challenging to rehabilitate himself. The Talmud states that a person, after repeating the same sin a number of times, no longer views the act as being sinful. And if we no longer consider something to be a sin, there is nothing to seek atonement for.

This is true when we speak about our relationship with God. There may be times when we view a transgression as not being that significant and we have few qualms about transgressing it. What we fail to realize is that sinning is like a slippery slope, as our rabbis write—one sin leads to another. Therefore, we need to be extremely vigilant in not placing sins in categories of less severe and more severe. Since transgressing a less serious sin may ultimately lead you to transgress a graver one. [230]

The butterfly effect is the idea that small, seemingly trivial events may ultimately result in something with much larger consequences—in other words, they have nonlinear impacts on very complex systems. For instance, when a butterfly flaps its wings in India, that tiny change in air pressure could eventually cause a tornado in Iowa.

This is also true when we speak of human behavior. Very rarely will a person commit a heinous felony; it usually starts with petty crimes, and once such behavior has become second nature, they will push the boundaries to commit graver forms of misconduct.

We therefore need to place safeguards around our behavior and actions and not fall into the false sense of security that what we are doing isn't all that

---

230. *Yaaroth Devash 2,1*

bad. While that may be true, we need to be conscious of the slippery slope that can take us to places we never ever imagined we would or we could go.

How do we stop the slide?

There are many approaches when it comes to enforcing law and order. Some may be more successful than others. One of the approaches is known as zero tolerance. The understanding is that if we discipline the person for a minor violation, this will discourage the person from committing more serious felonies.

We don't always see a police vehicle through our rearview mirror to keep us in check. Therefore, we need to self-regulate. It may be difficult and, at times, challenging, but it is an ideal we should strive for—and that is the benchmark of zero tolerance.

Big and Small

Reb Yehonatan shares a fascinating statement made by King David that was recorded in rabbinic literature. At first glance, the statement seems somewhat cryptic and difficult to comprehend: King David proclaimed that he did not fear a serious transgression because it was serious; rather, he feared a seemingly less severe sin because it was not as serious.

Reb Yehonatan explains King David's words to mean the following: King David was not worried he would transgress a severe sin, such as murder, God forbid. Because he knew the severity of the crime and the punishment, there was no way he would even contemplate such an act. However, he was concerned that perhaps he wouldn't speak nicely to someone and hurt their feelings. Compared to murder, such conduct is of course minor, and the punishment is definitely not the death penalty. Therefore, King David was wary of what might be considered a minor transgression because he might *inadvertently* say something he shouldn't.[231]

---

231. *Yaaroth Devash 1,5*

We all have a line in the sand that we will not pass. Many who don't keep kosher will not eat bacon. Others who drive on the Shabbat will not drive on Yom Kippur.

What is the rationale behind these decisions? We all want to maintain our connection with God. And we all want to feel that we belong. It simply becomes a question of what act will severe that bond?

If we would appreciate that any and every sin big or small creates a barrier between us and God, this would help strengthen our resolve in not differentiating between the so-called big and small transgressions.

Why Do We Sin?

The primary reason we sin is because we don't know that what we are doing is prohibited. And even if we are aware that it is sinful, we fail to realize the spiritual harm the sin will cause. Reb Yehonatan writes that if we would only know the damage sins causes, we would shed enough tears for them to create a stream.[232]

We all know that medicines need to be kept far away from tiny hands. They all have tamper-proof caps to keep the prying hands of little children out. We take similar precautions with adults as well. We place large signs that state, "Hazardous material. Keep out." And poisonous substances have large warning signs on the containers alerting us of the danger.

If sins are so harmful, why doesn't God make them difficult to access, like the medicine bottle or place glaring large signs warning us of how harmful they are?

One of the basic principles of the Jewish faith is free choice. We have been given the ability to choose between right and wrong. It is our prerogative to be either good or bad. If every time we did something wrong, we were hit by a bolt of lightning, no one in their right mind would do it. Hence, we would no longer be in a position to choose freely.

---

232. *Yaaroth Devash 2*

To give us the ability to choose freely, God placed no warning signs or obstacles in our path to prevent us from sinning. However, not for a moment should we be under the false impression that transgressing the word of God by eating nonkosher is any less harmful than consuming poison.

Why Do We Transgress God's Will?

Why would someone transgress the will of God? There is usually one of three reasons: The first reason is a lack of knowledge; the person doesn't know what they are doing is prohibited in the eyes of God. The second is a sense of grandeur, of entitlement; it leads the person to believe that they are not bound by the laws of God. The third is a desire for what is prohibited; this need far outweighs the repercussions from abandoning the will of God.

There are three approaches a person can take to ensure they don't sin: The first is to learn and study until you are well versed in the Torah and its laws. The second is to focus on a prayer that we recite twice a day, and that is the Shema "Hear O Israel the Lord our God the Lord is One."—where we proclaim that everything is an expression of Godliness and that God is everywhere. How then can we be haughty if we realize we are standing in the presence of God? The third is to be conscious of the fact that our time on earth is limited and eventually we will follow in the footsteps of all humanity that has preceded us and we will pass away. Reflecting on this will put things in its proper perspective, and we will not be driven by temporary transient pleasures.[233]

The reasons for sinning and how we can overcome them are applicable in our daily lives as citizens of the countries where we live. There are usually three reasons someone would break the law. He didn't realize that you can't turn right when facing a red light. He feels certain laws don't apply to him; he stands above the law. He needs to get to a very important meeting therefore he is allowed to speed. And finally, the temptation and desire are

---

233. *Yaaroth Devash 2*

*too great to overcome. He is hoping he doesn't transgress the Eleventh Com-
mandment: "Don't get caught."*

*To remain a law-abiding citizen, one needs to remember the same three
approaches mentioned above. There is a legal principle of ignorantia juris
non excusat (ignorance of the law excuses not). We may have a driver's
license, but before we begin to drive in a new country, we need to make sure
we know the rules of the road. Second, we are obligated by Jewish law to heed
the laws of the country we abide in. And, finally, we need to remember that
most people transgress the Eleventh Commandment and they get caught.*

Prevention

"Out of sight, out of mind" is a proverb suggesting that we generally
forget those of our friends and relatives we don't see often. Mind is a
mechanism very much attached to the here and now; it rarely looks
back unless there is need for it. This idea is clearly demonstrated in a
law recorded in the Torah pertaining to idol worship.

Generally, it is sufficient to simply nullify the idols of the heavens.
However, the idol known as Pe'or had to be physically destroyed. Why
wasn't it enough to simply nullify the Pe'or idol? The Jewish people
had transgressed and served the Pe'or idol. If they only nullified it, it
would remain intact. The concern was that the Jews might be tempted
to serve it once again. They therefore had to physically destroy it. As
the saying goes, "Out of sight, out of mind."[234]

*One of the methods used by law enforcement to test for intoxication is to
ask the person to walk in a straight line. If we aren't drunk, we can walk in
a straight line without veering to the right or left or tripping over our feet.
However, if we had to walk along the edge of a cliff, we would be cautious
and we would distance ourselves from the edge in the million-to-one situation that we would trip or mistakenly veer off the straight line and fall over
the edge.*

---

234. *Ahavat Yehonatan Re'eh*

Likewise, the rabbis felt there were certain Torah laws that we were somewhat lax in, and we didn't realize how close we were to the edge of transgression. Therefore, a rabbinic law was introduced as a safety net to safeguard the Torah.

God or Man

In the eyes of God, which sin is more severe: when we sin against God or when we sin against our fellow man?

In the times of Noach prior to the flood, mankind had become extremely sinful. They rebelled against God, and they caused great harm and financial loss to their fellow man. The rabbis share a fascinating insight into how God viewed their sins. God said, "When mankind rebels against me, I am willing to forgo my honor and I will not bring the flood. However, I cannot look the other way when I see mankind causing pain, suffering, and financial loss to their fellow human being." And it was at that point that God brought the flood.[235]

We can divide God's commandments into two categories: those between man and God and between man and his fellow man. Some people are very careful when it comes to their relationship with God. They will be extremely scrupulous when it comes to observing the Shabbat or eating kosher. And, at the same time, they feel no remorse in viewing the marketplace as a jungle where man eats man and the prohibitions such as not stealing and not causing damage are conveniently forgotten.

Then there are those who are extremely diligent in how they interact with their fellow man. Always being courteous and kind and at the same time being honorable in their business affairs. However, they fall short when it comes to the laws that are very much God centric, such as putting on tefillin daily and lighting the Shabbat candles.

The Ten Commandments were divided into two categories; on the first tablet were five commandments that spoke of man's relationship with God,

---

235. *Tiferet Yehonatan Noach*

while the second tablet contained five commandments between man and his fellow man.

We cannot arbitrarily decide which are more important; we need to try to excel in all of God's laws. However, we must remember that, on Yom Kippur, God does not forgive those sins that negatively impact our fellow man until we have sought forgiveness from whom we wronged.

Wealth and Poverty

The trappings of wealth and the struggles of poverty can lead a person to sin. If you are wealthy, the world is your backyard, and the pursuit of earthly and physical pleasures come to the fore. And, at the same time, spirituality and holiness become second fiddle. There is also the sense of entitlement that comes with wealth that could cause us to become extremely arrogant. On the other hand, the poor person does not have these challenges. He is too busy trying to put bread on the table to even dream of pursuing the trappings the world has to offer. Similarly, he doesn't believe he has anything to be conceited about.

Poverty as well can be a catalyst to sin. If we are poor and don't succeed at changing our circumstances no matter what we try to do, this may lead us to believe that God has abandoned us and that He isn't interested in caring and helping those who are down on their luck. Such an attitude would label us as a heretic and nonbeliever. However, if we are wealthy, we may not spend too much time thinking of God, but we definitely would not conclude that God has abandoned us.[236]

At times, we play God by labelling who is a good Jew and who is a bad Jew. What we don't consider is that when it comes to serving God, the wealthy have their unique challenges, as do the poor. And, unless we are God, we are not in a position to decide whose circumstances are more challenging. Therefore, we should always view a Jew favorably regardless of his financial standing.

---

236. Ahavat Yehonatan Shoftim

Litmus Test

If we are prone to unlawful behavior or have a predisposition toward consuming things that are extremely harmful to our well-being, how can we be assured if we have beaten the curse? For example, we drink way too much alcohol, and we can't seem to stop the urge to drink; how will we ever know if we have it under control?

Obviously, if we are living in a city where you can't purchase any alcohol, we will never know if we have slain our dragon. Only if we are living down the block from a liquor store and we are not tempted to purchase alcohol or we are at a party with an open bar and we don't slowly make our way over can we presume that we are on the road to recovery.

That is why we are instructed to eat on the eve of Yom Kippur to atone for the sin of Adam and Chava. They sinned by eating the forbidden fruit in the Garden of Eden. If we would not be consuming any food, how would we know that, if given the chance to eat, we will not be tempted to eat food that is not permitted. Therefore, we are instructed to eat on the eve of the holiest day of the year and demonstrate that even though we are eating, we are only eating kosher, thus annulling the sin of Adam and Chava.[237]

We are all familiar with the sayings "Don't put yourself in harm's way" and "Don't tempt fate." In the first instance, we should never put ourselves in a position where we might become compromised. For example, if we didn't always keep kosher and then we decided we would only eat kosher, the last place we should go is our once favorite nonkosher restaurant because the temptation may be too great. However, if by chance we do go that restaurant and we have absolutely no desire to sit down and order a meal, we can be confident that eating nonkosher food will no longer be a challenge.

---

237. *Chidushei Rabbi Yehonatan*

To Be Free

The Jewish people are living in a unique period, something we more than likely never experienced since the times of King Solomon when he built the first Temple in Jerusalem.

For the first time in more than 1,900 years, we have our own homeland and the right and the ability to self-govern. We have never been as affluent as we are now. There is virtually no country in the world where we are not permitted to openly practice our faith. The world of academia, of finance, of the arts, and of the sporting arena are open to us. The words "segregation" and "second-class citizens" are a thing of the past.

You would imagine that by living in such times, we would fully embrace our illustrious heritage and pursue a life enriched with Jewish ritual and observance. However, we know only too well that this is not the case. After the Holocaust, there were approximately 10.6 million Jews in the world. Nearly eighty years later, at the time of this writing, there are only approximately 15.2 million Jews. The numbers don't lie. One of the key factors for why we haven't reached pre-Holocaust numbers is due to assimilation.

Reb Yehonatan explains that King Achashverosh from the story of Purim had invited all the Jews to join with the rest of his subjects in great celebration and merriment. As a result, the Jews felt that the shackles of their servitude had been removed. They no longer saw themselves as second-class citizens and were now able to do and to live as they pleased. And this nearly led to their annihilation at the hands of Haman. Achashverosh understood that if you want the Jewish people to, God forbid, disappear, don't build ghettoes and bar them from leaving. On the contrary, open the gates large and wide, and they will assimilate on their own.[238]

---

238. *Yaaroth Devash 1,3*

Freedom brings with it its own peril. A great rabbi who spent many years in the gulag for being an observant Jew and for teaching Torah once remarked that the challenge of remaining a God-fearing Jew is more challenging in the West than it was in the former Soviet Union.

In Russia, whether you liked it or not, you could never forget that you were a Jew and that you were different from the rest of society—whether it was in terms of where you could live or the inability to attend higher levels of education or employment in certain fields. While living in freedom in the United States or any other country of the Western world, you can very easily disappear into the fabric of society and never be reminded that you are Jewish. Freedom is a God-given right that every human being should enjoy. Let us use our God-given right to ensure that God is right where He should be.

Idol Worship

Even the most nonobservant Jew would not serve idols. Our history is replete of Jews who gave their lives rather than being forced to serve idols. The Hebrew word for "idol worship" is *avodah zarah*, which means "worshipping a foreign entity." You don't have to actually bow down to an idol for it to be considered idol worship. Anytime you do something that is against the will of God is considered, to a lesser degree, a form of idol worship—since, by your actions, you are demonstrating that there is an existence or motivation outside of God that has your calling.[239]

Are we idol worshippers? The answer would obviously be no. It is hard for us to comprehend how any intelligent human being could have thought that by bowing down to a figure of wood or marble they would have their prayers answered. However, if idol worship is understood to mean serving something other than God, aren't we all guilty of idol worship to some extent?

---

239. *Yaaroth Devash* 1,17

We have all heard of the expression, "serving the almighty dollar." We are obsessed with making money and being able to afford more of what life has to offer. Try this experiment: if you were told that a certain person is extremely successful, what is the first thought that crosses your mind? If you immediately think how much the person is worth, then you have defined success in terms of wealth. And perhaps your response is indicative of the value and importance you place on financial success.

We may not serve idols made from marble and wood, but we are very tempted to serve idols in the form of the green dollar bill.

Sons

Like Father Like Son

The saying "like father like son" means that a man or a boy has the same attitudes as his father or behaves in the same way.

The Talmud records that, during the Temple period, there was a woman by the name of Kimchit, and she was blessed with seven sons. Each of her sons served as the Cohen Gadol (the High Priest). The Talmud relates that the rabbis asked her what great acts she accomplished to merit seven great sons.

Why did the rabbis assume that it was in the mother's merit that the sons turned out as they did? Perhaps it was in the merit of their father's behavior that all the sons became the Cohen Gadol. The rabbis asked specifically about the mother's behavior because they are of the opinion that how a boy will behave and conduct himself is very much dependent on the mother's conduct. "Like father like son" perhaps, but from the Torah's viewpoint, definitely, "like mother like son."[240]

A great rabbi once said that, just as wearing tefillin every day is a mitzvah, so too is it an absolute duty for every person to spend a half hour every day thinking about the Torah education of children. As parents, we need to realize that very rarely are our children guided and influenced by what we say. It is what we do that has the greatest impact on their character.

---

240. *Ahavat Yehonatan Tzav*

Soul

Eternal Battle

Every Jew has a positive (good) and negative (evil) inclination. The Talmud writes that we need to serve God with both of them. How do we serve God with our negative inclination?

Reb Yehonatan writes that we all possess an animal soul and a spiritual soul. The animal soul resides in our heart. This soul comes from the evil inclination, and it encourages us to pursue mundane physical pleasures. The spiritual soul descends from heaven. When the verse says, "And God blew into man's nostrils a living spirit," it is referring to the spiritual soul. And this is the good inclination whose desire is to only do good.

The tzaddik is able to transform his evil inclination into a positive inclination, and likewise, transform the animal soul into an intellectual soul. This explains how we can serve God with our evil inclination, by first changing it from evil to good.[241]

By way of analogy, the human body is like a country, and the two souls and inclinations are like two kings. Each king wants to rule and control the country. It does that by defeating the other king. Likewise, each soul wants to control and influence the bodies they reside in. It accomplishes this by defeating the other soul.

There are two ways for a king to defeat his enemy. The first is when the king is able to subdue the enemy until they are no longer considered a threat. A far greater victory would be if the king could harness the strengths and resources of his enemy by transforming the foe to friend. Similarly, Reb Yehonatan is impressing upon us that a righteous person is able to change his negative inclination and animal soul into a positive and spiritual soul.

---

241. *Chidushei Rabbi Yehonatan*

One Family

When God created Adam, He first formed a physical body. The body was lifeless. God then blew the soul into Adam via his nostrils. The human being is a composite of the physical and the spiritual. Reb Yehonatan writes that the souls of family members are linked and connected with one another. And when a family member passes away, it spiritually impacts all the family members.

He explains this by way of analogy: The body is like a receptacle and the soul is a lit candle that illuminates the vessel. Besides illuminating its own vessel, the candle sheds light on the vessels that are in close proximity. And when the candle is extinguished, the vessels surrounding the candle become less visible.

This, he says, explains an interesting law pertaining to a Cohen. A Cohen is prohibited to come in contact with a corpse. However, he is permitted if the deceased is one of his seven blood relatives. Why the distinction? When the Cohen loses a close relative, in a sense, part of the Cohen's light has been extinguished and he becomes somewhat impure. Since he is now impure, he is permitted to come in contact with his deceased relative.[242]

We are well aware of the medieval proverb that "blood is thicker than water." A person saying this is declaring that their loyalty to family is greater than their loyalty to anyone else.

Jewish law states if we have limited resources in giving tzedakah (charity), and we can either give the money to a relative or to a stranger, we should give the money to our relative. A great rabbi once called in a wealthy individual and shared with him the plight of one of the members of the congregation who was in desperate need of financial help. After giving a sizeable donation, the wealthy man inquired who this destitute person was. The rabbi answered, "It is your brother" and then he berated him for not being aware of his own brother's predicament.

---

242. *Ahavat Yehonatan Emor*

We should never forget that charity begins at home, because the souls of the family are intertwined one with the other.

Inner Workings

Part of the Jewish belief system is that we all possess a *neshamah* (a soul). And when a person passes away, the soul leaves the body and returns to heaven. Of course, the soul is not something physical that any of the five human senses can define. However, based on the written and oral tradition, our great Torah giants throughout the generations have given us a small keyhole into the nature of the soul.

Reb Yehonatan answers a number of questions pertaining to the soul.

When was the soul created?

While the Torah clearly states that Adam and Chava were created on the sixth day of creation, the holy souls of mankind were created on the first day of creation. And on the sixth day, they were inserted into Adam's and Chava's inanimate bodies and, as a result, came to life.

When does the soul enter the body?

The soul enters the body forty days after conception. The Talmud describes the fetus during the first forty days as "mere water." And, after forty days, the fetus begins to form.

When does the evil inclination enter the body?

There are two schools of thought: either at conception or at birth.

How many evil inclinations do we have?

We have two. The first seeks our downfall and ruin. The second expresses itself as negative character traits, such as anger.[243]

Imagine we were given a very expensive car and were told that we can use it free of charge until the owner asks for it to be returned. We will be forever thankful and indebted to the person who lent us his car free of charge. Since we don't know when the owner will ask for the car to be returned, we will do our utmost to keep it clean. We won't rely on taking it to a carwash once

---

243. *Ahavat Yehonatan Shoftim*

a week or once a month. We will strictly follow the rules of the road as we don't want to get any tickets or get into an accident and damage the car. To the best of our ability, we want to return the car in the same condition it was lent to us—and, if we can, return it even in a better condition.

A car takes us from point A to point B. A soul takes us from birth to the day of our passing. It stands to reason that we need to care for our soul more than we care for our car.

We may not see or feel our soul, but we know we have one. God lends it to us for our benefit. He can take it back at any time. We therefore need to do whatever we can to ensure that it is not exposed to impurity or the profane. We need to safeguard the soul so that it remains pristine clean at all times.

We may not be able to see our intellect, but we know we have one. Likewise, we may not see our soul, but we know we have one.

Healthy Self-Esteem

In one of Reb Yehonatan's sublime insights into human nature, he writes that we need to realize we are the children of royalty. We possess a Godly soul that comes from a very lofty place in heaven, and it descends into our bodies. And since we are the children of the King, we need to act accordingly.

He writes that the malady afflicting so many of our generation is that we have forgotten our soul component. Hence, we see no problem in debasing ourselves in all kinds of inappropriate behavior. We need to always be proud of our special status. And while haughtiness is the antithesis of spiritual endeavor, pride that stems from the knowledge that we have a soul is to be encouraged. It is what protects us from simply following the rest of society.[244]

A great psychiatrist who was a prolific writer once remarked that he wrote many different works all based on one central theme, self-esteem.

---

244. Yaaroth Devash 1,15

He explains that it is imperative for a person to have a healthy self-esteem to have a sense of self-worth. In Yiddish, there is a saying "es past nisht." Loosely translated, this means, "It is beneath your dignity; it is unbecoming of you to have acted in the manner that you did."

If someone does something inappropriate, we should criticize the act and not the person. If we belittle the person and tell them how terrible they are, it could evolve into a self-fulfilling prophecy. The person thinks to himself, "If everyone labels me as being rotten, I might as well be one." By criticizing the person, we are crushing them and taking away their desire and will to improve.

On the other hand, if we explain to the person his true worth and potential and how his behavior is simply unbecoming, we have empowered the person to be able to overcome his challenges.

We need to remember and be conscious of the fact that we are more than just flesh and bones; we possess a Godly soul. And if part of our very being is holy, pure, and spiritual, it would be inconceivable for us to even contemplate dragging it through the mud and dirt of unbefitting conduct. Reb Yehonatan writes that we are higher than angels; if that is the case, we need to act accordingly.

Speech

Stop Talking

We all know someone who would do themselves a favor by keeping their mouths shut. And, at times, we may think to ourselves that we also need to control what comes out of our mouths.

What ideas can we put into practice to enable us to be more conscious of what we say?

God created the world with words, as the verse says, "And God said let there be light." Man was the only one of God's creations that were gifted with the power and potential impact of speech. Man can speak words of comfort and joy or words of destruction and terror.

Our thoughts, in a sense, remain our private property. However, once our thoughts are verbalized, they create a new reality. Words of love create nurturing; words of hope generate positive action. This is alluded to in the Talmud statement, "A covenant is made for the lips." This is understood to mean the spoken word, even if unintentional, becomes fulfilled.[245]

It is unreasonable to tell someone to simply stop talking. However, it is reasonable to say, "Stop and think before you begin talking." Realize that just as God's words creates realities, so to our words create realities. Reflecting on these ideas will go a long way in helping us control what comes out of our mouth.

The Power of the Spoken Word

We are all aware of the power of the spoken word. Words can bring comfort, and words can be cruel. Words can heal, and words can harm.

---

245. *Yaaroth Devash 1*

There are four types of speech that are considered inappropriate. The first, one should not unduly flatter someone who is unworthy. Second, one should not utter falsehood. Third, one should not speak *lashon hora* (derogatory or damaging statements about an individual), and fourth, one should not indulge in foolish and idle chatter.

If a person feels an urge to indulge in one of the four inappropriate forms of speech, what should he do? Recognizing that it is nearly impossible to simply refrain from talking, he should channel the desire into a positive form of speech or behavior.

Channel the desire to flatter someone who is undeserving by flattering and praising God in your prayers.

The opposite of lying is being truthful. When one does *teshuvah* (repents), one needs to be completely honest about his inappropriate behavior. If he isn't truthful, he will feel no need to repent. Repentance is the path we must take to overcome the urge to lie.

A person speaks negatively about someone because he has animosity toward them. He needs to change his mindset and view the person positively. The finest example would be to give the person *tzedakah* (charity).

Recognize the amount of time wasted with idle chatter by utilizing the time to study Torah, God's wisdom.[246]

All of existence can be placed in one of four categories: the inanimate, vegetation, the animal kingdom, and mankind. What is interesting is that the Hebrew word used for "man" in this context is medaber, which translates to "the speaker." Speech is what defines the human and is that which contrasts him with the rest of existence. Speech is a God-given gift, a gift to be cherished and not squandered.

---

246. *Yaaroth Devash* 1,15

Suffering

Attitude

If we are here on earth, we will experience challenges, and we will face difficulties; no one is immune. A story is told of a group of people who were standing in a circle, each carrying their package of problems. They were instructed to place them in the middle of the circle. They were then told to take any package they wanted. Interestingly, they each took their own package.

Are there any tools we can use to help us deal with life's curve balls, which seem to come from nowhere, as if out of thin air?

Reb Yehonatan offers the following sage advice by way of analogy: A doctor informs his patient that he will have to drink a repulsive-tasting medicine on a daily basis to cure his medical condition. The patient doesn't deny that it tastes terrible; however, he is aware this is the only way he will be cured and is therefore very happy to take it. It is a case of short-term pain for long-term gain.

Likewise, said Reb Yehonatan, we need to internalize and understand that God is the source of all goodness and only good emanates from Him. And the trial we are experiencing will ultimately heal us and make us stronger. We should see the challenging times like the bitter medicine that has a positive outcome at the end.[247]

It is all a question of attitude.

A great rabbi suffered tremendously in his life. He was a frightful pauper; there was never enough to eat in his home, and his family was beset with all sorts of afflictions and illnesses. Yet he was always good humored and cheerful, and constantly expressed his gratitude to the Almighty for all His kindness.

---

247. *Chidushei Rabbi Yehonatan*

A student once approached him and asked, "How is it possible for a person to be so happy and joyful when life was so difficult and grim?"

The rabbi replied, "That is a very good question. I am very sorry, but I can't answer it. You need to ask the question of someone who has experienced suffering."

No one will deny that what Reb Yehonatan is teaching us and how the great rabbi viewed his life are indeed very lofty spiritual levels that are very difficult to attain. We may never be able to reach such a level of acceptance. But every step we take toward that ultimate goal will help us in dealing with life's struggles.

Sukkot

Eternal Message

Rosh Hashanah marks the beginning of the Jewish New Year, and ten days later is Yom Kippur, the Day of Atonement. A mere five days after Yom Kippur, we celebrate the festival of Sukkot. Throughout the eight days of Sukkot, we are instructed to leave our homes and dwell in a temporary abode called a sukkah. The sukkah is a structure that has no proper roof and is covered with vegetation. The gaps in the roof enable the person sitting in the sukkah to see the stars and, at the same time, allow the rain to enter.

It is true that the Jewish people have been called the wandering Jew, and for forty years, we traveled in the desert living in temporary dwellings, such as the sukkah. However, there must be a profounder reason why, at the beginning of the Jewish calendar year, we are instructed to spend eight days exposed to the elements by leaving our safe, secure home and venturing out to reside in a temporary dwelling.

The message of the sukkah is eternal. It is relevant not just for the eight days of the festival; it is pertinent every day of our lives. The sukkah is a temporary abode and its covering is such that through it you can see the stars in heaven. The sukkah is teaching us that our sojourn on earth is temporary, as no one lives forever, and that we need to turn to God in heaven for direction and inspiration.

Recognizing that life is transient not only impacts our spiritual growth but also affects our physical health. Reb Yehonatan suggests that there is a strong correlation between our forefathers living long lives and that they always dwelt in tents. Our forefathers never built permanent structures to live in. As such, they were not frightened of an oncoming enemy, as they could simply pack their tents and flee. They were also not worried about experiencing famine, as they could very easily relocate by uprooting their tents and move on. Thus, their lives were somewhat less stressful, and as a result, they lived longer.[248]

When we are stressed, the immune system's ability to fight off invaders is reduced, making us more susceptible to infections. What's more, there's a link between stress and heart attacks. These claims are backed by medical research.[249]

The source for a lot of stress and anxiety stems from financial worries and concerns. Whether it is a result of a lack of or a desire for more. If we would be able to put things in its right context and perspective and see the fleetingness of this physical world, this would go a long way in reducing our stress.

The sukkah is much more than a tent covered by leaves; it is an eternal message about how we should live our lives.

Transient Existence

The expression "There are no atheists in a foxhole" means that, in a time of crisis, people turn to God. Human nature is such that we take God for granted when our family is healthy and we are financially successful. It is when we face challenges that we remember there is a God.

The festival of Sukkot occurs every year during the harvest season when food is bountiful. The concern is, as we enjoy the fruits of our success, we might come to forget God. Therefore, we are instructed to leave the safety and comfort of our home and venture out and live in a sukkah. The sukkah symbolizes the frailty of life and the importance of remembering God during the good, not just during the bad.[250]

---

248. *Yaaroth Devash 1,6*

249. Dimsdale, Joel E. "Psychological Stress and Cardiovascular Disease." *Journal of the American College of Cardiology* 51, no. 13 (April 2008): 1237–1246. doi: 10.1016/j.jacc.2007.12.024.

250. *Tiferet Yehonatan Sukkot*

It is important to be able to put things in perspective; of course, this doesn't mean we should all become gravediggers. We are meant to serve God with joy and happiness; we would never be capable of that if we are always thinking about our demise.

But every so often it would be wise to reflect and think about our transient existence, realizing that we take nothing with us besides all the good we did while here on earth.

Teachers

Pay Them a Visit

In the times of the Temple, we were obligated to make a pilgrimage to God's home three times a year. And in the Messianic era, when the third Temple will be built, we will visit the Temple every Shabbat and every Rosh Chodesh (the first of the month). During our exile, when we have no Temple, is there an opportunity to experience the spiritual height of visiting the Temple?

When we visit our rebbe, our teacher, our spiritual guide, it is considered as if we have visited the Temple.[251]

Jewish law places great emphasis on the honor, respect, and awe that we must have for our teachers. Our sages declared, "Your fear of your teacher should be equivalent to your fear of heaven."

Our sages proclaimed, "Whoever disputes the authority of his teacher is considered as if he revolts against the Divine Presence. Likewise, whoever thinks disparagingly of his teacher is considered as if he thought disparagingly of the Divine Presence."

Therefore, during our exile, we are obligated to visit our rebbe as a remembrance of the pilgrimage that was normally made to God, since a great Torah scholar is in some measure equated to God. The greatest level of respect must be given to our teachers, and if we are thinking of misbehaving in class, remember visiting them is like visiting the Temple.

---

251. *Ahavat Yehonatan Shabbat HaChodesh*

Teaching

The Ultimate

What more could we wish for? Imagine a person has completed his mission here on earth and now his *neshamah* (soul) is in *Gan Eden* (the Garden of Eden). The neshamah is in a state of eternal peace, enjoying all that is truly perfect while basking in God's glory.

Could we wish for anything more? Reb Yehonatan says yes. The neshamah's greatest pleasure and what it wants to do more than anything else is to teach. It wants to teach those less knowledgeable about God, His Torah, and His *mitzvot* (commandments).[252]

While it is somewhat counterintuitive, research has shown that we are happiest when we are giving to others and not when we are receiving. What greater gift could we be giving to someone than the knowledge of God and His wisdom? Feeling inadequate in our knowledge of Torah and our ability to teach doesn't preclude us from sharing and giving the ultimate gift: the gift of knowledge. A great rabbi once said, "If you only know the first letter of the Hebrew alphabet and you meet someone who doesn't even know that, you should teach them that letter."

If we ever wanted to know what our souls are longing for more than anything else, it is to teach the word of God. And it is something each and every one of us, without exception, can do.

---

252. *Yaaroth Devash* 2,7

Tefillah/Prayers

One Good Deed Leads to Another

One of the basic tenets of Judaism is the belief in Divine Providence, that nothing happens by chance. What we experience and encounter is very much dependent on our actions and behavior. Reb Yehonatan, who was a master orator, writes that one of the themes he would regularly touch upon in his lectures was the importance of prayer. He says that if we concentrate properly during our morning prayers, we can be assured that during the course of the day, we will merit the opportunity to fulfill many of God's commandments, and we will be successful in our business dealings.[253]

Prayer is more than simply saying words. Whether it is the words that jump out at us from our siddur or the words that emanate from the depths of our soul, prayer is a recognition that God is listening to every word we utter.

Prayer is a God-given privilege; it is a gift from Above that allows a mere mortal, a finite creature, to communicate with the Supreme Being. It is a time we should cherish and utilize to its fullest.

No Talking

Imagine you are talking to someone of great importance, and you need them to do you a favor that no one else can. And as you are selling them your pitch, you begin talking to someone else. How successful do you think you will be? Or imagine you are on the phone with someone and you are telling them how great they are, but then you put them on hold mid-sentence. How sincere do they think you are if you could just put them on hold?

---

253. *Yaaroth Devash 1,4*

Reb Yehonatan says that, in a sense, this is what happens when we talk in the midst of our prayers. By talking while we are praying, this causes our prayers to become disconnected from God.[254]

A great rabbi once walked into a synagogue and remarked how the room was full of people's prayers. The congregants took that as a wonderful compliment. Later, the rabbi remarked that he was not trying to be complimentary at all. On the contrary, he was berating them in a subtle manner. You see, this synagogue was notorious for the amount of talking that took place during the service, and as a result, the prayers couldn't be elevated heavenward, and they remained trapped within the synagogue.

With God's Help

It is very common for Jews to conclude a statement with the words *bezrat Hashem* (with the help of God). As Jews, we recognize that without the help from the above, we would be unable to accomplish anything during the course of the day. Therefore, Reb Yehonatan emphasizes how important it is that we reflect on the day ahead in our morning prayers. We should pray that we be successful and that we accomplish our many tasks in an upright and noble manner.

Many may err in believing that these personal prayers must be said and expressed in the Hebrew language similar to the language of the *siddur* (the prayer book). Reb Yehonatan writes that if we are unfamiliar or unable to pray using Biblical Hebrew, we should pray in the language we are most comfortable with, and God cherishes every word that we utter.[255]

Prayer is referred to as service of the heart; it stands to reason then that the words we say should emanate from our heart. Words that we cannot comprehend can never come from the depths of our emotions.

---

254. *Yaaroth Devash 1,40*

255. *Yaaroth Devash 1,1*

Big or Small

We don't call the president's or the prime minister's office if our garbage hasn't been collected. Such matters are handled by our local council. Heads of state don't waste their time with such trivial and insignificant matters. They deal exclusively with issues that impact the country as a whole.

Reb Yehonatan writes that this is not how God interacts with the human being. In God's eyes, there is no distinction between a large mountain or a molehill. God wants to hear all our needs and wants. The appropriate place to insert our particular requests is in the blessing of the Amidah "Shema Koleinu," where we ask that God hears our voices.[256]

God is infinite; as a result, there is no distinction between a large or small amount. The distance between one and infinity and 100 and infinity is one and the same. In God's eyes, there is no difference between big and small.

I Said It Yesterday

One of the great challenges of formal prayer is that it can easily become very monotonous as we say the same prayers day in and day out and sometimes more than once on the same day. What can we do to ensure that our prayers remain faithful to the original text, on the one hand, and on the other hand, still feel fresh and alive?

Reb Yehonatan writes that we need to supplement our daily prayers with a personal prayer. Every day we should focus on another aspect of our lives. One day, we can focus on asking God to bless us with financial security; on another day, we may request that God grant us success in our studies. If we are unable to formulate our requests in the holy tongue, we should express our needs in our language.[257]

---

256. *Yaaroth Devash 1,1*
257. *Yaaroth Devash 2,12*

From a historical perspective, prayer was always considered a very personal and private moment between man and God. We were therefore encouraged to compose our own prayers. However, as a result of persecution and exile, Jews where no longer familiar and fluent in the ancient Hebrew language, and this impacted their ability to express themselves in a meaningful way. As a result, the Men of the Great Assembly formulated a standard set of prayers.

There is great value in having a standard set of prayers as set out in the siddur (the prayer book). A Jew can enter a synagogue anywhere in the world and feel at home and will be able to be part of the service. Second, the prayers have been formulated to contain all the spiritual states a Jew is supposed to attain during prayer. Yet, at the same time, we are encouraged to never lose that personal connection prayer affords us.

Layers of Interpretation

Have you ever wondered why certain individuals pray for a very long time? It isn't because they struggle to read and pronounce the words properly since people who pray at great length are usually great Torah scholars. It also isn't because they are saying the prayer for the first time, and it is new to them, as they have been saying the same prayer day in and day out, some for at least forty or fifty years.

The reason is that every prayer has layers upon layers of interpretation, and when a person prays, he can reflect on a multitude of insights on the same section. Or he may pray every day while reflecting on a different inspiring thought and understanding.

Three times a day we recite the Amidah, a prayer comprised of 19 blessings. In the second blessing, we acknowledge and thank God that there will come a time when all our departed loved ones will return. This unique period in human history will occur after the Messianic era and is known as the period of the Resurrection of the Dead—a blessing truly worth reflecting on.

Reb Yehonatan shares a fascinating elucidation of this blessing. One of the greatest gifts God gave mankind is the opportunity and the ability to do *teshuvah* (to repent), to rectify our past mistakes. Life is forward moving; we can never turn back the clock, except when it comes to teshuvah. God is telling us that if we are sincerely remorseful for our prior actions and we make a solemn commitment not to transgress in the future, He will remove and whitewash what we had done wrong in the past.

A sinful individual is considered as being disconnected from God and is therefore referred to as being dead while they are still walking the face of the earth. If this sinful person will do teshuvah and repent, God will no longer consider him wicked, and he will no longer be viewed as being dead.

The second blessing can now be understood to mean that we are thanking God for giving us the opportunity to rectify the sins of our past, and as a result, God has given life back to the dead.[258]

It is important to understand our prayers, and therefore many people feel more comfortable praying in a familiar language. What is important to remember is that the prayers were composed in Biblical Hebrew or Aramaic. And we are now reading a translation of the prayer in our native tongue. Thus, we are reading but one translation and understanding of the original text. If we really want to immerse ourselves in the world of prayer, we need to be comfortable reading and understanding the prayers in its original form. And then we can begin to explore the depths and the breadth of our prayers.

Teardrops

When we shed a tear from the depths of our heart, we may see that as a sign of weakness an inability to cope. We think the situation is hopeless, and we simply throw in the towel and the waterworks begin to flow.

---

258. *Yaaroth Devash 1,2*

When we talk of prayer, tears aren't a symbol of weakness; rather, they are a sign of connectivity, of longing to be one with God. The Talmud states, "All gates in heaven are closed except for the gates of tears." This is understood to mean that all the heavenly gates are guarded by an angel, while the gates of tears are guarded by God Himself.

When we pray, we need to realize that we are being given the gift of being able to talk one on one with God Himself. We need to be conscious of the fact that God is listening and He will answer our prayers. It is only natural then that we would begin to shed tears as our tears express the depths of our feelings.

God, who stands at the gates of tears, ensures that the gates remain always open.[259]

Depending on the situation and circumstance, tears may be expressing many different emotions. If you want to gauge whether your moments of prayer, your private time with God, are superficial and insincere or are genuine and heartfelt, check to see if you shed a tear.

Daily Prayer

Rosh Hashanah and Yom Kippur are considered the holiest days of the year. On Rosh Hashanah, it is decreed how the coming year will unfold for each and every one of us. And on Yom Kippur, the decision is sealed.

This is reflected in the various prayers that we recite on the High Holidays. If that is so, why do we pray to God on a daily basis for our needs if it has already been determined on the High Holidays?

By way of explanation, on Rosh Hashanah and Yom Kippur, God decides how much rain will fall. Where the rain will fall depends on our prayers and conduct during the course of the year. If we pray with sincerity and remain righteous, the rain will fall on our fields at the right time. However, if we are no longer worthy, then the rain will fall either on the mountains or during the wrong season.

---

259. *Ahavat Yehonatan Eicha*

The question we should ask ourselves is not how much money we will earn this year, but rather how much money will be left over after we have paid for all our essential expenses. We may earn a high wage, but during the course of the year, the fridge and washing machine, which are both fairly new, need to be replaced. Or there was a terrible storm and now the roof needs to be replaced.

We need to understand that none of these unforeseen expenses are by chance. It could very well be that, as a result of our prayers on the High Holidays, God had blessed us with a large income for the coming year. But, unfortunately, our actions during the course of the year do not warrant such a blessing of wealth. God, however, will not take back the blessing; rather, he will cause us to spend it on things that normally we wouldn't need to.

Remember, we need to count our blessings, and we need to make sure that the blessings are not being used to replace our fridge.

Tefillin

Constant Reminder

While we are obligated to fulfill God's commandments without questioning the purpose or reason for them, rabbis throughout the generations have attempted to offer insight and reason for the mitzvot, thus enhancing our performance of the mitzvah.

Reb Yehonatan reflects on the mitzvah of tefillin, in which every male over the age of thirteen straps a small leather box on his left hand called *tefillin shel-yad* and a similar-sized box on his head called *tefillin shel-rosh*. The hand symbolizes a person's activity and actions. The head symbolizes a person's mind and thought process. By wearing tefillin, in a very tangible way, we are reminded of how our very existence and everything we experience is part of the Divine Plan and that God is aware of everything we do and think.

It is for this reason that the rabbis instructed us to periodically touch our tefillin, and by doing so, we will remind ourselves of the deeper meaning of tefillin: to remember that God is constantly involved in the world and in our lives.[260]

To an outsider, many Jewish laws and customs may seem strange and perhaps even bizarre. When was the last time someone ordered matzah in a restaurant? Yet for eight days, leavened bread is out the window and matzah is a staple in our diet. Or how often do you see people blowing a ram's horn or shaking a palm branch and what looks like a lemon with some willows and myrtles? Not to mention, what must they think of eating in a hut with only foliage for cover for eight days? The list goes on and on. Tefillin is no exception. Anyone who has put on their tallit and tefillin on an airplane can attest to that.

---

260. *Yaaroth Devash 1,3*

However, once we begin to study and explore the deeper meanings of the mitzvot, we are exposed to such richness and depth, and what may have seemed strange and perhaps even odd, now makes perfect sense.

Teshuvah/Repentance

Too Far Gone

There may be times when we believe we are too far gone. We have reached the point of no return. And, if that is the case, we might as well go all out and enjoy things while they last.

Such an approach to life is ludicrous and has no basis in Jewish thought. We should never throw in the towel or give up. In God's eyes, every one of us can return no matter what has transpired in our lives to date.[261]

What an empowering thought. And at the same time, what a comforting thought. Most of us have things in our closet that we are not proud of. We are being told that, in a sense, we can go back in time and rectify our mistakes. And even if we feel that our closet is so full that we can't even close the door, we shouldn't become disheartened and wallow in a sense of helplessness. Rather, we should grab the opportunity we have been given to make amends for any inappropriate behavior in our past, knowing that it will be accepted.

Guiding Light

Much has been written concerning the necessary steps a person needs to take for his repentance to be fully accepted. The person needs to feel regret and remorse for his inappropriate behavior. He also must declare that his intention is not to repeat such actions a second time.

Reb Yehonatan adds another caveat in the teshuvah process. The person who is seeking God's mercy must teach and guide other

---

261. *Yaaroth Devash 1*

sinners in the appropriate steps that need to be taken to merit God's forgiveness.[262]

Why must we teach and guide other sinners on the path of repentance? We may suggest two reasons.

The first, we have all heard the phrase "Mind your own business." Many of us have had that phrase hurled at us, and at times, we have angrily said it to others. When it comes to Jewish observance, we need to appreciate that it is all one business. What you do affects me, and what I do impacts you.

The second, by way of example, if we were extremely overweight and discovered a new diet that changed our lives, wouldn't we wish to share it with anyone and everyone who was dealing with a serious weight issue? We need to have this attitude when we see our brother or sister struggling under the weight of sin and transgression. We need to help them navigate the path of return, just as we have successfully done so.

---

262. *Tiferet Yehonatan Nitzavim*

Thoughts

Controlling Our Thoughts

Yom Kippur is the holiest day of the year. We spend most of the day in the synagogue praying. We don't eat and drink for twenty-five hours. We do not wear leather shoes. For one day of the year, we remove ourselves from the physical world and become angelic. The need to elevate ourselves on this holy day extends not only to our actions and speech but also to our thoughts. We need to try, to the best of our ability, to control our thoughts, so that our thoughts should be holy and pure.[263]

How can we control our thoughts?

While at times it may be difficult and seem impossible, we can control what we say and what we do. Try talking with your mouth closed. It is going to be very difficult to do something wrong if you are sitting in a chair and you don't move. Our mind, however, is constantly thinking; it is something we have no control over. How do you stop thinking?

The first thing we need to acknowledge is that a human is always thinking. We cannot control what pops up in our minds. Many times, out of left field, we have these crazy ideas that are both inappropriate and unacceptable, and we have no idea where they came from. At that moment, we can do two things. We can choose to ponder and chew over it, or we can choose to say to ourselves, "Don't even think about it" and immediately begin thinking about something else.

By choosing to stop thinking inappropriate thoughts is what it means to have purity of thought. And, as challenging as it may be, we have the human capacity to achieve it.

---

263. *Yaaroth Devash 2,3*

Time

Every Minute Counts

We are all well aware of the statement "Time is money." We can measure a person's wealth in terms of whether it pays for the person to bend down and pick up a $100 bill. The mega wealthy make so much money per minute that they would be wasting their time and money to pick up the note.

What monetary value does a day have? Can we put a price on a day in the life of a human being? Reb Yehonatan suggests the following experiment: Ask a person how much money it would take for them to consent to passing away a day earlier than has been preordained? He writes that no matter how much money is offered, no one would take the deal. Life is of such intrinsic value that no price can be attached to it.[264]

At the funeral of a very great rabbi, one of his sons turned to his brother and said, "At least our father had arichat yamim (usually translates to mean long life). The brother in response questioned this assertion and asked, "how can you say our father lived a long life he passed away at a very young age?" The brother explained, when I said our father had arichat yomim I was taking these words literally. The literal translation of arichat yamim is long days.

While our father passed away a relatively young man. We can take solace with the knowledge that each and every day of his life he utilized to the fullest.

---

264. *Yaaroth Devash* 2,12

We can lose money, and we can make it back. We can lose our business, and we can start over again. There is one thing we can never get back—and that is time. We can never turn back the clock.

People say, "Time is money," but that statement is not accurate. Time is not money since money can always be retrieved. Time is life itself. Let us live life to its fullest.

Never to Return

In the opening verse of Psalms, King David writes, "Happy is the man . . . who has not sat in the company of ridiculers." The scoffer, the ridiculer, is a person who simply wastes his time, sitting around all day doing nothing with himself.

Reb Yehonatan impresses upon us that we need to be extremely diligent from falling into the trap of becoming a scoffer, as he considers it to be a terrible sin. He writes the greatest gift given to mankind is time. It is a commodity that should not be wasted. He offers a simple approach how we can sense the importance of time and not squander it. If we would think that the next minute, the next five minutes, or the next hour is our last moments on earth, how would we act, what would we do?

No doubt it wouldn't be wasted on silly and frivolous types of behavior.[265]

A great rabbi once said, "I hear people say, "We have an hour to kill. What should we do?" I tell them, "if you want to kill an hour, give it to me. I will use it."

We can all appreciate that if we would see someone destroying his own property or his own possessions for no reason, we would feel extremely sorry for them—perhaps even thinking that there must be something mentally wrong with the person.

---

265. *Yaaroth Devash 1,1*

Don't we realize that we are guilty of the same type of behavior? We may not go around breaking our furniture or smashing our car, and these are all things that we could easily replace. But don't we destroy our greatest possession, which can never be replaced, and that is time itself.

We are all familiar with the phrase, "Time waits for no man." Let us treat time with the respect it deserves and utilize it to the fullest.

Tithe

A Tax

In the times of the Temple, the Jewish people were obligated to give tithe from their produce. Tithe was given to the tribe of Levites, as the Levites did not receive a portion of the Land of Israel. Tithe had to be given to the poor, and a certain amount was taken by the farmers and eaten in Jerusalem. In the Messianic era, the Levites will receive a portion of the land and therefore will not need to receive tithe. Likewise, in the Messianic era, there will no longer be poverty among the Jewish people and consequently there will be no need to give to the poor.[266]

Once the Temple was destroyed, the level of obligation in giving tithe diminished. And when the third Temple is built, many of the tithes will become obsolete. While this may be true, the laws of tithe still need to speak and resonate within us in our daily lives.

As the saying goes, "In this world, nothing can be said to be certain except death and taxes." A certain percentage of our income is taken by the government as a tax. We have no choice in the matter. We can't say to the authorities, "I will pay when I get back from my vacation" or "It's been a tough few months, and I have decided I can't really afford to pay my taxes."

Similarly, when the Jews gave tithe to the Levite and the poor, it was viewed as a tax that had to be given.

We must never forget those who are less fortunate than we are, and while we may not be taxed, that doesn't negate our responsibility in helping the poor and the destitute. Remember, we always want to be a giver rather than a receiver.

---

266. *Ahavat Yehontan*

Torah

Effort

We are all familiar with the saying "Easy come, easy go" and the phrase "Anything worth having is worth fighting for."

Reb Yehonatan reflects that this is true when we speak about the study of Torah. We would be fooling ourselves if we thought that a superficial study of Torah would give us a true grasp of its depth and wisdom.

The study of Torah is more than just the accumulation of knowledge, such as the study of mathematics or the sciences. Our moral compass and our ethical behavior must be firmly rooted in the words of Torah that we study. "Life altering" is an appropriate phrase to explain the purpose of studying God's wisdom. Therefore, if we want it to impact our very essence, blood, sweat, and tears would be the modus operandi when it comes to Torah study.[267]

Many great rabbis are said to have removed their shoes and socks and immerse their feet in freezing cold water to ensure that they wouldn't fall asleep in the middle of their learning. Most of us are not at that level or even feel it is an aspiration worth striving for. However, such stories should be the impetus for us to try to be more committed and more devoted to our learning.

What to Learn When

Generally speaking, Jewish learning can be divided into two categories: the study of the Chumash (the Five Books of Moshe), known as the written tradition, and the study of the Talmud, known as the oral tradition. A student in an advanced school of Jewish study will plummet

---

267. *Tiferet Yehonatan*

the depths of the Talmud, analyzing and dissecting every word and nuance of the text. Many hours can be spent trying to comprehend a single line of the Talmud and its various commentary. The study of the Chumash, however, does not demand such intellectual prowess to grasp the meaning of a particular verse and its commentary.

Recognizing that *where* we learn impacts *how* we learn, Reb Yehonatan writes that when we are learning in depth, we need peace and serenity. We need to keep distractions to a minimum. However, when we are studying with less intensity, we don't necessarily need to ensure that our surroundings are serene and peaceful. He therefore suggests that when we are traveling, the hustle and bustle of the trip will not afford us the opportunity to study in depth; therefore, we should utilize the time productively by studying Chumash.[268]

How many of us would be willing to do the same thing over and over again if each time we did it we saw very little tangible results? I think very few. Reb Yehonatan was well aware of this basic human trait. He also recognized the importance of studying Torah whenever the opportunity presented itself. He therefore suggested that when we are traveling, we should learn Chumash. Because if we would learn Talmud, it is more than likely we would not fully understand what we had studied and also find it challenging to recall what we did learn.

Reb Yehonatan was very conscious of the damage that could be caused when we set ourselves up for failure. He was suggesting what we should learn and when we should learn it to ensure the best possible outcome from a learning perspective. However, this is true under all circumstances.

Supporters

There is nothing greater than the study of Torah. When we study Torah, we are in a sense connecting ourselves and enveloping ourselves in God's wisdom. One of the many beautiful byproducts of this is that

---

268. *Tiferet Yehonatan Voetchanan*

the Torah will protect us and prevent us from being influenced by the Yetzer Hara (the evil inclination).

Reb Yehonatan asks, "If not everyone is fortunate to be in a position to immerse himself in study, how then do they fortify themselves from the challenges presented by the evil inclination?" He answers that if the person will support those who are able to study, then in that merit, he will reap the benefits as if he had actually devoted himself to the study of Torah.[269]

In Judaism, there is a concept known as the "Yissachar-Zevulun" partnership. Yissachar and Zevulun were both sons of Yaakov, two of the twelve tribes. Yissachar and his descendants excelled in the study of Torah, while Zevulun and his progenies were extremely successful entrepreneurs. The two tribes realized that, on the one hand, they were lacking and, on the other, they had a commodity worth sharing. While Yissachar and his offspring devoted their lives to study, they were challenged when it came to providing for their families. While Zevulun and his children were extremely wealthy, they understood that Torah was missing in their lives. Zevulun said to Yissachar, "I will support your Torah learning," and Yissachar said, "I will share the merit of my study with you as a form of payment."

All forms of charity are important; high on the list is supporting institutions of Jewish learning. We may, in fact, be receiving more than we are giving. It is a win-win investment.

Exile

Reb Yehonatan emphasizes the centrality and significance of Torah study. He writes that the very purpose of creating the world was for the Jewish people to study Torah. He also writes that the reason for our lengthy exile is because we have failed to ensure that the Torah is

---

269. *Yaaroth Devash 1,1*

paramount in our lives, and as a result, we have forgotten so much of it.[270]

We live in a world where Torah study is so accessible. So much traditional Jewish literature has been translated into English. The internet has a plethora of Jewish content that you would need more than one lifetime to study. We owe it to ourselves to explore the richness and beauty of our tradition. And the more we expose ourselves to its teachings, the more we will fall in love with it and our faith.

A Daily Exercise

Over the centuries, any historian worth his salt will have tackled the question of Jewish survival. The mighty empires of ancient times no longer exist, but the Jewish people who have endured anti-Semitism throughout its bloody history, enduring the Crusades, the pogroms, the Inquisition, and the Holocaust, are miraculously still here.

The answer is the study of Torah. The Jewish people's everlasting connection with God's Torah, God's wisdom, has ensured that we remain immortal. Recognizing that our nation's very existence depends on the study of Torah, can there be a legitimate excuse for a person not to learn Torah on a daily basis?[271]

Have you ever heard someone say, "I ate yesterday. There is no need to eat today"? Of course not. Without sustenance, we could not live. Just as our physical self needs to be fed, our spiritual self needs to be nourished. The soul receives its nourishment through the study of the Torah.

A simple line that we can use to encourage us to learn is, "If I ate today, then I must learn today."

---

270. *Yaaroth Devash* 1,2

271. *Yaaroth Devash* 2,16

Table Time

How much time should we spend eating? In Ethics of the Fathers, it states, "Desire not the king's table." The table of kings can be understood to mean that one should not spend an excessive amount of time eating one's meal, as was the common practice of royalty. Rather, one should preoccupy themselves with more important matters, such as the study of Torah.[272]

Animals eat to have strength to work. Animals work so they will be fed, and they sleep to have energy to work. We can go through life living the same cycle. We work to be able to buy food. We eat to have strength to work, and we sleep to have energy to work. There must be more to life than living the cycle of work-eat-sleep. We must have a purpose that is worth living for. By studying God's Torah, we will find our purpose and our calling.

Strength in Numbers

It is preferable to learn in a *Beit Midrash* (a house of study) together with other people. When a person learns alone and reflects on his achievements, the learning may actually increase his haughtiness. However, when one learns in a Beit Midrash, the other learners will reprimand him if they notice any bad traits, such as arrogance, thereby keeping him on the straight and narrow.[273]

For the vast majority of Torah scholars, independent study was never considered an optimum way to learn. We always learn with a chavruta (a learning partner).

The Talmud relates that Reb Yochanan and Resh Lakish were learning partners. When Resh Lakish passed away, Reb Yochanan's students attempted to find him another learning partner. Unfortunately, Reb Yochanan was unhappy with all of the various rabbis with whom he began

---

272. *Ahavat Yehonatan Vayechi*

273. *Yaaroth Devash 2,3*

to learn with. When asked why, he explained, "When I learned with Resh Lakish, he argued and disagreed with everything I said. My new study partners agree with everything I say. I don't need people to agree with me. I need a study partner who will challenge my position and argue with my opinion."

What Should We Learn?

The Torah is comprised of many different parts. Each piece needs to be studied, and there are many different ways to learn a particular section.

Rabbi Yehonatan was very adamant that while the Torah is vast and there is so much to learn and all styles of Jewish learning are important, we must place emphasis and focus on learning practical Halacha (Jewish law). We need to learn the laws that relate to our daily lives such as tefillin, tzitzit, tefillah, brachot, and Shabbat. He felt people were not giving sufficient time to studying these parts of the Torah.

Rabbi Yehonatan was bemoaning the fact that while people could be great Torah scholars, if they don't learn the laws relevant to daily conduct, how will they be able to ensure that they are keeping these laws properly and leading a proper Jewish life?[274]

We all want to be good people. We all want to be law-abiding citizens. Imagine that we move to a new country and begin to drive. If we don't know the rules of the road, we have no idea if what we are doing is right or wrong. We could, without realizing, be driving on a one-way street in the wrong direction. We all would agree that a good driver knows the rules of the road.

Similarly, we all want to be good Jews. The first step we need to take in our journey is to study and be knowledgeable in Jewish law.

Become a Teacher

Reb Yehonatan bemoaned the fact that the study of Torah had declined in his times, that it was very difficult to find a place to learn,

---

274. *Yaaroth Devash* 2,5

and that young men had to travel great distances to study Torah. He therefore encouraged *talmidei chachomim* (Torah scholars) to become educators.

Reb Yehonatan writes that the tzaddik in *Gan Eden* (the Garden of Eden) yearns for the opportunity to teach Torah to others even though he is basking in God's glory. When the tzaddik teaches those less knowledgeable, he is emulating God.

Why is the tzaddik considered to be emulating God when he teaches?

God had no need to create the world. Why then did He?

God is the ultimate source of goodness, and the nature of goodness is to do good. Therefore, God created the world to bestow goodness on all of existence. Similarly, by teaching those less educated, you are bestowing upon them goodness.[275]

If Reb Yehonatan felt that the knowledge of the Torah had diminished in his times, what can we say about the times we live in today? And if Reb Yehonatan felt an urgency in encouraging Torah scholars to become educators, how true would that sentiment be today?

We aren't all cut out to be teachers and educators. That doesn't absolve our responsibility to share our knowledge with others. If there is a fire, we may not be trained firemen, but that doesn't mean we can't help out. It's a situation of all hands on deck.

There is a raging fire among the Jewish people, and that is ignorance. We need to put out that fire, and it needs all hands on deck to do it.

How to Serve God

Many faiths and religions believe that the path to attaining spirituality and holiness is to remove ourselves from this physical world. The less we occupy ourselves in the pleasures of the world, the closer we will come to God. There are certain sects that inflict upon their adherents

---

275. *Yaaroth Devash 1*

bodily pain such as lashing. Others will live a life of solitude, having no contact with another human being. Certain groups will refrain from eating as much as possible and when they do, they subsist on grains and the like.

God's laws do not seek to cause a person pain and anguish; on the contrary, God's laws are deemed to be pleasant. The one time of the year when God commands us to fast is on Yom Kippur. To ensure we have enough sustenance to fast without being ill affected, He commands us to eat the day before to help us during the fast.[276]

How should we view the world and all it has to offer?

That which God has prohibited, such as the eating of nonkosher, is something we must not do. However, if we eat kosher and we make a blessing prior to eating, and with the energy we receive, we serve God, we have elevated the food. We can take the mundane, the unholy, and turn it into something of profound holiness. We can take the hide of a cow and turn it into parchment on which we will write the Torah. We can use the marvels of the internet to broadcast a live Torah class, literally to the whole world, in an instant.

We should not view the world as the antithesis of Godliness and holiness but rather as a conduit to revealing God's presence in the world.

With Song

Have you ever entered a library, especially a research library, and the first thing that hits you is the overbearing silence? You can cut the silence with a knife. We feel like we shouldn't breathe just in case our breathing will distract someone.

Let us contrast that with what we would experience when we enter a Beit Midrash (house of study or yeshivah study hall) that is full of young budding scholars learning diligently. The first thing that strikes you is the noise. It is so noisy that you can hardly hear yourself think.

---

276. *Yaaroth Devash* 1,11

Why the disparity when it comes to study? Why in one place you would need earplugs while in the other you have to check twice to make sure the person across the aisle is still breathing?

The noise in the house of study is rooted in an educational pedagogy found in the writings of Rambam. He writes that one of the key methods to remember and recall what we have learned is by learning in a raised voice.

Reb Yehonatan encourages the Torah student to not only study and learn aloud but also learn with a sweet melody. The reason he gives is quite ingenious. Everyone is drawn to and affected by listening to a pleasant tune. If we learn with joy and sing the words with a pleasant melody, hopefully this will attract the listeners and they too will want to explore what it is about the learning that makes a person burst out into song.[277]

Someone once made a somewhat tongue-in-cheek remark. They said that if you are an observant Jew and you are miserable, hide in a closet. There is a lot of truth to this statement. Have you ever walked down the street and saw or encountered someone who didn't have a smile on his face and looked miserable, and you said to yourself, "I want to be just like him"?

Misery likes company, but we don't want to be the company. We want to be like the person who is very happy and always has a smile on his face.

Reb Yehonatan is impressing upon us how important our actions are, perhaps even more important than our words. And we can greatly influence people by how we conduct ourselves. Learning with a sweet melody may encourage the listener to explore what is making us happy.

If you are observant and miserable, don't hide in a closet; just work on becoming happy.

---

277. *Yaaroth Devash 1,2*

Torah Literature

Respect

We have always been known as the people of the book. We give great deference to God's holy books. When, God forbid, a Torah falls on the ground, the community needs to fast. When we accidently drop a *sefer* (book of Jewish learning), we instinctively pick it up and kiss it. Our reverence for the sefer extends even after the book is no longer useable, the letters have faded over time, or the pages have been torn or missing due to its constant use. There are specific laws about how the sefer can be discarded; it cannot be simply thrown into the trash can.

Reb Yehonatan writes that throwing the used book with its holy words into the garbage is tantamount to casting the name of God into the bin, and this will cause the person who does so to suffer great financial losses.[278]

Even though the book can no longer be used, it retains its sanctity and needs to be respected accordingly. If this is true when it comes to an inanimate object, then this is definitely the case when it comes to the Jewish people. Every Jew possesses within them a spiritual soul, a spark of Godliness. It is something that is innate; it is not dependent on what we do or don't do.

People don't have a "use by" date. Old age or being incapacitated does not take away a person's intrinsic value or holiness. We need to be conscious of this when dealing with our senior citizens. Remember, hopefully one day we will be the senior citizens.

---

278. *Tumim Choshen Mishpat* 27

Trust

In God We Trust

"In God we trust" is the official motto of the United States. This motto was placed on all United States currency. What does "in God we trust" mean? How does trusting in God influence and impact our daily conduct?

The Hebrew word for "trust" is *bitachon*. The Prophet Jeremiah writes, "Blessed is the man who *trusts* in the Lord; the Lord shall be his *trust*."

Using the word "trust" twice in the verse leads us to the understanding that there are two types of trust. The first is that one needs to be of strong conviction that God will save him from any harm he may encounter during his lifetime. A higher form of trust is when a person feels that God has already saved him from any impending danger.

To live a life anchored on either type of trust is no easy task. However, living such a life will give the person a strong sense of security and well-being.

There are two schools of thought when it comes to understanding what it means to have bitachon (trust in God).

One approach is to know that God controls everything and that nothing happens in this world without God's consent. At the same time, we also know that God is the source of all goodness. Therefore, everything we experience, even those moments that seem to be negative and challenging, must be good because our trust in God is so intense; we simply can't visualize it due to our limited understanding of the Divine plan.

Another approach, one that is more demanding, is to trust God that everything we understand to be good and what we desire will truly eventuate.

Both approaches will help us reach a level of serenity and peace, as we are placing our trust and our future in the hands of the truly benevolent God.

Finding the Key

We are all familiar with the term, "the key to success." We then spend the rest of our lives searching for that key. A more important key we should be searching for is the key to receiving God's blessing and kindness.

What is the key?

The Torah is replete with verses that answer this sublime question. King David in Tehillim (Psalms) writes, "Neither shall any of those who hope for You be ashamed." King David is teaching us that those who place their hope in God will never feel ashamed as God will always answer their prayers. The key word is "trust." When a person places his complete trust in God, his prayers will be answered.

Human experience seems to challenge this notion. How often do people say, "I believe in God, I trust God, and yet all my needs have not been met."

Why is this so?

We need to distinguish between earthly and physical needs and desires and spiritual ones. A person who has complete and total trust in God that God will shower him with great wealth and materialistic success will not necessarily experience the outcome he desires. However, a person whose trust in God centers on his spiritual needs and his desires permeate from his soul, such trust will never be in vain. God will answer his spiritual yearning, and the person will be surrounded by God's kindness.[279]

A great rabbi once explained the difference between emunah (faith) and bitachon (trust).

---

279. *Ahavat Yehonatan Eicha*

If we are faced with a problem, we can have faith in God that he will help us overcome our problems. However, having bitachon means that we don't think there is a problem in the first place. If we truly trust in God's goodness, we would understand that we don't encounter obstacles in our lives; rather, God is presenting us with opportunities.

Tzaddik/The Righteous

Judgment

The well-known proverb "The bigger you are, the harder you fall" means that the more successful someone is, the more challenges he will have when something goes wrong. Judaism has a somewhat different understanding of this phrase. By way of example, two children misbehave; though they do the same exact thing, their punishments are not the same. Why is this so?

One child was older, and he should have known better. The older child may be disgruntled and upset that they were treated differently; however, to the parent, it makes all the sense in the world to discipline our children depending on their age and intelligence. This is actually how God disciplines the Jewish people. The greater and more righteous a person is, the more God will be careful and demanding when examining his behavior.

Moshe had been the faithful shepherd of the Jewish people for close to forty years. He led them out of Egypt, he stood on Mount Sinai, and he received the Torah. During the years the Jewish people wandered in the desert, it was in Miriam's merit that their water supply miraculously came from a rock. After the passing of Miriam, the water ceased. God instructed Moshe to speak to the rock so that it should once again continue to give water. Instead, Moshe struck the rock, and as a result, his dream to enter the Holy Land had been shattered.

It seems rather harsh that Moshe would be denied the ultimate reward of entering the Promised Land simply for disobeying God on only one occasion. Why the discrepancy in terms of punishment?

Reb Yehonatan explains that the greater a person is, the more he is looked up to and respected. People instinctively want to emulate the person and walk in his footsteps. And since his behavior and actions affect and impact so many lives, he is judged more severely.[280]

A fundamental Jewish belief is that we can never say we live in a vacuum and my actions have no consequences other than to myself. In Jewish law, there is a principle called mar'it ayin—that certain actions, which should be permitted, are prohibited merely because other people could mistake what we are doing for something else that is prohibited.

One of the reasons for this injunction is that it may cause people to view one negatively, believing the person had sinned. For example, according to Torah law, the blood of an animal is forbidden to eat, but the blood of a fish is permissible. However, according to the principle of mar'it ayin, it is forbidden to eat the blood of fish, as an onlooker may believe the blood being eaten is from an animal, and the person eating the blood is a sinner, when in fact that isn't true.

A second reason is based on the teachings of Reb Yehonatan: that we need to be conscious of the fact that people are looking at our behavior and acting accordingly.

We may not be Moshe, but each and every one of us should strive to become a role model for others. Our actions and conduct will either lead people down the path of sin and iniquity or up the path of morality and righteousness.

Seeing

We are all familiar with the saying, "Seeing is believing." It is said to mean that if you see something yourself, you will believe it to exist or be true, despite the fact that it is extremely unusual or unexpected. Sight is one of the five senses and is extremely powerful. What we see not

---

280. *Yaaroth Devash 1*

only validates what we had previously thought was mere conjecture but also impacts and affects our emotions. We can become scared, excited, or worried by what we see.

Reb Yehonatan adds that seeing something can impact us spiritually. He writes that the tzaddik is a holy and righteous person, and when we gaze at his countenance, we are seeing an expression of holiness, and as a result, we become enveloped with blessings and holiness.[281]

It is self-understood that we need to be extremely careful about what we allow our children to watch. Many studies have shown that allowing our children to watch violent movies or play violent video games has a very negative effect on their behavior.[282] They will be more prone to violence, and their respect for authority, parents, and teachers will diminish considerably.

A great rabbi took it one step further and writes that even before a child reaches the age where they can comprehend and understand what they are looking at, we need to be very careful about the images they see. He therefore felt that the animals pictured on the babies' clothing or those the child plays with should be only kosher animals.

Indeed, there are some who have the custom that a pregnant woman will not go to a zoo so that she will not see a nonkosher animal, as this may spiritually harm the fetus.

Being Seen

Reb Yehonatan writes that not only when we see a righteous person are we affected and impacted, but it is equally true that when a tzaddik or a great Torah scholar gazes upon us, it is a cause for blessing.[283]

---

281. *Yaaroth Devash* 1,12

282. American Academy of Child and Adolescent Psychiatry. "Video Games and Children: Playing with Violence." AACAP.org. June 2015. Accessed March 3, 2022. www.aacap.org/AACAP/Families_and_Youth/Facts_for_Families/FFF-Guide/Children-and-Video-Games-Playing-with-Violence-091.aspx

283. *Yaaroth Devash* 1,12

We are familiar with the idea of ayin hara (the evil eye). Very often people will say, "Bli ayin hara" to avoid being affected by the evil eye. A great rabbi once remarked that the evil eye has within it a burning energy, and man can be harmed by one who has that burning power because this type of eye can burn like fire that burns.

In a similar vein, the tzaddik has the spiritual energy via his penetrating vision to transfer blessings to those he sees.

Giving Is Receiving

Reb Yehonatan compares the righteous to a spring. The more water you draw from the spring, the more it will replenish. Such is the life of the tzaddik; the more the tzaddik gives, the more he receives in return.[284]

This is true not only for the tzaddik; this is true for each and every one of us. It may seem counterintuitive; however, as studies show, we are happier when we are giving than when we are receiving.[285]

A great rabbi once instructed one of his followers who was suffering from depression to try to help someone every day; the more people he helped, the better he would feel.

His Words Live On

Reb Yehonatan shares a fascinating insight. He writes that if we repeat the teachings or the words of a saintly individual who has passed, the righteous person's soul becomes clothed in those words, and it is as if the tzaddik is standing next to us. This, he explains, is how we are to understand the words of the prophet who says that the righteous live

---

284. *Tiferet Yehonatan Vayeira*

285. Huffington Post. "Giving, Rather Than Receiving, Leads to Lasting Happiness: Study." December 20, 2018. Accessed March 3, 2022. www.huffpost.com/archive/ca/entry/giving-creates-happiness_a_23623679.

in two worlds. They live in the eternal world after their passing, and at the same time, they live in the physical world by virtue of us repeating their saintly words.[286]

We may not be a great Torah scholar who has left immense writings or a tzaddik whose saintly words have been transcribed for posterity. But that doesn't mean we can't have a lasting impact that will affect generations to come. If we lead an ethical and decent life, if we are benevolent and kind, if we are charitable and giving and we imbue our children with these qualities, and they in turn instill these qualities in their children, then in a sense we live on via our descendants.

The question is no longer, "Do we make a difference?" the question is, "Will we make a difference?" And only we can answer that question.

Eternal Connection

While the tzaddik is alive, he is constantly showering blessings upon others. This does not cease upon his demise. How do we continue to receive the blessings of the departed?

Repeating their words of Torah or spiritual insights impacts the part of the soul that remains eternally attached to their gravesite. This part of the soul will then connect with the higher levels of the soul and ultimately cause the tzaddik's blessings to pour forth.[287]

If we stop to think for a moment, one of the strangest things we do is visit the gravesite of a departed loved one. And even stranger, many talk to the grave, and perhaps the strangest of all, there are those who leave behind an invitation to a family wedding or bar mitzvah.

Why is this strange? Because we are going to a slab of marble and a lifeless body that will be reduced to nothing more than bones over time. There is no one there who is listening, so who are we talking to? On a cold, overcast

---

286. *Yaaroth Devash* 2,7

287. *Yaaroth Devash* 1,16

wintry day, instead of trekking out to the cemetery in our winter coats and umbrellas, braving the elements, why don't we sit around the warm fire in the living room with a warm drink and reminisce about our departed loved one?

Reb Yehonatan makes sense of why we do what we do, and in fact, it is not peculiar at all. We are not going to an inanimate piece of marble that is covering decaying flesh and bones. We are making a pilgrimage to the site that contains part of the eternal spirit of our loved one. A spirit that is as much alive as it was when its home was the physical body of our dearly departed. As such, there is then no better place to connect with the departed than where they are buried.

Opportunities

The Messianic era will usher in a new world order. One of the radical changes that will occur is that we will no longer have a *Yetzer Hara* (evil inclination). We will no longer be tempted to sin, and we will be preoccupied in the service of God. This era will be true utopia. It therefore is somewhat surprising that the rabbis write that the righteous will lament the fact that there is no longer the challenge of the evil inclination.

Reb Yehonatan explains that when we are confronted by the evil inclination and we are able to subjugate it, we are rewarded for the accomplishment; this is something we will not experience during the Messianic era.[288]

No one goes through life plain sailing; we each have our own struggles and challenges to face. We have absolutely no control over what life has in store for us. We cannot choose our fate or destiny. The only thing we can choose is how we will react to a given situation and how we will navigate life's ups and downs. This will very much depend on our attitude and frame of mind.

---

288. *Ahavat Yehonatan Devorim*

We can view the challenges we encounter as obstacles or opportunities. We need to look at life's trials as being opportunities.

As the saying goes, "What doesn't kill you makes you stronger." This notion has a scientific basis. Stressors, if not too large, result in growth. Many biological systems require stressors for growth. For instance, bones increase in size or density after the stress of lifting heavy weights.

Of course, we pray and beseech God that we should merit the coming of the Messiah and strife and war will be things of the distant past, but until that happens, let's view life as a series of opportunities from which we can grow.

Anonymity

Reb Yehonatan makes an interesting observation: he says that there are righteous individuals in every generation. The distinction between the generations is in how they respect the righteous. In earlier times, the righteous were praised and respected, while in the latter generations, they were not held in such great esteem, and as a result, the righteous preferred to remain anonymous.[289]

If you want to insight into a society or a group of people, look at who they honor and respect. This is true for a country as well. If you want to ascertain the moral standing of a country, look at how they care for the elderly and the less fortunate.

People who do not value and respect people of fine character are really passing judgment on their own moral standing.

Never Forgotten

Life is fleeting; life is transient. In the scheme of things, our time on earth is seemingly of little significance. Therefore, we all want to leave a legacy, something we will be remembered by. Many fall into the trap

---

289. Ahavat Yehonatan Eicha

of believing that the wealthier they are, the more they will be remembered. They see that, throughout their lives, they are honored and respected, and people seek their advice. They erroneously assume that the same honor and respect will be afforded their name after their passing. However, once they have passed, their memory passes with them.

A tzaddik, a person who dedicates his life in honoring the Torah, lives a life worth emulating. When he passes away, his noble character did not die with him. The impetus of following in the tzaddik's footsteps did not stop with his passing. The tzaddik remains very much alive in people's hearts and minds.[290]

Perhaps we wonder why a wealthy person who only accumulated his wealth and did not give charity is forgotten after he dies. The answer is, he is forgotten while he is still alive. Have you ever noticed what happens when a very wealthy person loses all their money? He is no longer honored, he no longer seats on the dais, and people no longer seek his advice on matters of importance. Why is this so? The magnate was not being honored for what he is but rather for what he has. If he no longer has, then who he is not worth respecting.

It is a very sobering thought to know that with our passing, our memory passes as well. We all want to be remembered. And we can be, by focusing our lives on improving who we are and not in accumulating what we have.

X-ray Vision

Many of us who have a very strong prescription for glasses; when we remove them, we can't see anything that is more than five feet away. We obviously realize that nothing has disappeared. The objects are still there; we just can't see them. Likewise, when we use a microscope, we are astonished to see what the world contains that our naked eye is oblivious to.

When God created the world, he began by first creating a number

---

290. *Yaaroth Devash 1,12*

of spiritual worlds, and in each descending spiritual world, God's presence was further concealed. In our world, we don't see God. The Divine is concealed. That does not mean He isn't present. Our rabbis teach us that God is constantly recreating the world, and if He would cease to recreate, the world would cease to exist. The world is a manifestation of Godliness.

However, the tzaddikim of each generation, due to their holiness, are able to see what the average person cannot. They are able to see the *Shechina* (God's revelation). It is as if they are wearing glasses that allows them to see God in a revealed manner.[291]

Little Yossele was attending public school. One day, the teacher asked his students if any of them had seen God. The students responded that they had not. "See," said the teacher, "if you cannot see God, it means He doesn't exist." Yossele tentatively rose from behind his desk and, in a timid voice, asked the class, "Is there anyone here who has ever seen the teacher's brain?" The students began to giggle and said, "No." In a loud voice, Yossele proclaimed, "Then we must say the teacher is brainless."

We may not be on the spiritual level of a tzaddik to actually see Godliness with our naked eye. However, we should not be blind to the fact that every aspect of existence is imbued with spiritual energy.

A great rabbi was walking through the forest with his students. He pointed out a leaf that had just blown off of a tree, floating down to rest on the sun-parched dirt road. The rabbi told his students that this leaf falling off the tree at this particular time and landing in this specific place was orchestrated by God. He asked his students to lift the leaf off the ground, and there was a worm dying in the summer heat; the fallen leaf had given it back its life, providing comfort and protection from the sun.

---

291. *Tiferet Yehonatan Vayelech*

Power of Prayer

When the righteous pray, their prayers immediately ascend to heaven. On the other hand, for the Jew who has yet to reach such spiritual heights, his prayers would first need to pass through the Temple in Jerusalem. After the destruction of the Temple, the prayers of the Jew attach themselves to the prayers of tzaddikim, and both sets of prayers rise together as one.[292]

Judaism does not believe in the concept of an intermediary between man and God. We pray to God and to no other entity. What then is the role of the righteous in terms of our prayers?

By way of analogy, you desperately need a bank loan and therefore need a meeting with your bank manager. You have a dear friend who is the bank's largest client; it would stand to reason that your friend will have a better chance of getting you an appointment than you could on your own. You may even ask your friend to plead your case for you. However, you realize that your friend does not have the power or authority to issue the loan. That decision rests with the bank manager. Likewise, we don't pray to the tzaddik. Rather, we ask the tzaddik if we can piggyback our prayers on his prayers or ask him to pray to God on our behalf.

Permission to Die

In his eulogy for his father-in-law, Rabbi Yitzchak Shapira (the Head of the Beth Din in Bohemia), Reb Yehonatan said something rather extraordinary. He said that God cannot take the soul of tzaddik unless the tzaddik agrees. When a tzaddik senses that he has fulfilled his life mission, he will allow God to remove his soul. Similarly, God will not do anything to a tzaddik that is against his will. On the other hand, a wicked person has no say when he will pass away.[293]

---

292. *Yaaroth Devash 1,9*

293. *Yaaroth Devash 1,16*

There is a misconception when it comes to an understanding of what it means when we say someone is a tzaddik. We read the stories in the Torah about Abraham and Sarah and about Moshe and Aharon and the many others. We know they were very holy people, but we assume that their holiness can be quantified in terms of our own spiritual level. By way of example, the world record for the 100 meters is at present 9.58 seconds. We could probably run it in 20 seconds, give or take a few seconds. The person who holds the world record is only twice as fast as we are. We could be under the impression that the same is true when we gauge the spiritual contrast between ourselves and the tzaddik—that the tzaddik is perhaps only ten times as holy as we are.

According to Reb Yehonatan's understanding of the interaction between the tzaddik and God, it becomes evidently clear that there is no correlation or parallel between the tzaddik and the regular Jew in terms of their level of holiness. It is as if we are not running the same race.

When studying the narratives recorded in the Biblical texts, it is imperative that we understand that these giants are not simply twice or even ten times as fast; they are running a completely different race.

Why Die?

A tzaddik devotes his life to educate the Jewish people and inspire them to come closer to God. Why then would a tzaddik agree to pass away when he knows that he can still accomplish so much?

God causes the body of the tzaddik to experience great pain and suffering; the soul sees and senses this. The soul cannot bear to see the tzaddik's body enduring so much agony and grief, and it therefore requests that God take his soul to alleviate the suffering of his body.[294]

Jewish mysticism believes that the ultimate spiritual experience will occur after the resurrection of the dead and the soul will be reunited with its body. Why does the body need to experience such revelations of Godliness?

---

294. *Yaaroth Devash* 1,16

During the person's sojourn on earth, it wasn't just the soul that served God; the body served God as well. The body was the vehicle by which the soul was able to express itself. It therefore stands to reason that the body needs to be rewarded together with the soul. The body not only contains holiness but also becomes holy. We must therefore honor and respect our bodies and do whatever we can to ensure that our bodies don't endure pain and suffering.

We also need to appreciate that we don't own our bodies. Our bodies are a gift from God and therefore we need to give them the utmost respect and never willfully cause them any harm.

Feeling the Pain

Nothing is of greater value than life itself. Barring three commandments, all laws are voided if a person's life is in danger. Yet, there are times when a tzaddik will request that God take him before his time. A tzaddik cannot bear to see the suffering of the Jewish people, and he would rather die than live in a world where his brethren are in pain and anguish.[295]

King Solomon was considered the wisest of all men. He was once asked, "How should we view a two-headed person? Is it one person since there is one body or two people as there are two heads?" King Solomon answered that they should bring a pitcher of hot water and pour it over one of the heads. If the other head feels pain, then it is one body. If, however, the second head exhibits no pain, then we know they are two separate people.

Most of us are not on the spiritual level of a tzaddik, preferring to die than to see others suffer. However, we need to be sensitive to the pain of another. Two men were sitting in a bar, and one asked the other, "Are you my friend?" The response was, "Of course." He then asked, "Do you know what is hurting me?" The response was, "No." The person who had posed the

---

295. *Tiferet Yehonatan Yitro*

questions said, "If you were truly my friend, you would know why I am in pain."

May we be blessed with a long life. And may we live a life that is in tune with the needs of others.

Legacy

The tzaddik's holiness extends to his possessions. While a tzaddik is still alive, anything that he has built or constructed can never be destroyed. It can only be destroyed after his passing. This explains an interesting facet concerning the destruction of the first Temple. The Temple was built by King Solomon; however, the gates and the doorways were constructed by his father, King David. When the Temple was destroyed, the gates miraculously sunk into the ground and were preserved.

Why were King David's gates rescued?

The Talmud states, "King David the King of Israel lives for eternity." Since King David, in a sense, is still alive, all that he built cannot be destroyed. However, the rest of the Temple was constructed by King Solomon, and once King Solomon passed away, it became possible for it to be destroyed.[296]

We traditionally wish one another, "Till 120," meaning that we should live until the ripe old age of 120. We don't wish each other that we should live forever. Living for eternity is something we will only experience during the Messianic era. We understand that there is no permanence to our existence. We therefore try to ensure that we leave behind a legacy, something we will be remembered by.

Being blessed with children and raising them to follow in the footsteps of our ancestors perpetuates our memory, and we live on through them. We can donate charity to build institutions and thereby always be connected with them even after 120 years.

---

296. Ahavat Yehonatan

There is another way to extend our lives beyond 120: when our behavior and actions influence others to become closer to God. By doing so, we live on in their lives and their descendants' lives till the end of time.

We Can All Lead

Our forefather Yaakov was blessed with twelve sons. Each son became the head of a tribe. When two people married who were from different tribes, the offspring would be considered a member of the father's tribe.

The law was that the head of the Jewish people in Israel had to be a descendant from the tribe of Yehudah. Even though we normally ascribe lineage dependent on the father's tribe, if one's mother was from the tribe of Yehudah even though one's father wasn't, he could be appointed head of the Jewish people.

That explains why Nadav and Avihu felt that they would succeed Moshe and Aaron and lead the Jewish people into the Holy Land. While Nadav's and Avihu's paternal lineage was the tribe of Levi, their maternal lineage was the tribe of Yehudah. Thus, they had the necessary ancestry to become the next leaders of the Jewish people.[297]

We may not descend, either via our father or mother, from the tribe of Yehuda, but that doesn't negate our ability to take on a leadership role. We are all capable of becoming a leader. At the onset, it may be challenging, but there is nothing more rewarding than the knowledge that we have impacted the lives of others.

A great rabbi once remarked, "Good leaders create followers; great leaders create leaders. We should strive not only to become a leader but also to influence others to become leaders.

---

297. *Yaaroth Devash 1,1*

Tzedakah/Charity

Just Give

The rabbis write that in the merit of giving charity, we will merit the final redemption. Why is this commandment singled out as the mitzvah that will usher in the Messianic era?

To properly fulfill a mitzvah, two things must occur: the first is the actual performance of the mitzvah. You must physically put on the tefillin. It isn't enough to contemplate the spiritual heights we reach when we put them on. The second is, when we put on the tefillin, we need to know why we are putting them on. We must ensure that we have the proper intention and understanding when performing the mitzvah.

The only mitzvah that does not require both the act and the thought is the mitzvah of giving charity. When a person gives charity, it makes no difference to the poor person why he was given the money. As long as he has money to survive, he doesn't really care what the person was thinking when he gave him it.

Many times, we do the commandments without the correct intentions or with no intention at all. In such a situation, the mitzvah would be lacking. The only mitzvah where this does not apply is the mitzvah of giving charity. You don't need to have any intention when giving charity. Therefore, in the merit of giving charity even without cause or reason, we will merit the final redemption.[298]

The local priest, Father Smith, has had a string of robberies. He goes over to his very dear friend Rabbi Cohen and asks him if he ever had a problem with robberies.

---

298. *Ahavat Yehonatan Eikev*

"Not really," replies Rabbi Cohen. "We have this thing we put on the door-post called a mezuzah and it protects our homes from harm."

"Could I please have one for my front door," asks Father Smith. "I'm desperate for a solution."

A few weeks later, the priest knocks on the rabbi's door with the mezuzah in hand. The rabbi asks if he was still experiencing break-ins.

"No, no," the priest assures him, "no robberies."

The rabbi is puzzled. "So why are you giving it back?" he asks.

Father Smith sighs. "I dunno," he says. "Ever since I hung it up, the doorbell doesn't stop ringing. Each time a different man is standing there, saying the same thing, 'Tzedakah please—and it is costing me a small fortune.'"

It is well documented that the Jewish people are from the most benevolent and charitable people that exist. It is something that is ingrained within us from the times of Abraham when he welcomed the three angels portraying themselves as Arabs into his tent.

The rabbis state that if a Jew is not charitable to his fellow human being, we should question his lineage.

Keep It a Secret

If we have a choice whether to be a giver or a receiver, we would all choose to be the giver and not the receiver. Everyone has a sense of self-esteem and self-worth. No one wants to feel that they are beholden to others for their needs. It would be devastating if a person's financial predicament and crisis would become public knowledge. Therefore, Reb Yehonatan writes that when we give charity, it should be given in the most discrete manner possible.[299]

---

299. *Medrash Yehonatan Shmot*

Maimonides writes that the highest level of giving charity is helping a person to become self-sufficient similar to the Chinese proverb, "If you give a man a fish, you feed him for a day. But if you give him a fishing rod, you feed him for a lifetime." The second level is when both the giver and receiver remain totally anonymous. The giver has no idea who he is giving to, and the receiver has no inkling from whom he is receiving.

Our rabbis describe financial security as being like a wheel at times; we are at the top of the world and money seems to be growing on trees ripe for the picking. However, the wheel can turn very quickly, and we can find ourselves at rock bottom amd in need of the assistance of others. We should be conscious of this when we give to those in need that there may come the day when we will be the receiver and not the giver.

Why We Give

Why would we give away our hard-earned money? Perhaps we believe that, by giving charity, God will protect us from misfortune, or by giving charity, God will bestow upon us an abundance of blessings.

Reb Yehonatan writes that we should fulfill the will of God and give charity with no ulterior motive, and it is our intense love of God that is driving us to give away our hard-earned money.[300]

How do we know if we are in a healthy and strong relationship? If we don't keep tabs. When it isn't based on a system of give and take, where the other person gives and we just take.

Very often you will hear people say, "I love fish." They don't love fish; otherwise, they wouldn't eat fish. They love themselves, and that is why they eat fish.

If we are in a relationship because of what we can get out of it or what we can gain from it, such a relationship is nothing more than an exercise in self-interest and self-gratification.

---

300. *Ahavat Yehonatan Re'eh*

The same can be said in respect to fulfilling God's commandments. If our sole motivation is to reap God's rewards and blessings, are we really serving God or is it nothing more than self-worship?

The Poor of the Temple

For close to 2,000 years, we have been yearning for God to bring the Messiah and rebuild the third Beit Hamikdash. Three times a day in our prayers, we beseech God that the Temple should no longer be a dream but rather a reality. There is no holier site for the Jewish people than the Temple Mount.

It is therefore fascinating that Reb Yehonatan is of the opinion that giving money to the poor takes precedence over giving money to build the Temple. He explains that is the reason King David did not merit to build the first Temple. During King David's lifetime, there was a terrible famine in the land. King David had set aside a large amount of money for the building of the Temple, and he did not use enough of those funds to alleviate the suffering of the poor. Therefore, he wasn't given the honor of building the Temple. And that honor was bestowed upon his son, King Solomon.[301]

The Talmud inquires, "Why did God create a multitude of the same species while only creating Adam and Chava?" The response given is to impress upon humanity that, if we save the life of one single human being, it is as if we have saved the whole world, and if, God forbid, someone takes the life of another human being, it is considered as if he has destroyed the whole world.

Judaism views human life as being of intrinsic value. The crime and the punishment of taking the life of a young healthy human being and the life of a person who has only minutes to live is the same. Is it any wonder than that God wanted the money designated for His home to be given to the poor?

---

301. *Ahavat Yehonatan Shekolim*

Perhaps the life message being taught is, if we have limited resources in terms of giving charity, do we give it to a building fund or to feeding the poor? The answer is now crystal clear.

Prioritize

One of the challenges people of means face is how to prioritize their donations to worthy causes. Reb Yehonatan reflects on the following common occurrence. If you would ask a wealthy individual to donate a large sum of money to purchase a *Sefer Torah* (Torah Scroll), they wouldn't hesitate. However, if you will ask them to give that money to a widow or an orphan, they may decline.

Reb Yehonatan argues that this makes no sense since the law is that we are permitted to sell a Torah for the needs of an orphan. It stands to reason then that when faced with a choice between donating to the purchase of a Torah or supporting an orphan, we should support the orphan.[302]

Every fundraiser will tell you that it is easier to collect funds for a new building than it is to collect money for its upkeep. People like to see something tangible for their money. People like seeing their name proudly displayed on the front of buildings for all to see.

While such acts of charity are to be highly applauded, Reb Yehonatan is gently reminding us that we must never lose sight of the fact that feeding the widow, the orphan, and the destitute is the highest form of giving. Let us never forget that we sell a Torah to help the orphan.

For God's Sake

In truth, God Himself could feed and sustain the poor; however, God wants to give us the opportunity of meriting to fulfill this mitzvah. Our rabbis state that the world's continued existence is dependent on the Jewish people giving charity. Reb Yehonatan offers a very insightful

---

302. *Ahavat Yehonatan Tzav*

310   🔥   Sparks of Wisdom from Rabbi Yehonatan Eybeshitz

understanding into the mitzvah of giving tzedakah. He writes that when we give charity, we are in a sense laying out the money for God, as God should be supporting the destitute. God, in turn, will repay us in this world and in the world to come. In the world to come, He will repay the amount we laid out. And, in this world, we will receive the reward for our actions.[303]

What an empowering idea that when we give charity, we are laying out the money for God. Yet at the same time, giving away one's hard-earned money is not easy to do. The Talmud teaches us that when we give charity, we shouldn't think that, as a result, our bank balance will diminish; rather, we should view it as a wise business investment. As our rabbis explain, not only will God repay the money we give to charity but He will also add to what we have given. In fact, we are taught that God begs us to test Him in this matter.

From this perspective, giving charity may not be that challenging after all.

No One Is Poor

Reb Yehonatan makes an interesting observation: When the Jewish people left Egypt, they were all extremely wealthy. How then were they able to fulfil the mitzvah of giving charity? He answers, by giving money toward the *Mishkan* (Tabernacle) and giving sacrifices, the Jewish people fulfilled the mitzvah of giving charity.[304]

More than likely, the only time in our history when there were no poor people was during the forty years the Jews wandered in the desert. We therefore have no excuse in not giving charity. However, what we can learn from Reb Yehonatan's insight is that giving charity for the building or upkeep of a Torah Institution was the Jewish people's first act of charity.

---

303. *Yaaroth Devash 1,7*
304. *Yaaroth Devash 1,7*

Tzitzit/Fringes

Caring Makes All the Difference

There are many mitzvot we have been unable to fulfill since the destruction of the Temple. There are other mitzvot we can only partially fulfill since the destruction. One such mitzvah is the mitzvah of wearing tzitzit. A man should wear a four cornered garment, and, in each corner, he needs to attach fringes.

In the times of the Temple, the tzitzit were comprised of four threads. Three threads were white, and the fourth thread was dyed a unique bluish color called tekhelet. Unfortunately, we are unable to make the dye for the *tekhelet,* and we have had to replace this thread with another white thread.

Reb Yehonatan writes that while we may not be able to wear the tzitzit as our ancestors did, we can be rewarded as if we did. How is this possible? If we truly lament our misfortune that our tzitzit are incomplete, and we anxiously await the time when we will be able to do so, God will reward us as if we were wearing the tekhelet thread.[305]

Nothing against dentists, but I would imagine that most of us wouldn't be that upset if the dentist called to reschedule our appointment to a later date. How we react to a missed opportunity or to a canceled event will very much tell us how precious and significant that occasion meant to us.

If we tried our best but could not complete a God-given task or we lived in a time or place where a mitzvah could not be performed, how does God view this? Will we be penalized or perhaps there is a route we can take and be rewarded?

---

305. *Yaaroth Devash* 2,2

It depends. If God will see how upset we are that we couldn't do the mitzvah, He will reward us as if we had. If, however, we will smile and rub our hands together in glee that another commandment has fallen by the wayside or we are apathetic to the whole thing and we show no emotion at all, it stands to reason that God will not reward us.

Don't Overlook

Reb Yehonatan laments the fact that, in his lifetime, men were not as scrupulous when it came to the mitzvah of wearing tzitzit as they should be. He felt that men were willing to compromise on the kashrut (standard) of the tzitzit to save a few pennies, knowing full well that with a little more money, they would be able to purchase tzitzit of the highest quality. He also was concerned that the coats the men were wearing had four distinct corners and would need to have tzitzit attached to them. He writes that this issue could be easily overcome, yet the men did not take the matter seriously enough.[306]

Imagine if we were invited to a royal dinner. We would make sure that every stitch of clothing would be in pristine condition. Our shoes would be polished until we could see our reflection in them. We would take pride in what we were wearing because we were meeting royalty.

We need to be conscious of the fact that we are always in the presence of royalty. God is constantly in our midst. We need to make sure that the clothes we need to wear, such as tzitzit or tefillin, should be of the finest and the most beautiful, even if it means paying a little bit more for them.

Wear Them with Pride

There is certain apparel that are distinctly Jewish. The tzitzit is one such garment. Reb Yehonatan writes that we should be proud of our

---

306. *Yaaroth Devash 1,2*

Jewish identity. And we should wear our tzitzit in a manner that makes them visible to passersby.[307]

As a nation, we have a lot to be proud of. Our contribution to Western civilization is immeasurable. This is most eloquently and powerfully articulated by John Adams, second president of the United States, when he writes, "I will insist that the Hebrews have done more to civilize men than any other nation . . . fate had ordained the Jews to be the most essential instrument for civilizing the nations."

The values and principles of the modern world find their roots in Jewish teachings. As historian Paul Johnson writes in his national bestseller A History of the Jews *(Harper Perennial, 1988):*

"Certainly, the world without the Jews would have been a radically different place. Humanity might have eventually stumbled upon all the Jewish insights. But we cannot be sure. All the great conceptual discoveries of the human intellect seem obvious and inescapable once they had been revealed, but it requires a special genius to formulate them for the first time.

The Jews had this gift. To them we owe the idea of equality before the law, both divine and human; of the sanctity of life and the dignity of human person; of the individual conscience and so a personal redemption; of collective conscience and so of social responsibility; of peace as an abstract ideal and love as the foundation of justice, and many other items which constitute the basic moral furniture of the human mind. Without Jews it might have been a much emptier place."[308]

It stands to reason then that we should be proud of our Judaism, and we should display it with great enthusiasm.

---

307. *Yaaroth Devash 1,2*

308. Paul Johnson. *A History of the Jews.* Harper Perennial, 1988.

Unity

The Power of One

One of the many sacrifices brought in the Temple was known as the incense offering. The Torah records that when the Jewish people were afflicted with a plague, Aaron the High Priest offered an incense sacrifice, and it curtailed the plague. What is unique about the incense offering that it can stop a plague in its tracks?

The Hebrew word for "incense" is *ketoret*. In Aramaic, the word *ketoret* means "a knot." You join two strings together when you make a knot. When the Jews are united as one, the plague will cease. If, however, the Jews remain separate and there is no harmony among them, the offering of the incense sacrifice will be of no consequence. [309]

When we are united, even the angel of death cannot harm us. The second Temple was destroyed because we, as a people, were not united; there was unwanted hate between one Jew and another. To rectify this sin, we need to find common ground with our fellow Jew, and we have to foster unwanted love between one another.

The Trees Know It

Unity is of the utmost importance in the eyes of God. There is nothing more beloved by parents than to see their children getting along with one another. In our prayers, we refer to God as our Father in heaven. There is nothing more beloved by God than to see His children, the Jewish people, living in peace and harmony together.

Reb Yehonatan develops this understanding by reflecting on the episode of Adam and Chava in the Garden of Eden. Adam and Chava both ate from the Tree of Knowledge and, as a result, were banished

---

309. *Ahavat Yehonatan Devorim*

from the Garden. The Tree of Knowledge symbolizes exile, pain, and suffering.

There was another tree in the garden: the Tree of Life. The Tree of Life, as its name implies, is symbolic of redemption, holiness, and spirituality. Reb Yehonatan therefore writes that if the twelve tribes had been living in harmony, they would have been attached to the Tree of Life. Tragically, this was not the case, and the Jewish people had forged a bond and became connected with the Tree of Knowledge.[310]

We have been in exile for close to 2,000 years since the destruction of the second Beit Hamikdash (Temple). The first Beit Hamikdash was destroyed because the Jewish people transgressed the three cardinal transgressions: idol worship, prohibited relationships, and murder. After the destruction of the first Temple, we were exiled for seventy years. The second Temple was destroyed because of unwanted hate between one Jew and another Jew. The severity of this sin is clearly demonstrated by the length of our exile.

The way to end our exile is to rectify our errors and mistakes by increasing our love and connection with our brothers and sisters. If we use the analogy of a person being swept down a raging river and needing to grab on to a protruding branch, Reb Yehonatan is teaching us to grab on to the branch of the Tree of Life, and we will be saved. But if we are holding on to the Tree of Knowledge, we will continue to remain floundering in the raging waters of exile.

What Is Considered True Unity?

We could argue that when two opposite forces learn to coexist, we have created a sense of unity. However, at best, this would be considered a superficial form of unity.

In our prayers, we extol God by reflecting on the fact that God makes peace in the heavenly worlds. What type of peace are we referring to?

---

310. *Yaaroth Devash* 1,12

The rabbis explain that God causes fire and water to coexist. Fire and water are mutually exclusive, and the fact that the fire remains fire and the water remains water and they can both exist together as one is truly miraculous.

Reb Yehonatan feels that this understanding of unity and coexistence does not describe unity in its purest, most sublime form. He writes that when God makes peace in the heavens between fire and water, what happens is that fire takes on the characteristics of water and water takes on the nature of fire.

As admirable as it is, the willingness to coexist cannot be the definitive understanding of true unity. The highest level of unity is when each person is willing to embrace the very nature of the other person, when each person is willing to change their outlook and perspective to be in sync with the other individual.[311]

No one can deny the very lofty form of unity that Reb Yehonatan ascribes to. And, at the same time, no one will deny how truly challenging it would be to reach such a point. We think to ourselves that simply coexisting with others is difficult enough and that is a goal worthy of aspiring to.

However, that doesn't mean we shouldn't attempt to take even baby steps toward Reb Yehonatan's understanding of unity. What we need to do is put ourselves in the other person's shoes, to try to see things from their perspective, to try and understand what is motivating them, what is driving them.

We may never see eye to eye with the other person; however, by attempting to view life through their sight and vision, we may be drawn closer to their outlook and ultimately to them as well.

---

311. *Yaaroth Devash 1,5*

Water

Water and Fire

Two of the most powerful and at times destructive elements of nature are fire and water. Between the two, water is more powerful. We can stop a raging fire by dropping more and more water on the fire until it is extinguished. On the other hand, water cannot be curtailed, and theoretically speaking, there is nothing that can stop a raging tsunami.

The nature of fire is to continuously rise and go higher. The nature of water is the exact opposite; water moves and gravitates to the lowest possible point. If we would describe fire and water in terms of character traits, we would say fire symbolizes haughtiness, since fire seeks to grow taller and higher similar to a person who is haughty. Water, on the other hand, symbolizes humility, since water seeks to find the lowest point possible.

As water is more powerful than fire, so too is the character trait of humility the most powerful and important trait a person should strive to reach.[312]

In an ingenious manner, Reb Yehonatan looks at the nature of the world and finds avenues for self-improvement and self-development. He was an intellectual giant who was able to see and discern things that the average person could not. That doesn't mean we cannot or should not look at the incredible world God created and see if there are any messages we can glean in our journey toward self-improvement and self-development.

---

312. *Yaaroth Devash 2*

Wealth

If I Were a Rich Man

One of the blessings in the Amidah is a request for financial wealth. How much money should we ask for? What would be considered a fair amount?

Reb Yehonatan discusses this issue and also spends a considerable amount of time discussing how we accumulate our wealth. He writes that we should pray to God that our livelihood should not be a result of illegal business transactions. We shouldn't steal; we shouldn't infringe on another person's means of income. Our business ventures should not lead to jealousy or disagreement.

What should we aspire to in terms of our wealth?

The main reason we should want to become wealthy is to help the unfortunate, the downtrodden, and the needy. We should channel our financial successes to support the Torah scholar who is down on his luck. Reb Yehonatan states that when we give charity, it is as if we have brought a sacrifice to the Temple.[313]

While standing in line at the bank with his mother, waiting for the next available teller, a young boy pointed to the teller and said, "He must be very wealthy! Look how much money he is giving to the people." With a big grin on her face, his mother replied, "That isn't his money. The money belongs to the bank. He is simply distributing the bank's money." We too should consider ourselves God's bank teller, and it is our solemn responsibility to ensure that the money doesn't remain in our pockets but is distributed equitably to those in need.

---

313. *Yaaroth Devash*

Display or Hide? That Is the Question

Reb Yehonatan shares a very profound understanding concerning how we should view our financial successes and whether or not we should display it. To demonstrate his viewpoint, he shares the following story from the Talmud:

During the Roman occupation, a key leader of the Jewish people was Rabbi Yehudah, the Prince. Rabbi Yehudah was extremely wealthy, and when his son married, he held a lavish affair. Certain segments of the society wondered how he could make such a fancy wedding when we no longer had the Temple. The Talmud explains that Rabbi Yehudah viewed his wealth as a gift from God, and he was trying to impart a very important message to the Jews living in those times. The lesson was that God takes care of those who lead an observant lifestyle, and by living such a lifestyle, God will bless them with great joy and serenity.[314]

Judaism places great emphasis on the why, why we do things. Two people can drive the same expensive car, but one should be shunned and the other lauded.

If someone buys an expensive car to show off his wealth and make others envious as he drives around town, such behavior is nothing to be proud of and is to be shunned.

The one who should be praised is the person who prays in the synagogue three times a day and can be found in the house of study every morning and evening. He is displaying his wealth to dispel the false narrative that religious Jews cannot be wealthy in a modern and secular society. He is trying to impress upon others that spending time in prayer and study doesn't diminish their ability to do well monetarily, and on the contrary, there may be a very strong correlation between the hours devoted to prayer and study and financial success. If this is what motivates a person to drive an expensive car, he should be praised.

---

314. *Ahavat Yehonatan*

For No One

We are well aware that, at times, there can be animosity by the poor and downtrodden toward the wealthy and the successful. This disdain takes on all stripes and colors. In his astute understanding of human nature, Reb Yehonatan writes that perhaps the worst expression of bitterness is when the poor person wishes that all wealthy individuals would lose every penny they have and be as poor as a pauper.[315]

Hopefully we don't fall in the category of being poor, and our survival is not dependent on the whims and wishes of others. However, that doesn't mean we are immune to such negative thoughts. Unfortunately, human nature is such that it is quite common for a person to think. "If I can't have something, no one else should have it either," rather than thinking, "I wish we could both have it."

In Yiddish, there is a word that succinctly embodies this very negative attitude: fargin; we don't fargin someone. We can't bring ourselves to be happy with someone else's successes. It really is a terrible trait to have and one that we need to work on dispelling over time.

Blessing or Curse

Is wealth a blessing or a curse? For that matter, is poverty a blessing or a curse? The answer to both questions is that it depends on our perspective and how we deal with its particular circumstances.

A person who is wealthy and doesn't need to worry or stress about putting food on the table or paying the bills will have a clear mind and will be able to focus totally on serving God and studying His Torah. On the other hand, wealth brings with it great challenges. The wealthier we are, the more we tend to indulge in worldly pleasures and the more we feel entitled to what the world has to offer.

Likewise, a person who is poor faces his own challenges. On the one hand, a person who is poor will be preoccupied with etching out a

---

315. *Ahavat Yehonatan*

living and will not have the time or headspace to devote himself to God and His Torah. However, a poor person is more than likely to be humble and living a more spiritual lifestyle.[316]

As the story goes, two salespeople are sent to Africa in the nineteenth century to sell a well-known brand-name shoe to the natives. After a week, one salesman comes back and says, "Forget it, the natives don't wear shoes." The next day, a cable is received from the other salesman: "Send me 15,000 pairs of shoes immediately. There is a huge market here. No one is wearing shoes."

Reb Yehonatan is impressing upon us that if we are looking for excuses, we can find them, and if we are looking for opportunities, we can find them as well. In fact, every situation can either be an opportunity or an obstacle to spiritual growth. It is simply a question of perspective.

---

316. *Tiferet Yehonatan Nitzavim*

Wisdom

Who Is Wise?

At one time or another, every human being will wonder how smart they are. For a fleeting moment, we may even contemplate we may be as brilliant as Albert Einstein. Many of us will take IQ tests to see what are IQ level is. In truth, before we take a test to gauge our intelligence, we first need to ask ourselves, "How do we define intelligence?" and "What makes a person wise or intelligent?"

There are conflicting ideas on how intelligence and wisdom are measured. Rabbi Yehonatan offers the following scale for a person to use when attempting to discover their level of intelligence and wisdom:

A wise person is someone who can see beyond the superficial, who can see beyond the here and now and ascertain if what they are seeing is intrinsically good and noble. A person who needs a benchmark of evil to conclude what should be considered righteous and holy cannot be counted among the wise men of the city.[317]

This definition of wisdom and intelligence may seem rather simplistic and basic. We all know the difference between right and wrong. We all know how to distinguish between good and bad. We don't have to be a rocket scientist to be able to do so.

However, if we look back at human history, we see certain behaviors that were considered normal and acceptable being viewed with disdain a few generations later. We also see the opposite: actions that were viewed as immoral were embraced as normal only a few generations later.

Only a truly wise person, one steeped in profound wisdom, can see something for what it truly is. The passage of time will not define what is intrinsically good. Such wise individuals are few and far between.

---

317. *Yaaroth Devash 1*

Work

"Work" Is Not a Dirty Word

We are all familiar with the saying "Hard work never killed anyone." Many prefer to focus on the second part of the saying, "But why take the chance?"

How does Judaism view work and making a living?

Some of the greatest rabbis mentioned in the Talmud were tradesmen. They were blacksmiths, tailors, and cobblers. Rambam was the personal physician of Saladin.

The Talmud states that "one who benefits from his hard labor is greater than a God-fearing person." This statement cannot be taken literally. Does the Talmud then suggest that if you work hard, you have reached the zenith of spiritual endeavor, and you stand head and shoulders above the God-fearing individual?

Rather, the Talmudic statement is understood to mean that if a person earns a livelihood and does not want to rely on charity and, at the same time, is God-fearing, such a person is held in higher esteem than someone who is God-fearing and relies on the generosity of others.[318]

The purpose of our existence is to reveal God's presence in the world. We live in a time that there is no field in academia in which a Jew cannot participate. Long gone are the days when Jews were banned from attending higher levels of education. This is also true in the world of politics. An observant Jew who reaches the pinnacle of success is glorifying the name of God. He is demonstrating that being observant is not an obstacle to succeeding in any endeavor he may aspire to. As such "work" is not a dirty word. Rather it is a word that affords us the opportunity to glorify God.

---

318. *Chidushei Rebbi Yehonatan*

Worry

Days or Years

We have all heard of the expression, "Take it one day at a time." It is usually said to someone who has experienced great loss or tragedy. We tell the person not to think about the future and, instead, just try to get through the day, one day at a time. And, if circumstances are such, we may suggest taking it one hour at a time. And once they have gotten through the hour or day, then they can set their goal to survive for the next hour or day.

Reb Yehonatan suggests that this approach is advisable and beneficial, even when life is smooth sailing. Though things may be good now, we may be constantly scared that we will someday go bankrupt and lose everything we worked so hard for or we may be constantly anxious about our family's future, nervous about what our children and grandchildren will have to endure and confront in the coming years. Living with such a mindset and attitude, besides being "blessed" with endless sleepless nights. our lives will be truly miserable.

What Reb Yehonatan suggests is that we take it one week or one month at a time. Since these periods of time are fairly brief, our fears can be better assessed and managed. And once the week or month has transpired, we can then begin to focus on the coming week or month.[319]

Only a fool disregards what tomorrow may bring. However, worrying about what will be in ten years' time is equally as foolish. There are many approaches to deal with constant and, at times, debilitating worry.

One approach is to fortify our trust in God. We need to say to ourselves, "If God is capable of directing nearly eight billion people, He surely can look after me."

---

319. *Yaaroth Devash 1,5*

And, in truth, does worrying make a difference? Is God really in need of our worrying about how He is going to run our affairs and solve our problems? Or will He succeed in finding good solutions even without our worrying? We all know the answer, so stop worrying.

Glossary

Abarbanel/Don Isaac Abarbanel/The Abarbanel (1437–1508): a Portugese rabbi, scholar, Bible commentator, philosopher, and statesman

Abraham: First of our forefathers

Aharon: Brother of Moses

Aliya: Literal translation *to go up*; commonly used to describe one who immigrates to Israel

Amidah: Literal translation *standing*; the core of every Jewish worship service (also referred to as the Shemonei Esreh)

Av: Fifth month of the Hebrew calendar.

Av Bet Din: Head of the Jewish Judicial Court

Avihu: Son of Aharon, nephew of Moses

Baba Metziah: One of the sixty-three tractates of the Talmud that comprise the Oral Tradition

Bar Mitzvah: Literal translation *son of the commandment* (A boy turning thirteen is considered to have reached his bar mitzvah and is considered an adult.)

Beitza: Literal translation *egg*; one of the sixty-three tractates of the Talmud that comprise the Oral Tradition

Beit Hamikdash: The Temple (There were two temples. The first built by King Solomon stood from 957 BCE–586 BCE, and the second built by Ezra and Nehemiya stood from 516 BCE–70 CE.)

Beit Midrash: House of study

Book of Samuel: A book in the Bible by Samuel the Prophet (1056–1004 BCE)

Brachot: Literal translation *blessings*; the first of the sixty-three tractates of the Talmud that comprise the Oral Tradition

Brit Milah: Circumcision of an eight-day-old boy

Chasidic Hat: Type of headwear worn by Chasidic Jews

Chava: Eve; the first woman

Cheshvan: Eighth month of the Hebrew calendar

Chuppah: Canopy under which the bride and groom stand during the wedding ceremony

Cohen (pl. Cohanim): A priest from the tribe of Levi who served in the Temple; a position of paternal descent

Elul: Eleventh month of the Hebrew calendar

Ethics of the Fathers: A section of the Oral Tradition that presents a series of ethical principles articulated by the rabbis whose legal opinions appear elsewhere in the Mishnah

Etrog: Citrus fruit used during the festival of Sukkot

Hashem: Literal translation *the Name*, referencing God

Hillel: One of the most influential rabbis in Jewish history (Born circa 110 BCE, he was the head of the House of Hillel, which eventually became the primary academy for Torah study prior to the destruction of the Second Temple.)

Jeremiah (650–570 BCE): A prophet

Job: A prophet

Jonathan: Son of King Saul, close friend of King David

Kabbalah: Jewish mysticism

King Achav (871–852 BCE): Seventh King of Israel

King David (1010–970 BCE): Second King of Israel

King Saul (1021–1000 BCE): First King of Israel

King Solomon (970–931 BCE): Third King of Israel

Kippah: Head covering worn by Jewish males

Kreisi U'Pleisi: Scholarly work written by Reb Yehonatan on the second section of the Code of Jewish Law, dealing with the laws of Kosher

Lulav: Palm branch used during the festival of Sukkot

Matzah: Unleavened bread eaten on Passover

Mezuzah: Literal translation *doorpost*; a small parchment scroll upon which the Hebrew words of the Shema are handwritten by a scribe (Mezuzah scrolls are rolled up and affixed to the doorposts of Jewish homes.)

Moed: Literal translation *festival*; the second section of the Mishna (Oral Tradition), primarily dealing with the laws pertaining to Shabbat and the Festivals

Mordechai: Leader of the Jewish people during the events that led to the story of Purim

Miriam: Sister of Moses

Mishnayot: The first major written collection of the Oral Torah (The Mishnah was redacted by Rabbi Yehuda, the prince at the beginning of the third century CE.)

Mitzvah/Mitzvot: Commandment/commandments

Nadav: Son of Aharon, nephew of Moses

Proverbs: Holy text written by King Solomon

Psalms: Holy text written by King David

Pidyon Haben: Ceremony marking the redemption of the first-born male at the age of thirty-one days

Purim: Holiday that commemorates the saving of the Jewish people from Haman, an official of the Achaemenid Empire who was planning to have all Persia's Jewish subjects killed, as recounted in the Book of Esther

Queen Esther: A young Jewish woman who lived in the Persian diaspora who found favor with the king, became queen, and risked her life to save the Jewish people from destruction, as recounted in the Book of Esther

Rabbi Shimon ben Lakish/Reish Lakish (circa 200–275): Regarded as one of the most prominent scholars of the second generation, the other being his brother-in-law and halachic opponent, Rabbi Yochanan

Rabbi Shneur Zalman of Liadi (1745–1812): The founder and first rebbe of Chabad, a branch of Hasidic Judaism; author of the Tanya and the Shulchan Aruch

Rabbi Yochanan (200 CE–279 CE): Regarded as one of the most prominent scholars of the second generation, the other being his brother-in-law and halachic opponent, Reish Lakish

Rambam/Rabbi Moshe ben Maimon (1138–1204): Author of many scholarly works studied to this very day

Rosh Hashanah: Jewish New Year

Seder: Literal translation *order*; held on the first two nights of Passover, consisting of a festive meal and certain rituals

Sefer: Book

Shabbat: Literal translation *rest*; seventh day of the week, Saturday, a day of spirituality and holiness

Shammai (50 BCE–30 CE): The most eminent contemporary of Hillel (Shamai founded a yeshivah called the House of Shammai.)

Shema: Text from the Torah that is recited twice a day during the morning and evening service (One of the most important prayers, the Shema incorporates the themes of the Oneness of God and love of God.)

Shemonei Esreh: Literal translation *eighteen*; refers to the Amidah

Shechita: The ritual slaughter of meat

Shoah: Holocaust

Shofar: Ram's horn blown on Rosh Hashanah, the Jewish New Year

Shulchan Aruch: Code of Jewish Law

Shu"t: Respona, a collection of a particular rabbi's questions received and answered

Shul: Synagogue

Sukkah: Hut-like structure with foliage as its roof

Tanya: An early work of Hasidic philosophy by Rabbi Shneur Zalman of Liadi, the founder of Chabad Hasidism, first published in 1796

Tefillin/phylacteries: Two small black boxes (each containing four different sections of the Torah) with leather straps worn by males over the age of thirteen during the morning service (one above the forehead and the other on the bicep opposite the heart)

Tevet: Tenth month of the Hebrew calendar

Talmud: Literal translation *study*; the work that comments and expands upon the Mishnah (Oral Tradition)

Torah: Constitutes the Five Books of Moses

Tzaddik: Righteous person

Urim V'Tumim: Scholarly work written by Reb Yehonatan on the fourth section of the Code of Jewish Law, dealing with financial matters

Yeshivah: School for young men focusing on the studying of the Written and Oral Tradition

Yom Kippur: Day of Atonement

Yaakov/Jacob: Third of our forefathers

Yehudah: Son of Yaakov (The kings of Israel descended from the tribe of Yehudah.)

Yidden: Jews

Yitzchak/Isaac: Second of our forefathers

Zeraim: Literal translation *seeds*; the first section of the Mishnah (Oral Tradition), primarily dealing with the laws pertaining to agriculture

Zohar: A foundational work in the literature of Jewish mystical thought known as Kabbalah, written by Rabbi Shimon bar Yochai in approximately the second century

Acknowledgments

This is the second book I have written based on the teachings of Rabbi Yehonatan Eybeshitz, one of the greatest rabbis of the eighteenth century. Reb Yehonatan was as at home with the Talmud (oral tradition) and Shulchan Aruch (code of Jewish law) as he was in discussing philosophy and worldly affairs with kings, princes, and heads of the church.

In this endeavor, I am most fortunate to have been blessed with such wonderful partners as Richie and Julie Gerber. They relentlessly pursue their vision, and through the grace of Hashem, I am privileged to be part of it.

Julie is a direct descendant of Rabbi Yehonatan Eybeshitz. She and Richie are passionate about exploring their ancestor's life and learning his profound thoughts and ideas. Reb Yehonatan's writings are, of course, in Lashon Hakodesh Hebrew, making it in a sense a closed book for the English-speaking world. The Gerbers have tasked me with transcribing and elucidating Reb Yehonatan's writings, a responsibility I do not take lightly. The Gerbers are to be commended for their desire to share this treasure chest of knowledge and inspiration with the broad populace.

Our paths would never have crossed if it wasn't for the input of my dear son-in-law Rabbi Ephraim Duchman, a special *yesha koach* (thank you), Ephraim.

This book as the previous one has been greatly enhanced by the highly professional team The Book Couple: Carol Killman Rosenberg for her editing skills and Gary Rosenberg for the beautiful cover and layout. A great rabbi once said that Jewish books need to aesthetically appealing and easy on the eye. Carol and Gary, you hit the bull's-eye.

I would like to dedicate this book to my wonderful children and grandchildren. They all continue to be a great source of nachas for myself and my late wife, Rivkie a"h, in olam ha'emet. The greatest nachas Rivkie and I have is seeing how they have established their own homes and the way they are raising their children in the manner they saw in their home and the homes of their grandparents.

I would also like to dedicate this in memory of my beloved family members who have passed away. While they are no longer present in this physical world, their memory and their shining example live on in their children, grandchildren, and great grandchildren.

My late wife, Rivkie, who passed away on the 19th of Adar 2 5774 (2014). Rivkie was a respected Rebbetzin and a devoted teacher. Her warmth and friendliness, humor and vibrancy, authenticity and compassion touched the lives of all who crossed her path. However her greatest achievement was the way she raised our six beautiful children.

My late father Reb Meir Barber, who passed away on the 18th of Elul 5779 (2019). He was one of the pillars of the Sydney *frum* community. My father was a Holocaust survivor; he spent most of the war years with his family in Siberia. He was a child when the war broke out, never really having the opportunity of studying in a yeshivah. However, after the war, he ended up in Bergen-Belsen. He attended a yeshivah that had been established in what was once an infamous concentration camp. Prior to coming to Australia, his family received a bracha from a great tzaddik that he would have *dor yeshurum um'vorach* (Blessed offspring) who will continue in the righteous path of our tradition. May this blessing remain with his descendants for generations to come. He eventually made his way to Sydney, Australia, and in his small suitcase, he brought with him one of our family's great treasures. He brought his Gemorah with him. On the first page, it says his name and the name of the yeshivah, *Sheirit Hapleito* Bergen-Belsen. Perhaps this encapsulates the secret of Jewish survival. The recognition of the inseparable bond between the Torah and the Jewish people. It speaks of the strength of the Jewish people that even in our darkest hours we continue to learn and teach G-d's Torah. That Gemorah continues to inspire his children, grandchildren, and great grandchildren.

My late father-in-law Rabbi Asher Halevi Heber who passed away on the 8th of Nisan 5780 (2020). He merited that the Lubavitcher Rebbe and Rebbetzin were the *kevaterin* (they carry the baby to the bris) at his bris in prewar Paris. For over forty years, he was a beloved teacher in Manhattan Jewish Day School. It was astounding to hear and read the accolades his students shared with the family at the time of his untimely passing. Many had been in his class more than thirty years before, and they were still able to recall so much of what he had taught them and how he had inspired them to lead Torah-observant lives coupled with a great thirst for the study of Torah.

My beloved uncle and aunt Reb Shabsi and Rebecca Kornwasser; my uncle passed away on the 2nd of Adar 5772 (2012). He came from an illustrious family of Radomsk Chasidim. He was an everlasting link of the Chasidic world of prewar Poland and the Jewish world I grew up in in Australia. His stories of Chasidic life in Sosnowiec and his heroic self-sacrifice for Torah and Mitzvos during the Holocaust inspire me to this very day.

Rebbeca Kornwasser passed away on the 21st of Shat 5779 (2019). Auntie Becca, as she was affectionately called, was beloved by everyone. She was imbued with great *simchat hachayim* (love of life), which she shared with all who knew her. One could say she lived to give. She had a heart of gold and only saw the good in people.

To my dear mother, Esther Barber, and my dear *shviger* (mother-in-law), Nechama Heber. May you both find a level of solace in seeing the beautiful generations you are both the proud matriarchs of. May Hashem bless you both with many years of good health and be *zoche* (merit) to greet *Moshiach Tzidkeiynu b'karov mamosh* (the righteous Messiah speedily in our days).

Publisher's Acknowledgments

From Julie and Richie Gerber

Our hearts burst with joy as we publish *Sparks of Wisdom,* our second book based on the writings of our brilliant ancestor, Rabbi Yehonatan Eybeshitz. As everyone knows, publishing a book is a group effort, and we have been blessed with a wonderful, supportive team that has helped us to make this possible every step of the way.

Rabbi Efraim Duchman, Director of Development for Cholel Chabad, has been with us since the beginning, offering advice and solutions to our problems. We can proudly say that he is an integral part of our work and has become a good friend.

With deep gratitude, we acknowledge the extraordinary work of translator and author Rabbi Yacov Barber, who keeps going the extra mile in his translations, interpretations, and enlightened writing. Rabbi Barber, this has been a truly uplifting collaboration!

Many thanks to The Book Couple, Carol Killman Rosenberg and Gary Rosenberg, for helping to make this book what it is.

Thanks to Tim Sample for creating Gerber's Miracle Publishers' logo.

We believe in miracles, and we thank Rabbi Havelin of the Chabad House in Hamburg, Germany. His assistance has been nothing short of miraculous. He took the photograph of the menorah on the cover of this book. That very menorah was once used by Rabbi Yehonatan Eybeshitz when he was the head rabbi of Hamburg.

Much of our motivation to publish the works of Rabbi Yehonatan Eybeshitz can be traced to the Rebbe's own comments. The Lubavitcher Rebbe, Rabbi Menachem M. Schneerson, of blessed memory has spoken many times about our illustrious forefather. The Rebbe cites a quote from Rabbi Yehonatan Eybeshitz and his inspired writings stating:

"True Torah scholars are not just writing their own ideas. They are writing Torah knowledge gifted to them by Hashem"[320]

And finally, we profoundly thank Hashem for guiding us to this moment in our lives. We know He has miraculously brought into our lives all the people mentioned and made many circumstances possible to make Rabbi Yehonatan Eybeshitz's ideas available to the world at large. Baruch HaShem, Thank You, G-d!

In Loving Memory of our parents:

**Ana Ejbszyc Meler and Isaac Meler
Pearl and Sam Gerber**

---

320. *The Lubavitcher Rebbe Hadran al HaRambam parshat Vayigash 5749 footnote 67 quoting Reb Yehonatan from his scholarly work "Commentary on Tokfo Cohen" section 124.*

Index

due process, 134
dwellings, 258–259

earth, 47, 149, 163–164
    See also world
eating, 72, 181–182, 244, 286
echod. See one
education, 186–187, 199
egg yolks, 176–177
Egypt, 46, 126, 215
Egyptians, 23, 60
Eizenshtate, Meir, 4
elderly, 122, 191, 223, 288
Elijah, 226
Eliyahu of Vilna, 163
embalming, 60–61
embarrassment, 62
Emden, Yaakov, 6
emotions, 16, 78, 146
    See also specific types
emunah. See faith
envy, 89–90
Esau, 35, 121, 171, 172, 200
Esther, Queen, 215
Ethics of the Fathers, 41, 151, 168, 283
eulogies, 220–221
evil, 12, 69, 75
evil eye, 89, 295
evil inclinations. See Yetzer Hara
exile, 57, 63, 81, 82, 118, 174, 224,
    281–282, 316
Eybeshitz, Elkeli (Shapiro), 4
Eybeshitz, Yehonatan, 3–10
    accusations by Yaakov Emden, 6
    amulets by, 8
    Halacha and, 9
    Kreisi U'Pleisi, 4, 7–8, 9
    personality, 7–8
    preaching of, 98, 99, 217
    pronouncements, 10
    refusal to seek endorsements, 105
    students of, 7

study sessions of, 5
his Torah study, 7, 8
on Torah study, 10, 162
Urim V'Tumim, 5
writings, 3–4, 5, 7–8, 9

faith, 64–65, 291
families, 71, 158–159, 250–251
fargin, 321
farming, 232
Fasilberg, Avraham, 5
fasting, 286
fear, 66–67
fetuses, 251, 294
fire, 317, 318
fish, 68, 72
flattery, 69, 255
flood, 242
food, 41, 70–73, 81, 156, 244
    cycles, 176–177
    kosher, 73, 176–177, 244, 286
    nonkosher, 70, 73, 190, 240, 286
forgiveness, 20, 51–52, 60, 83, 135,
    154–155, 188, 272–273
free choice, 74–76, 92, 239–240
freedom, 245–246
friendship, 20, 37–38, 77, 139, 160
fringes. See tzitzit
funerals, 61
future, 325–326

Gan Eden. See Garden of Eden
Garden of Eden, 12, 171, 315–316
garments, 111, 161
    four-cornered, 312, 313
    spiritual, 24
    tearing of, 161
    tzitzit on, 312–314
gehenom. See hell
Genesis. See Bereishit
gevurah, 34, 48–49, 83, 208
giving. See charity

About the Author

Rabbi Yacov Barber was born to Holocaust survivors. He is the father of six children and a proud grandfather. He has lived and studied in Israel, Canada, and Melbourne. He is currently living in New York. Having received both Rabbinic Ordination and Judiciary Ordination, he has also completed courses in palliative care, mediation, family violence, and arbitration.

Rabbi Barber is an internationally acclaimed motivational speaker and a much sought-after communicator on ethics as well as spiritual and personal growth. He has lectured across the United States, Europe, Australia, and Canada.

He is the author of *Generation to Generation: Insights into the Haggadah, Wit & Wisdom: Sermons on the Weekly Torah Reading*, and *Pearls of Wisdom*, a translation of insights of Reb Yehonatan Eybeshitz on the weekly portion and the festivals.

Visit his website RabbiBarber.com

www.ingramcontent.com/pod-product-compliance
Lightning Source LLC
Chambersburg PA
CBHW071136130626
46553CB00004B/1394